Just Care

by the same author

Just Schools
A Whole School Approach to Restorative Justice
Belinda Hopkins
ISBN 978 1 84310 132 1

of related interest

Restorative Justice
How It Works
Marian Liebmann
ISBN 978 1 84310 074 4

Understanding Looked-After Children
An Introduction to Psychology for Foster Care
Jeune Guishard-Pine, Suzanne McCall and Lloyd Hamilton
Foreword by Andrew Wiener
ISBN 978 1 84310 370 7

Working with Gangs and Young People
A Toolkit for Resolving Group Conflict
Jessie Feinstein and Nia Imani Kuumba
ISBN 978 1 84310 447 6

Street Wise
**A Programme for Educating Young People about Citizenship, Rights,
Responsibilities and the Law**
Sam Frankel
Foreword by Bishop Tim Stevens
ISBN 978 1 84310 680 7

The Pocket Guide to Restorative Justice
Pete Wallis and Barbara Tudor
ISBN 978 1 84310 629 6

A Short Introduction to Attachment and Attachment Disorder
Colby Pearce
ISBN 978 1 84310 957 0

Anger Management Games for Children
Deborah M. Plummer
Illustrated by Jane Serrurier
ISBN 978 1 84310 628 9

Just Care

Restorative Justice Approaches
to Working with Children in Public Care

Belinda Hopkins

Foreword by Jonathan Stanley

Jessica Kingsley Publishers
London and Philadelphia

First published in 2009
by Jessica Kingsley Publishers
116 Pentonville Road
London N1 9JB, UK
and
400 Market Street, Suite 400
Philadelphia, PA 19106, USA

www.jkp.com

Library of Congress Cataloging in Publication Data
A CIP catalog record for this book is available from the Library of Congress

British Library Cataloguing in Publication Data
A CIP catalogue record for this book is available from the British Library

ISBN 978 1 84310 981 5

Printed and bound in Great Britain by
Athenaeum Press, Gateshead, Tyne and Wear

Contents

This book is dedicated to Veronica Hart, whose idea it was to write this book, and who would have been its co-author had her personal circumstances not dictated otherwise.

Acknowledgements

I would like to thank Veronica (Ron) Hart, to whom this book is dedicated, first and foremost. Ron was the first manager of a residential children's home to implement a restorative approach and has been a tremendous inspiration to others around the UK. It was she who read my first book, *Just Schools* (Hopkins 2004), and encouraged me to write a book about residential child care. We had hoped to write the book together, but unfortunately Ron's personal circumstances conspired to make her very busy elsewhere. Ron did, however, design a questionnaire which she circulated round the whole of the Hertfordshire care team – the first county-wide service to be trained in restorative approaches. She invited them all to say what they would like to see in a book about restorative approaches. I am very grateful to them all for helping me to plan what needed to be in the book. I trust I have got it right.

In fact Ron's change of circumstance meant I needed to reach out to a lot more people for help, and the book could now be called a team effort. I wrote to every Youth Offending Team in England and Wales and asked for contacts in residential homes that were using restorative approaches. Many people replied with offers of help, and although I did not have time or resources to follow up every phone call or visit I am deeply touched by the support I have had from YOTs all over the country and also very grateful.

From these initial enquiries I was put in touch with some wonderful managers of care homes who invited me to come and visit. My first thanks go to Dave Ayres and his team in Derbyshire, Mike Ormerod from Salford Youth Offending Team, Lindsay and her team at Station Road, Leanne and her team at Godfrey Road (both Salford Homes), and Wendy Bowen, Andrew Nixon and their colleagues in Downham Market – all of whom gave me such a warm welcome when I visited.

I also want to thank those dedicated readers of early chapters of the book, who gave me such useful and encouraging feedback – Martin Kelly, Jean Maddox, Lynn Knowles, James Easton, Steve Searle, Fiona Allen, Chris Hill, Alistair Coutts, Philip Skedgell, Kathy Bates, Francesca Form, Kate Wells, Janet Evans, Nicola Watson, Christopher Makin, Gordon Murray and Simon Smart. My dear friend and colleague Caroline Newton deserves a huge 'thank you'. After breaking her foot in heavy snow she dedicated herself to reading the whole book and to giving me very detailed feedback. I am delighted to have been able to help her while away the hours in such an entertaining way.

I also want to thank Richard Newcombe, John Clark, Wendy Thompson, Alison Glover, Les Fletcher, Brian Littlechild, Jonathan Stanley, Chris Igoe and Jennifer Armstrong, all of whom have offered support in different ways – giving me suggestions, information regarding policy and protocols, further contacts and useful case studies. Any misunderstandings about what they have shared with me are all my responsibility – I am grateful for their generosity.

Last-minute help came from Richard Hendry and his colleagues at Safeguarding Communities, Reducing Offending (SACRO) in Scotland, who helped to clarify the situation there when the police are called out to residential settings. I would also like to thank Tim Chapman and Jim McGrath who responded to my help for clarification on the Northern Ireland situation in similar circumstances, again at very short notice.

Closer to home I want to say a big 'thank you' to my amazing office manager Tracy Parsons, who has been running the business practically single-handed for months – probably even more smoothly than when I am there to distract her! My training team have perhaps wondered why I was not in touch quite as regularly as I should have been while they have been out and about running all the training courses. Thank you for your understanding – I hope this new resource will help you to refresh your skills and understanding and make you even more brilliant than you all already are.

Finally, on a more personal note, I want to thank my daughters Molly and Bryony, and my husband Michael, for the incredible support and encouragement I have had in these last intense months as the deadline loomed nearer. The book could not have been written without you – and I cannot thank you enough.

Foreword

The restorative approach is now firmly established as one of the distinctive strands of residential child care practice in England. There are excellent prospects for its implementation across the residential sector globally, and the grounds for practical optimism are to be found within these pages.

This book will be of interest beyond the residential sector. In these times of integrated children's services and a common approach to the care of young people, this book will also be of use to a wide range of readers, including foster carers and supervising social workers, youth justice workers, educational psychologists and professionals in child and adolescent mental health services. Teachers, especially designated teachers, may also want to match their learning from other publications from Jessica Kingsley Publishers, notably *Just Schools* by the same author, Belinda Hopkins.

An overview of research carried out by the National Centre for Excellence in Residential Child Care, entitled *What Works in Residential Child Care* (available at www.ncb.org.uk/whatworks), identifies the foundations needed for positive care: culture, theory of practice, clarity of purpose and a relational and non-institutional approach. As this book shows, a restorative-inspired approach meets all of these foundations.

Any approach to positive care needs to prove itself in the daily life of residential child care. This is testing ground unlike any other area of children's services. The fact that restorative approaches are flourishing shows that they speak to the daily needs of children, young people and grown-ups in residential settings. They provide, as Leslie Hicks in her work on management of residential child care observes, 'a way of explaining' (Hicks 2007). Using a restorative approach allows an understanding of a situation and, equally important, a method of moving onwards that makes it possible to sustain the all-important relationships.

Restorative approaches comprise one of the distinct strands developing within the residential sector. There are connections to other developments too:

Strand	Connection to restorative approaches
Social pedagogy	'head, heart, hands'
Solution-focused	achieving consensus
Attachment	relationship being essential
Therapeutic child care	inner and social worlds
Pillars of Parenting	bonding between parent and child
Social learning theory	behaviour, not the person

Belinda Hopkins draws on many sources as she describes the creation of a distinctive restorative practice. There are currently few places to go for training in restorative approaches (there is a list at the end of this book), and it is important to select the most appropriate for your use. In such a situation, what is needed is a readily available reference that offers an approachable introduction to restorative justice, such as this book provides.

The book is both a description of restorative approaches and an instruction manual for implementation. The book is written from an English perspective but will have resonance with others globally, especially those from other 'strands' who are looking for a resource from which to incorporate restorative methods.

A simple yet profound perspective is required for a restorative approach; close observation of what is in front of you, and your place within it, along with a relational and contextual engagement.

Restorative approaches cannot be implemented by one charismatic leader in residential settings. Team and group work are essential in a setting where shared responsibility and group living is the therapy.

Winnicott wrote of daily living being the most therapeutic aspect of residential child care. An understanding of restorative approaches helps us consciously to structure an environment around the needs of a young person, providing the support they need in order to become the person that they want to be. A 'whole environment' – one that provides a culture of enquiry in which equally valued young people and grown-ups operate as social actors and subjects rather than objects – encourages the development of a 'whole child', with a unique identity and boundaries, who is able to learn to live within his or her own skin. The development of this culture is an achievement. It cannot be produced by interventions, benign or otherwise. A restorative approach avoids prescriptive interventions, and instead advocates 'holding the space' in a containing/facilitating environment where young people may come to feel safely nurtured.

The book features extended sample dialogue that brings situations to life and will be useful for individuals reading the book as a self-study tool. It shows how restorative approaches are achievable in everyday terms – not a practice for a special few in a rarified setting – something we can all do.

Exercises are presented as a step-by-step guide to implementation, and the restorative world is opened in manageable amounts. You will be encouraged to test yourself: there is understanding of the fact that you need to do some practice to refine your understanding and judgement, and ample examples are provided of how to overcome commonly encountered obstacles and conundrums – you will be learning from others' mistakes, including Belinda's, honestly shared.

Many residential child care practitioners or carers of children will use quick, informal 'in the corridor' or 'street RJ' (as it is described here) restorative approaches. These are complemented by sections on formal approaches which outline defined stages that need to be followed.

Also included are the little things that count: safety, location, logistics, welcomes. The inclusion of these shows the proactive thinking that is being role modelled for us all as prospective restorative practitioners. The book also features offshoots of restorative approaches, such as use of the 'daily circle', which would be useful in any setting, whether or not you plan to use the approach deliberately.

One of the closing chapters focuses on multi-agency and organization-wide implementation, awareness and skill-building, but perhaps most important is that Belinda uses the final chapter to 'bring it all back home'. 'Home is where we start from,' said Winnicott, and in the journey we take in this book we are provided with enough wisdom and insight to see how we can do what is described here for ourselves.

It is not possible to write about this book without also writing about Belinda Hopkins. She has her finger on the pulse and is outward facing, an ambassador 'walking the walk and talking the talk'.

Meeting her is to come into contact with the very embodiment of all that is restorative, committed to opening up rather than closing down. Meeting her, one is struck by the active listening in all she does, the amount of reflecting and absorbing. She links knowledge to experience, shares that of herself and others, that which works and, no less important (and this shows her modesty), that which does not. How often do we get to learn from others' mistakes, openly shared? It is a mark of the person and of this book.

These pages are a distillation of Belinda's learning thus far. Readers will note not only the breadth of her knowledge and the way she makes it accessible and practical, but also her active engagement with interested parties from all over the country. The number of people acknowledged in this book shows her belief in the fruits of collective endeavour. Her ease in communicating with people across children's services makes this a book that is both for and from those who will use it.

There may be moments, as you read this book, when you appreciate that Belinda is writing from the perspective of an experienced practitioner, but, as she modestly tells us, she was not always such, and she is writing for the person she was as much as the person she is now. What makes this book special is that Belinda offers it to us as equals in the process. Such humility comes through her commitment to making the restorative ideal a reality.

Jonathan Stanley
Coordinator of the Children's Residential Network,
NCB (National Children's Bureau)

Chapter 1

Restorative Justice and Restorative Approaches – Setting the Context

Introduction

Children and young people in public care have inevitably been through, and are often still going through, some very difficult life experiences. Their lives are likely to have been adversely affected by their experience of some combination of poverty, unemployment, poor housing, family conflict and breakdown, health issues and social isolation (Francis 2008). They will therefore have a high level of complex needs and their behaviour will often present extraordinary challenges. What these young people need above all is loving care, but the title of this book – *Just Care* – is not intended to be a facetious and simplistic reminder of this fact to residential and foster carers. Caring describes what we do, as well as how we feel and respond, and the day-to-day interactions in residential settings demand skilful care in the active sense, as well as unconditional caring in the emotional sense. The title *Just Care* is intended to combine the notion of justice and fairness with both the active and emotional senses of the word 'care'.

The book offers practical suggestions for those working with children in care, drawn from the experiences of working with young people in educational contexts using restorative approaches. These approaches are underpinned by the philosophy, values, principles and practices of restorative justice. The book is for staff in residential homes and schools and also for foster parents, who I hope will find the more informal restorative approaches useful for day-to-day life with the child or children in their care.

Much of the book focuses on responding to conflicts, and also to challenging, antisocial and at times violent and destructive behaviours. However, an important message throughout the book is that for these responses to be effective, they need to be consistent with, and informed by, an underpinning ethos and a set of values and principles that influence day-to-day interactions among all members of the residential home, school, unit or foster family. These values and principles emphasize the importance of relationships above all, and whereas 'restorative justice' tends to be associated with responses to wrongdoing, antisocial or criminal behaviours, 'restorative approaches' embrace both the making and maintaining of relationships, as well as repairing these when they are in some way damaged through harmful behaviours. In other words, restorative approaches include proactive as well as reactive concepts and strategies.

In researching the book I have been in contact with lots of people who have experience of the residential child care sector – local authority managers, care home managers, residential social workers, youth justice professionals, police officers and magistrates. Regrettably, the voice of young people themselves is missing. Despite my requests to those working professionally in the field, I was unable to include any quotations from young people, and I do hope that subsequent publications will remedy this situation. Residential staff are very enthusiastic about restorative approaches and attest to their positive impact on their charges as well. However, we do need to hear from the young people themselves.

This chapter sets the context for what is to follow. It considers the reasons for increased interest in using restorative justice in residential settings, and the gradual evolution of interest beyond the single intervention known as a 'restorative conference' to the wider application of 'restorative approaches'.

A very brief history of the development of various models of restorative justice practice is provided, but since this book is predominantly about practice, readers with a particular interest in the history and theories of restorative justice are encouraged to read more widely from the growing body of excellent literature in the field. Suggestions for further reading are found at the back of this book.

Throughout the book links will be made between specific restorative approaches and the wider residential child care literature and research. However, once again it is emphasized that the book is essentially practical, and there is undoubtedly much more to be written about the theories underpinning restorative work in residential contexts.

Early interest in restorative justice – focus on reducing offending

In recent years there has been increased interest in using restorative approaches in residential child care settings, based on the philosophy and practice of restorative justice. This innovative approach to dealing with conflict, antisocial behaviour and criminal behaviour has been increasingly used in the youth justice field in the UK since the late Nineties and the approach is now being trialled with adult offenders as well. The evaluations of this approach have been positive and suggest that the opportunity for offenders to meet with those against whom they have offended in a facilitated meeting can make an impact on their future offending behaviour, and also meet the needs of victims for closure (Shapland *et al.* 2006, Shapland *et al.* 2007, Sherman and Strang 2007). The reduction in re-offending behaviour and the desire to reduce the extent to which looked-after children are criminalized in the first place have been two of the reasons why those working in the looked-after sector have been drawn to restorative justice (Willmott 2007).

Statistics show that young people in residential child care are disproportionately represented in the criminal justice arena (Department for Education and Skills 2006a, NACRO 2003a, NACRO 2003b). This situation has arisen not only because children in care are more likely to offend because of the numerous risk factors they have often been exposed to (NACRO 2005), but because the disruptive behaviours of the children have resulted in a call from staff to the police. Up until recently, because of current guidelines enshrined in the National Crime Recording Standard (Home Office and Association of Chief Police Officers 2002) and the protocols involved, when police officers are called out to an incident they have felt obliged to record the incident as an offence – to 'crime' it.[1] This can then lead to an arrest and a reprimand, final warning or a court appearance following bail (NACRO 2003a). Probably neither the staff concerned, nor the police involved, would wish for such an outcome. However, without training in alternative strategies, or because of organizational pressures, staff often turn to the police in desperation. (Chapter 8 discusses further the need to change policy and procedures so that restorative responses can be integrated into agreed organizational practice.) Using a restorative approach instead can divert children in care away from the criminal justice system by ensuring that the incident is dealt with by staff in such a way that both the wrongdoer and those affected reach a mutually agreed way forward without recourse to the police (Willmott 2007). (Chapter 8 will discuss restorative options even after police intervention, which in serious incidents may well be appropriate.)

In Scotland and in Northern Ireland the situation has been, and to some extent still is, similar – at present if the police are called out to a residential unit the young person is likely to be charged. In both countries, however, what happens following the charge is changing as Youth Justice services in both countries begin to adopt more restorative practices, and this is discussed further in Chapter 8.

In Scotland, following a charge, the route was always somewhat different anyway. If the young person is charged, then the case is passed to the Reporter to the Children's Panel. The Panel is a unique Scottish institution made up of three trained lay people, which has always been welfare based – and so a young person is unlikely to receive a punitive or custodial response except in exceptional cases, if there is deemed to be a public safety risk.

Assuming the Reporter feels there is sufficient evidence to proceed, and that the charge is not contested, the Reporter may make a diversionary referral to a Youth Justice service for appropriate support or intervention. Alternatively the referral may

---

1   See Chapter 8 for a discussion of how this situation is rapidly changing as the Home Office reconsiders crime recording and sanctioned detections.

go to the Children's Panel. The Panel members will take reports and meet with the child, their carer and other relevant professionals, and reach a 'disposal', with various possible options, including a referral to the Youth Justice service, if this has not already happened. Although this route may be less punitive, until recently there were not options to put things right between those affected.[2]

An ex-teacher from a residential special school, one of the people who has been giving me useful feedback on this book, wrote:

> I would wholeheartedly recommend the use of restorative practices (RP) in residential schools. You are right to be concerned with the issue of offending and young people in care building a portfolio of police charges. I can think of several occasions where I was assaulted myself (to varying degrees, and generally pretty minor) where there was no automatic system within the school to deal with the system restoratively. My feeling, and that of many other staff in this situation, whether a victim or not, was that the young person needed to see some kind of consequence for their behaviour, and that in the absence of anything else, a phone call to the police was the only action available. I don't think it is up to the 'victim' to initiate restorative work; there must be a system already in place that will automatically deal restoratively with this type of situation. I'm not saying that young people must never be charged by the police, but the use of RP would definitely reduce the number of offences reported, and have a much more satisfying outcome for all involved.
>
> *Alistair Coutts, former teacher in a residential special school*

The ripple effects of criminalizing young people

It is worth considering what the 'justice route' means, not just for the young people involved but also for staff and other residents in a care setting. For the sake of argument, imagine a scenario in which a young person reacts angrily to something a member of staff asks them to do, and ends up lashing out and hitting the staff member. The member of staff, angry and hurt (and the more so, perhaps, because they are on the night shift without much support), rings the police. As discussed, the police officer has often felt obliged to record the incident as an offence – to 'crime' it. The young person is therefore formally arrested, taken to a custody centre and charged.[3]

---

2   This section has been adapted from some informative paragraphs offered by Richard Hendry and his colleagues at SACRO for which I am very grateful.

3   Chapter 8 discusses how the police and the Youth Offending Team in different areas have tried to minimize the criminalization of young people with locally agreed protocols that seek to get round the current inappropriate guidelines. It also offers the promise of long overdue, common-sense changes.

It is possible that even in the time elapsing between the incident and the arrival of the police, much has changed – perhaps the young person has calmed down and apologized. Perhaps the member of staff has accepted their apology. Nevertheless a process has been set in motion, and the ensuing arrest and charge will do nothing to help the relationship between young person and staff, and could have repercussions in the residential home because of others' judgement about whether the police should have been called or not.

Following the charge, if the young person is bailed to court, there will be some lapse of time before the young person's first court appearance, and again, this delay will not be easy for anyone in the residential home. There may be little chance for the member of staff or the young person to move on and repair their relationship, with the court case hanging over their heads, even if they wanted to. It can be a stressful time for everyone – with other conflicts and challenging behaviour happening because of the stress and the uncertainty.

Unfortunately the legal system around the protagonists may well be polarizing the situation anyway. Defence lawyers are likely to argue for psychological assessments on the young person, which may not only delay court proceedings but also boost the young person's sense that they were blameless. Indeed, defence lawyers are often likely to argue in court that their client is not at fault, owing to their extenuating circumstances. Making this case in the young person's hearing will not be helpful in encouraging him or her to become accountable for their behaviour. It is likely to antagonize the member of staff, who needs the young person to acknowledge the harm caused in order to be able to move on themselves. In effect the adversarial process ensures that both the young person and the member of staff feel like the victim, the former because their defence lawyer is emphasizing their difficult situation and past problems, and the latter because there seems no chance of the young person taking any responsibility for what happened, since this is proscribed by the defence lawyer's protocols.

Worse still, it could be part of the defence lawyer's case that the member of staff was at fault and mishandled the situation. (If by any chance the case is dropped on its passage through court, this can also leave the young person feeling invincible and the person harmed resentful at the lack of accountability.)

While the case is unresolved at the court level, the ripples of harm can spread out and infect other people in the residential home, with sides being taken. The young people may be angry at the member of staff for calling the police in the first place. Staff may be divided about whether the police should have been called out at all, and yet also frustrated because of the lack of options available to them in such circumstances.

Meanwhile, magistrates themselves feel frustrated at seeing young people in care for apparently trivial incidents that would not be considered criminal matters in the case of young people were living with their own families.

To be fair, what magistrates may not appreciate, as they read through long sets of case notes, is that the apparently 'trivial' incident may have been the straw that broke the camel's back for a hard-pressed member of staff in the home, who had found no

> I have often felt that quite a number of cases brought to court by children's homes could be dealt with internally far better through restorative justice. One such example was a girl who, out of anger and despair because her mother would not speak to her on the phone, damaged a door. Another involved a boy who kicked and dented a care worker's car after an argument with the person. These sorts of offences are carried out by young people in great need of care, and of support , in the process of seeking a restorative settlement, particularly as the parties will continue to live together and the harm needs to be quickly healed.
>
> *A magistrate in Somerset*

other strategy that worked to change the young person's behaviour. However, this is why restorative options are as much for the benefit of staff as of the young people.

Although magistrates would argue that children in care are dealt with promptly, delays of months between an offence and the sentence are not uncommon. Such delays can be highly detrimental, since a young person may well be making huge efforts to reform in the interim, and indeed may long ago have forgotten what had led up to the incident in the first place. Even if they were fortunate in repairing their relationship with the member of staff originally affected, the sentence, when it finally comes, could be a huge blow to their progress and cause fresh damage to their relationship, not only with the member of staff most involved but with other members of staff in the home.

Because of the negative impact, on both the young person and the staff, of going down this 'justice route', it is not surprising that the inevitable tensions, stress, unanswered questions, resentment and continuing unmet needs on all sides can lead to other incidents, and the young person may find themselves in increasing trouble, in part because the issues that needed to be dealt with initially have never been addressed. Clearly there is something very wrong with this state of affairs and something needs to change.[4]

Case study

One incident springs to mind: after a serious incident that affected the whole community within a residential home, the wrongdoer had a long wait for sentencing and he could not cope with his guilt or the rest of the community. He dealt with his guilt and fear by abusing alcohol and damaged every relationship

---

4   Fortunately changes are in progress at the level of police involvement, and new restorative practice for minor disturbances and conflicts is being piloted as I write this book. These are discussed further in Chapter 8. These changes make the case for a restorative approach within the residential setting even more urgent.

he had in some way. He went on to commit more criminal acts and at the time of sentencing had not moved on from the initial incident.

In my view, if restorative approaches had been known to the staff and young people within the residential home, I would hope the outcome for this young person and others involved would have been more positive and healing.

From restorative justice to restorative approaches

The criminalisation of young people, and the negative impact on all concerned, led to an interest in the use of restorative justice by those working in care settings. Initially, in the early years of the new millennium, 'restorative justice' was often used as a synonym for 'restorative justice conferencing', and it was training in the facilitation of conferences that was offered. This formal process is predicated on a model that usually involves

- both 'victim' and 'offender' (sic) meeting in the company of their immediate community (parents or carers) and anyone else directly affected by the incident

- everyone present recounting their perspective on the situation and their feelings

- everyone discussing what they need in order to move on as individuals, and also how things can be put right.

This formal process can be highly effective. It does, however, require a commitment of time for preparation, since the facilitator needs to meet with every participant individually beforehand and the meeting itself can be quite lengthy.

Although this book will say more about the formal conference process later (in Chapter 6), most of it will focus on the less formal restorative approaches and their contribution to relationships improving day-to-day in residential settings. Whilst restorative justice in its formal sense can and does make a contribution in care settings, it is in its less formal aspects, described as 'restorative approaches', that it can have most impact and address many of the issues and challenges currently facing the residential child care sector. One particular concept that is gaining ground in residential settings is that of 'social pedagogy', and it will be argued that day-to-day restorative practice provides a framework for care staff to operationalize socially pedagogic principles, especially in challenging situations. This will be further discussed in later chapters.

It may be useful to provide some background into the development of 'restorative justice' *per se*, and then consider the wider concept of 'restorative approaches'.

The origins of restorative justice

In his foreword to my book *Just Schools* (Hopkins 2004) Guy Masters draws together four different strands that he believes contribute to the development of what is referred to as 'restorative justice' in many countries today. Each of these strands contains within it certain key features which help to illustrate the essential essence of what restorative justice is all about.

One strand is the story of Mark Yantzi and Dave Worth, Mennonites working in the criminal justice system in Kitchener, Ontario (see Figure 1.1). In 1974 they dared to do something different when dealing with two young men who had vandalized the property of 22 residents in a nearby town.

Figure 1.1 Origins of victim–offender mediation

They proposed the idea of arranging for the men to meet their victims and make amends for what they had done. Unprecedented as it was, the judge administering the sentence made this possible by giving his permission for something new to be tried. The young men were taken to the house of each family and in almost all cases, following face-to-face dialogue with those affected, there was a positive outcome and reparation was agreed and carried out. The meetings had a dramatic effect on the two young men and on the lives of many of the victims, and was the beginning of a Victim–Offender Reconciliation Programme (VORP) that spread through Canada, to the United States and then to Europe (Peachey 1989, Zehr 1990) (see Figure 1.2). In recent years one of the young men recounted how his life was changed by the meetings, and he now, many years later, works as a volunteer for a VORP scheme (Yantzi 2004).

Another important strand (Figure 1.3) has been the development in New Zealand of the Family Group Conferencing (FGC) model for dealing with youth offending, enshrined in the youth justice system since 1989 as the preferred way of dealing with any offence other than the most violent crimes (McCold 2001). This approach

Figure 1.2 Spread of victim–offender mediation

developed as a result of Maori communities expressing their distress with the way their young people were finding themselves, disproportionately, on the wrong side of the law and then incarcerated far from friends and family. This approach contrasted strongly with traditional Maori practice of sitting in circle with their community to share together what had happened and find ways forward together (Consedine 1995). This included the wider community becoming accountable for what might be behind the young person's wayward behaviour, and helping to reintegrate the young person back into the community.

Figure 1.3 Origins of family group conferencing

The third strand developed from the second, since the New South Wales Police Force in Wagga Wagga developed their work with young offenders (and, later, older offenders), inspired by the New Zealand model (Figure 1.4). Sergeant Terry O'Connell visited New Zealand to learn more about family group conferencing and then, supported by John Macdonald and David Moore, developed what has become known as 'the scripted conferencing model' (Moore and O'Connell 1994).

Figure 1.4 Influence of family group conferencing spreading to New South Wales

In this model some key questions are asked of all those affected by an offence:

- What happened?

- Who has been affected and how?

- How can we put right the harm done?

Terry was invited over to the UK in the mid-Nineties to share his experiences of using his version of the conference with police officers and other agencies, and this led to a surge of interest in restorative justice in the UK (Figure 1.5). His model also influenced practice in some areas in the USA.

The fourth strand comes from Canada, where First Nation communities, especially in the Yukon, have developed sentencing circles; these involve the community in deciding the appropriate sentence and way forward for a young offender, endorsed by the judge, who also takes part. Zehr (1990) points out the value of involving the community in dealing with its own problems and the potential this offers to building relationships between people and communities.

In fact it has become clear that many indigenous communities around the world have some variant on community problem-solving, often with community members sitting together in a circle sharing their stories and their ideas for resolving issues that have arisen. Circle processes for community building and problem-solving have also influenced restorative work in the United States, and various models of restorative practice are developing there (Figure 1.6). Whilst some practitioners have been

Figure 1.5 Influence of restorative conferencing spreading beyond Australia

Figure 1.6 Indigenous practice of using community problem-solving approaches widespread

inspired by the Australian 'scripted conference' model and its attendant theories (McCold and Wachtel 2002), others draw inspiration from indigenous circle traditions (Pranis 2001).

Each of these four strands have key themes in common:

• a chance for all sides to tell their own story – so that those harmed get a sense that the harm they have suffered has been acknowledged and recognized, but also so that those in the wrong can tell their own story

• an opportunity for gaining clarity and understanding, and for developing empathy – answers to questions have proved in research to be an unmet need of many victims in the traditional justice system (e.g. Why us? Did we do something to deserve this? Will it happen again?)

- recognition that all those affected have needs which must be acknowledged and addressed for real healing to take place

- ownership of the conflict by those immediately affected and, by dint of negotiation, ownership of the agreement over reparation

- an opportunity for those in the wrong to put things right, and therefore earn their way back into the community and perhaps be forgiven, not only by this community, but by themselves.

Implicit in these themes are certain key values and principles – self-determination, collaboration, flexibility, equality, non-discrimination, non-violence, fairness, respect, empowerment, trust, honesty, voluntarism, healing, personal accountability, and inclusiveness (Barton 2003, Quill and Wynne 1993, Restorative Justice Consortium [RJC] 2004).

Elements of all four of the strands have been developing in various ways around the world, and in the UK in particular. Victim–offender mediation has been used in the UK for many years by voluntary services working closely with the police, probation services and Victim Support. These early victim–offender services inspired the development of nationwide community mediation services for neighbourhood and community conflicts. Many of these services began working in schools developing peer mediation programmes. Family group conferencing has been used in its therapeutic form by social services for many years, to address deep-seated needs of a young person and their family. In some areas, however, it is also used in conjunction with, or integrated into, the restorative conference model. In such circumstances it is recognized that the harm caused by a young person's behaviour needs to be addressed, and that, while there may be victims who would benefit from the process, the young person responsible for the harm also has deep needs which need to be addressed.

The use of circles to involve communities of various sorts in making decisions affecting their lives and for developing a sense of community has a long history amongst those working in residential care and therapeutic settings.

The restorative justice conference

It is the success of the scripted conferencing model that has perhaps had the most significant impact in the development of the concept of restorative justice in the UK in the last ten years. This success is in large measure due to the enthusiasm with which the Thames Valley Police, under the leadership of the then Chief Constable Charles Pollard, adopted restorative justice in their work with young offenders from the late 1990s. For the police 'restorative justice' became, and in some cases still remains, synonymous with the scripted conference process originally developed by O'Connell, Moore and Macdonald (in Moore and O'Connell 1994).

This process, relying heavily on a written script, is underpinned by some key theories that were retrospectively developed to explain why the process is effective (Braithwaite 1989, Nathanson 1992). The process is predicated on the involvement of an impartial facilitator, at least one clearly identified offender who acknowledges responsibility for what they have done, and at least one victim willing to attend. The meeting also involves significant people in the lives of both offender and victim, their immediate community, who are likely to have been affected by what has happened. Furthermore the offender's supporters would also be people whose respect and regard the young person craved and whose disapproval of what he or she had done would be significant and undesirable.

Useful as this conferencing process has been and continues to be, the identification of restorative justice with this scripted model has, in my view, hampered the development of a much more useful application of restorative justice principles – what we will describe in this book as 'restorative approaches'.

In residential care settings, for example, staff trained in the conferencing model swiftly discovered that the more formal process was less useful than they had first hoped, because most of the incidents they needed to address flared up quickly and needed immediate attention. More often than not there was no clear-cut case of 'offender' and 'victim' but simply two people in conflict, each blaming the other. They therefore began to request training in a range of less formal processes which were nevertheless informed by the philosophy of restorative justice. Their experiences using these processes have gradually led to a realization that the approach required a cultural shift in the way staff and young people interact on a day-to-day basis, and that the benefits of using such an approach could go far beyond the narrow remit of reducing potentially offending behaviour.

Initially this more flexible approach was not as widely known in care settings, and indeed it is hoped that this book will address what has been a lack of available resources to help staff in care settings to learn more about the far more useful set of strategies known as 'restorative approaches'.

Restorative approaches

In the late 1990s, as the Thames Valley Police was championing the use of restorative justice conferencing for youth offending, I was offering training in school and residential contexts with my own version of restorative justice – a synthesis of four elements which I saw as linked by the same key themes and the same values and principles that underpinned the various historic strands of restorative justice described earlier. These four elements were:

1. proactive relationship and community-building

2. interpersonal conflict management

3. mediation

4. restorative conferencing.

It seemed obvious to me that a process like conferencing would be far more effective in a community context such as a school or residential home, if the values and principles on which it was based, the skills used to deliver it and the outcomes it sought to achieve were built into the fabric of the institution as well.

I was inspired by the work of Howard Zehr and Harry Mika, who began to look at the whole paradigm of traditional criminal justice and suggested that a fresh set of lenses was needed (Zehr 1985, Zehr 1990, Zehr and Mika 1997, Zehr and Mika 1998). To my mind this 'paradigm shift' was needed just as much in school and residential settings, where disruption and wrongdoing, even when these stemmed from interpersonal conflicts, were being dealt with as a discipline issue requiring sanctions (Hopkins 1999b).

The term 'restorative justice' began to outgrow its usefulness in educational contexts. It had become too tightly connected to the conferencing model. Instead I began to use the term 'restorative approaches' – a broader term that indicated a much broader conceptualization of what was needed in a community setting such as a school, a residential home and even in families (Hopkins 1999a).[5]

My early attempts to illustrate the breadth of this concept included the use of the restorative pyramid model – in order to explain that key values and principles underpinned all restorative skills and that these skills in turn informed specific restorative processes (Figure 1.7).

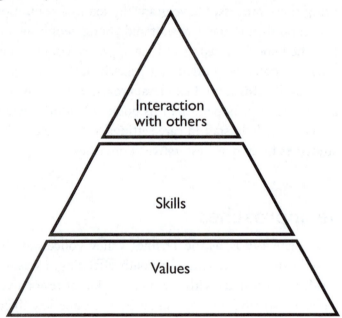

Figure 1.7 Restorative justice practice underpinned by values and skills

_____

5   The phrase 'restorative justice' continues to be a useful term when helping people to see the links between what is happening in criminal justice settings and places such as schools, residential homes and even families – where behaviour is still often managed using sanctions and threats of sanctions.

However, this book is going to use a different approach – by making the case for five key themes which underpin all restorative approaches and then weaving these themes through every chapter.

The five restorative themes

I spend much of my time delivering training courses to those working with young people in a variety of contexts, as does my excellent team of trainers. We are constantly evolving new ways to explain what restorative approaches are and how to integrate them into daily life – both professional and private. For us restorative justice and restorative approaches are not just what you do, but how you are. What follows are the five key themes that inform our practice – as trainers and as people. These will be explained and elaborated on further in Chapter 2 and will inform all the chapters describing practice.

These themes are derived from the original four strands of restorative practice mentioned earlier. They are also enriched by our increasing understanding of both the power of narrative and of the influence of thoughts and self-talk on emotions, which recent developments in cognitive psychology have helped to elucidate.

Theme 1: An appreciation of, and respect for, individual perspectives

In any given situation everyone will have a unique experience, and their perspective will differ depending on numerous factors including their personality, their mood at the time, previous experiences, the way they encode the world, their learning style, and so on. An understanding and respect for these differences has informed indigenous circle practices for generations (Pranis 2001).

Theme 2: A commitment to developing mutual understanding by making explicit the link between thoughts, feelings and behaviour

Our interpretation of an event, informed by all the different factors mentioned above (personality, experience, etc.) and probably many more, will influence our emotions in any given moment and these emotions will impact on how we respond or react in that moment. This insight underpins cognitive psychology and cognitive behavioural therapy and informs solution-focused therapy and pro-social modelling.

An understanding of the link between thoughts and feelings is considered to be an important aspect of emotional literacy and emotional maturity. Giving people an opportunity to reflect on their own inner dialogue at any given time, and the emotions this gives rise to, can help them understand how they behave, or behaved, in certain situations. By the same token, hearing from others what was going on for them at a given moment helps to develop an understanding of the reasons for their behaviour in certain situations. Empathy consists of being interested in these connections and able to acknowledge and respect them.

Theme 3: A focus on harm and how to repair this harm; on the effect of an action and who has been affected

As Howard Zehr (1990) writes in relation to crime: 'Crime is a violation not of rules, but of people'.

The focus of reactive restorative work is on the harm caused and how those involved can find ways to repair the harm, whether this is in terms of the damage caused to person and property, or to relationships and community safety. In less serious cases the focus is still on the way in which a given situation has affected or is affecting those involved. Hence questions about harm, effect and affect are central to a restorative process, to develop and encourage an awareness of who has been affected and how.

To be mindful of the impact of our behaviour on others is the mark of a considerate, empathic and respectful person and this proactive aspect of Theme 3, which needs to be part of daily life in the residential home or family, is discussed further in Chapters 2 and 8.

Theme 4: An appreciation of individual needs

In any situation different people will have different needs. Failure to understand and appreciate our own and others' needs in our interactions with each other can lead to conflict (Rosenberg 1999). Without surfacing these needs, mutual understanding and empathy cannot be achieved. However, interestingly, a key insight in restorative work, offered by Peta Blood in her restorative work in Australia, is that both the harmed person and the harmer have similar needs. We have found it useful to encourage people to consider their own personal needs for moving on as a preliminary to discussing and agreeing practical strategies for meeting these needs.[6]

Theme 5: Accountability in terms of repairing harm and putting things right, and shared ownership of problem-solving and decision-making by those involved

This theme comes through strongly in all four of the historical strands influencing restorative practice – the importance of involving those who have been affected by an event or situation in finding ways forward, but also in considering their role in what has happened. In his seminal article 'Conflicts as property' Nils Christie (1977) highlighted the tendency in modern times for those in authority to steal the conflict away from those to whom it belongs and seek to have ownership of the solution as well. He also points to the tendency to impose these solutions on those people, who

---

6   Mediators sometimes differentiate between 'position statements' that those in conflict can sometimes make – in the form of demands – and the underlying 'interest' informing the position statement. I prefer to use the term 'need' in this context.

would have been better placed to find ways forward for themselves. The challenge for those in authority to share their power of decision-making is immense.

There can be a risk when things go wrong that the perceived wrongdoer is the only person held to account. Ownership of decision-making and joint problem-solving often leads to a reflection by those present at a restorative meeting about whether they could do things differently in the future to avoid similar incidents happening again – a reflection which amounts to a 'blame-free' way of sharing accountability. The restorative approach therefore creates opportunities for shared accountability where appropriate (and it is not always appropriate).

A working model

As explained previously, on pages 25–26, the four elements of a restorative approach in an educational and/or residential setting are:

1. proactive team and community-building

2. interpersonal conflict management

3. mediation

4. restorative conferencing.

These four elements all have in common the five restorative themes outlined above and summarized here:

1. unique perspectives

2. linking thoughts, feelings and behaviour

3. harm, effect, affect and repair

4. needs

5. accountability; empowerment; collaborative problem-solving.

Figure 1.8 illustrates what I mean by a restorative approach in an institution or organization, showing how the four key elements all share the same five key restorative themes.

In addition to this working model, which helps to differentiate a 'restorative approach' from the purist notion of 'restorative justice' and restorative conferencing, this book is going to use the metaphor of a die as a way of organizing the chapters on practice.

The dice metaphor

I plan to consider how the five key themes can inform various kinds of interactions, interventions and processes in terms of how many people are involved, rather than

Figure 1.8 Restorative approaches

how serious or formal the situation is (which is also how our training courses are organized). I hope this helps to clarify what 'being restorative' is all about and how the five themes can support all our interactions, including our own internal dialogues.

I use the metaphor of a die, with each facet on the die signifying how many people are involved. The facets with one, two or three spots on them are used to refer to a single person, two people and three people respectively. Beyond this, however, I use the spots more metaphorically. The four-spot facet is used to refer to small, informal groups of people (between four and eight), the five-spot facet is used as a metaphor for the formal restorative justice conference, and the six spots are a metaphor for working in circle in various ways – for community-building, problem-solving, group meetings, to name a few. The die has its spots arranged in a different way from a conventional die, since I would arrange all the spots to fit within a circle, as though all those involved in any of the meetings or conversations described were seated on or around a circular rug.

Each of the next seven chapters is characterized as shown in Table 1.1.

Each chapter builds on the ideas and skills from the previous one, and so reading Chapters 2–7 in succession will help develop understanding. In some chapters there are suggested activities for using with staff, and maybe also with the young residents, to develop greater understanding of what living and engaging restoratively means for them. These are adapted from training materials we use, and have proved successful and thought-provoking in residential as well as educational settings. They are also being adapted for the training of foster parents. Some useful reference sheets are reproduced as photocopiable pages in the appendices at the back of the book.

Table 1.1 Chapters 2–7 – the die: symbol and metaphor

⚀	Chapter 2	The restorative mindset
⚁	Chapter 3	Restorative enquiry – for active listening, developing empathy, encouraging communication and cooperation
⚁	Chapter 4	Restorative enquiry – for use in interpersonal conflict
⚂⚃	Chapter 5	Mediation or mini-conferencing – semi-formal approaches
⚄	Chapter 6	Conferencing – formal approaches
⚅	Chapter 7	Circles of various types

Conclusion

The five restorative themes will inform every interaction, from the most informal to the most formal, and will be relevant for both proactive and reactive responses and behaviours. The way dialogues are managed in small or large groups may well be similar, whether responding to some kind of serious situation or simply engaging in the day-to-day exchanges that occur when people agree, disagree, joke, complain, protest, celebrate, discuss, enquire, gossip, chat, and pass the time of day. The simple structure suggested for mediating between two people in conflict can be adapted for informal spontaneous interventions, as well as formalized in more serious situations. This simple structure also informs the larger group model presented as a 'conferencing' model when more people are involved.

Issues that have particular relevance to residential child care settings – in particular the issues of facilitator impartiality and attachment – are raised in various chapters as appropriate. Similarly, the application of various restorative approaches in foster settings is themed throughout the book.

Chapter 8 considers the importance of multi-agency partnerships and the development of frameworks, policies and procedures for ensuring a consistent restorative approach across an authority. Chapter 9 offers suggestions for implementation and sustainability of a restorative culture within a residential home or school. The Epilogue concludes by reflecting on the wider implications of the restorative approach described in this book – and suggests further applications for this humane and effective way of living and working in communities, and in society at large. This book does not claim to be the definitive book for those working restoratively in the residential care field, but it is the first – and as such will hopefully lay down the foundations for others to build on, in the same way that my book *Just Schools* (2004) has done in the field of education.

Chapter 2

The Restorative Mindset

Introduction

This chapter lays the foundation stone for living and working in a restorative way, namely the restorative mindset – a way of thinking about other people, about interpersonal relationships, about leadership and community, and about conflict and wrongdoing – that informs what we think and do. Acting restoratively is not about working from a script or a pre-ordained formula one moment and then addressing another issue in a different way. A restorative mindset helps people to act in a consistent way – not always getting things right, and indeed maybe sometimes choosing *not* to act restoratively – but at least recognizing this as a conscious choice and as an exception to the norm.

Developing a shared 'restorative mindset' enables a staff team to work together, knowing that there will be consistency between them and across shifts, if an issue arises that takes time to resolve. It also means that the young residents know that they will be treated in a similar way by every member of staff, and consistently by each of these members of staff. Furthermore, the restorative mindset is catching, as is the language that flows from it – such that concepts such as 'harm' and 'need' become recognized and shared, considered and acknowledged by staff and residents alike. In effect developing a shared mindset is the first step towards developing a shared restorative ethos and culture. Within a foster family the same consistency of practice is also important.

The chapter begins by establishing that 'restorative approaches' are first and foremost about relationships, and so the most essential component of a restorative mindset is the commitment to building, nurturing and, when they go wrong, repairing relationships. This does not mean avoiding conflict for the sake of peace, but being competent and confident to address issues as they arise and find ways forward that repair and even strengthen relationships. The link between values and practice is teased out in a suggested activity to use with a staff team or with a group of foster carers.

The chapter then introduces two important ideas – both sometimes referred to as 'paradigm shifts' – major changes in the way people think about an issue. The first idea involves a shift in the way we think about accountability when things go wrong, and the second invites us to think about our role as adults in our daily interactions with young people and in our use of power and control.

Finally the chapter brings together the five restorative themes once again and offers a framework for the inner dialogue that keeps our mindset restorative.

Relationships

When 'restorative justice' was first introduced to the UK there was, to my mind, an over-emphasis on process – even the definition of restorative justice most commonly adopted was about a process:

> Restorative justice is a process whereby all the parties with a stake in a particular offence come together to resolve collectively how to deal with the aftermath of the offence and its implications for the future. (Marshall 1998)

I believed that what was most significant about restorative justice was what it had to offer communities like schools and residential homes in terms of values, principles and skills and a new approach to the making, maintaining and repairing of relationships. My contribution to the field was a model that many people have found very useful in introducing a restorative approach into their community and which served as a basis for discussion amongst those exploring restorative justice as a philosophy and a way of engaging, rather than simply as a reactive process (Figure 2.1).

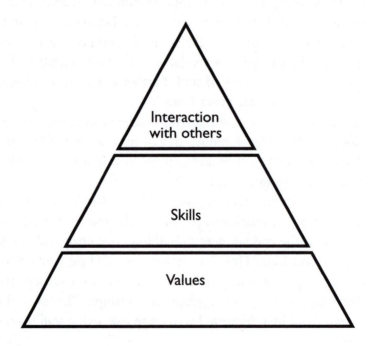

Figure 2.1 Relationships pyramid

Activity 1 describes how a team new to restorative approaches could begin to consider their current set of values and skills, how they contribute to the existing ethos in their team and in the residential home, and whether current practice in responding to conflict and challenge is using strategies that model and teach the values and principles subscribed to by the team.

ACTIVITY 2.1
LEARNING OBJECTIVES

- to identify the values that underpin a commitment to the making, maintaining and repairing of relationships
- to consider what is currently happening in participants' working environments, and to what extent these values and skills are in evidence and are being encouraged and developed
- to identify any lack of consistency
- to identify any training or development needs
- to illustrate the links between restorative approaches and existing strategies for developing attachment, resilience, emotional literacy and pro-social skills.

Begin by drawing Figure 2.1 on a large sheet of paper and suggesting that good relationships are at the heart of effective work with young people in care. People generally agree. The next part of the activity involves the group being asked a question by you, discussing it in pairs, and then a feedback in the round with one person from each pair sharing the fruits of their discussion. First draw another pyramid – but leave the sections blank for contributions (Figure 2.2).

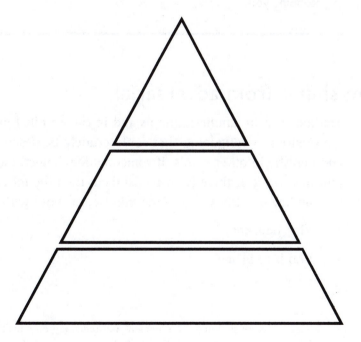

Figure 2.2 Relationships activity – values question

- **Question 1**: What are the values that underpin a commitment to making, maintaining and, when things go wrong, repairing relationships?

- Using a talking piece (see page 143), go round the circle inviting suggestions for key values that would be important. Write these in the bottom blank section of the pyramid.

- **Question 2**: If a visitor came to your residential home/school/house what would be the outward evidence that these values informed day-to-day activities?

- After a few minutes, using the talking piece, go round the circle inviting suggestions.

- **Question 3**: What skills need to be developed in a residential home/school/ foster family – amongst adults as well as young people – so that they are able to build, maintain and repair relationships?

- After a few minutes, using the talking piece, go round the circle inviting suggestions, and write these into the middle blank section of the pyramid.

- **Question 4**: What is currently happening doing to develop these skills (a) in the adults[7] and (b) in the young people? It may also be useful to think about whether such skill development could be offered to parents as well.

- After a few minutes, using the talking piece, go round the circle inviting suggestions, and write these on either side of the middle section of the pyramid.

- **Question 5**: When you deal with misbehaviour or conflict, is your response informed by the values we have discussed and are you using the same skills we have discussed? Look at Table 2.1 and after some private reflection discuss your answers with a partner.

- **Question 6**: If you were unable to answer 'yes' to every question, what was stopping you?

Paradigm shift – from adversarial...

Traditionally, in families, schools and in the criminal justice system there has been a response to wrongdoing that could crudely be described as 'name, blame, shame and punish'. In other words, if someone does something wrong, then they must be punished for it. If there is no punishment then the miscreant has 'got away with it'. Certain key questions inform the mindset of those with the power in such settings:

- What happened?

- Who is to blame?

---

7   It may be worth stopping for a moment and reflecting on which adults present had any training in relationship management, conflict resolution or dealing with challenging behaviour in their initial training – the chances are that very few have had such training.

Table 2.1 Checklist for responding to misbehaviour or conflict

When you deal with misbehaviour or conflict, is your response informed by the values we have discussed and are you using the same skills we have discussed?	
• Do you invite young people to give you their perspective?	yes/no
• Do you express sincere curiosity about their thoughts and feelings during the incident and since?	yes/no
• Do you ask them to think who else may have been affected or involved?	yes/no
• Do you encourage them to identify what needs to happen to put things right?	yes/no
• Do you invite them to think about what their own needs are for closure and repair?	yes/no
Do you manage to refrain from:	
• using your body or tone to threaten or show disapproval?	yes/no
• giving your own opinion about what has happened?	yes/no
• taking sides?	yes/no
• assuming you know what has happened?	yes/no
• telling people what to do?	yes/no
• offering unasked-for advice?	yes/no
• insisting people apologize and make up?	yes/no

- What is the appropriate response to deter and possibly punish those at fault, so that they will not do the same thing again?

The first question, *What happened?* is based on the belief that something factual happened, some essential 'truth', and that this can be discovered by interviewing or even interrogating whoever was involved or whoever witnessed the event. Words such as 'interview', 'interrogate' and 'witness' give away the origin of this approach – the criminal justice domain, requiring people to be detectives! In this approach discrepancies are viewed as suspicious, inconsistencies are considered proof of dishonesty and written testimonies acquire the status of evidence, often with priority given to statements given by those with higher age, rank or status.

The second question, *Who is to blame?* is informed by the belief that when something bad has happened there must be a culprit or culprits. 'Dealing with the situation' comprises first identifying this guilty person, or people, and laying at their feet the blame for what happened. The third question, *What is the appropriate response to deter and punish?* is based on the belief that accountability comprises being punished, and that punishment will deter both the miscreant and others from repeating the wrongdoing. This latter belief is adhered to despite evidence to the contrary. Sanctions and the threat of sanctions are rarely sufficient to deter further wrongdoing – a fact about which much more will be said.

These questions are deeply entrenched in thinking across the planet and can be seen in knee-jerk responses by one country's administration on another. If a less powerful country decides not to support its more powerful ally in a particular stance, then reprisals can be swift in the form of trade embargoes or withdrawal of diplomatic links. The same mindset is at play – 'You have behaved in ways we do not like so, as we are more powerful than you, we are going to make you suffer'.

It is a bullying mindset – an appalling example to give young people who are likely to be bringing up their own children. Indeed, this traditional approach to misbehaviour leads to absurd situations where, for example, young people who have bullied others are responded to by adults simply reproducing the bullying behaviour in their punitive response. No alternative model is provided to break the cycle of power and control. Behaviour 'management' policies are often developed in terms of how to react to undesirable behaviours, as opposed to how to develop and encourage desirable behaviours. (More will be said later about proactive behaviour policies and effective ways of addressing bullying.)

...to restorative

Restorative practitioners bring a different set of questions to bear on any situation of conflict or wrongdoing.

- What's happened?

- Who has been affected or harmed, and what do these people need in order to move on?

- How can everyone who has been affected be involved in repairing the harm and finding a way forward?

The first question, *What's happened?* looks deceptively similar to the first, traditional, question. However, its intention is very different because it is informed by the first and second restorative themes mentioned in Chapter 1:

1. everyone has their own unique story or perspective on any given situation

2. each of us interprets events in particular ways, and at any given moment our interpretation impacts on our emotional response.

So when we ponder to ourselves what is going on or what has happened, the curiosity is not around what may or may not actually have happened, if indeed this is even possible to ascertain, but what each individual person involved has *experienced*. To illustrate this shift in thinking, an activity like 'The Cloth' can be a light-hearted and yet thought-provoking way to encourage reflection amongst staff and residents.

ACTIVITY 2.2

ILLUSTRATING THEME 1: THE CLOTH

- Lay a large, interestingly patterned cloth haphazardly on the floor in the middle of the circle.

- Ask 'What do you see? I see...' (Demonstrate by giving an imaginative example to encourage creativity.)

- Go round the circle and invite people to say what they see. Some people may be more imaginative than others but it is important to welcome and value all responses, from 'I see a dragon/bird/monster/desert island' to 'A cloth on the floor'.

- After one round invite everyone to stand up and move round the circle about six places.

- Again the facilitator asks, 'What do you see? I see...' Invite people to say what they see this time, going round in turn as before.

- Finally ask 'Who was right?' and then 'What has this activity got to do with restorative practice?' and invite a brief discussion in pairs.

- Have a final go-round with each person sharing their ideas.

The second question, *Who has been affected or harmed, and what do these people need in order to move on?* constitutes a major shift in focus – from 'who is guilty' to who may have been harmed, and from appropriate sanctions to the needs that people have to feel better. This question links the third and fourth restorative themes, making a connection between unmet needs and the harm that these can cause. In any given situation, if people's needs go unmet, are ignored or indeed wilfully trampled on, they are likely to have experienced some kind of harm – within themselves or in relation to their connections with others.

There is a very thought-provoking activity which can help people understand that in any situation involving conflict or deliberate harm, both sides are affected and may need similar things as a result (Blood 2002). The activity can be a useful one for developing understanding about Themes 3 and 4.

ACTIVITY 2.3

ILLUSTRATING THEMES 3 AND 4: HARM AND NEED

- Invite people to think of a time when they were harmed by someone else – and define harm in terms of emotional, mental or physical harm – so feeling hurt, offended, insulted, threatened, let down, attacked, left out – these would all be included.

- Invite people to work in pairs and share what they personally need when harmed in this way.

- Invite contributions in the round and write these on a single flipchart entitled 'What do I need when I have been harmed?'

- Cover this sheet and then explain that at times we also, inadvertently or sometimes on purpose, cause others harm. What do we need then?

- Invite people to work in pairs and share what they personally need when they have harmed others.

- Invite contributions in the round and write these on a new piece of flipchart entitled 'What do I need when I have caused harm?'

- Reveal the previous sheet and invite comparisons. Inevitably there will be much similarity.

- Make the point that this activity alone can help people to understand that when people are in conflict (when both sides feel harmed themselves and blame the other for causing it), or when there is a clear-cut case of harm with at least one person feeling harmed, the needs are similar on both sides – and yet so often neither side's needs are properly addressed. It is not for nothing that in the criminal justice field the case for restorative justice is made as much for the benefit of victims as of offenders, because victims benefit so much from a chance to have all the needs identified in this activity met.

Table 2.2 records the most common answers I and my team have received over many years of doing this activity with participants on our training courses.

Table 2.2 Needs when harm has been caused

What do I need when I've been harmed?	What do I need when I've harmed someone else?
• an apology	• to apologize
• an empathetic listener	• someone to talk to
• amends made	• time to put things right
• the other person to understand what has upset me	• to make it up to them
• to be respected	• a chance to explain to the other person and myself
• to be allowed to have emotion	• to feel better about it and about myself
• support and positive reinforcement	• to be forgiven
• reassurance it won't happen again	• to reassure them and myself that it won't happen again
• to draw a line underneath it.	• to get back on friendly terms.

More traditional, punitive, approaches to wrongdoing rarely create a situation where the needs expressed above can be met. When a young person behaves in a way that is challenging for a member of staff, for example, there is likely to be harm experienced on both sides unless both people feel heard and understood. There is a possibility that the relationship between the two will be adversely affected, and this will affect the way they work together in the future. The key to making progress is the realization that all those involved are likely to have similar needs and to use this as the basis for moving forward. How to do this will be explored in later chapters, but the restorative mindset is one that focuses on this notion – putting things right by identifying the unmet needs of all those involved, as far as possible.

The third question, *How can everyone who has been affected be involved in repairing the harm and finding a way forward?* encapsulates the fifth restorative theme, and both paradigm shifts: defining accountability in terms of putting things right, rather than punishing and being punished, and empowering those involved to decide how this should be done, rather than imposing a solution.

Power over, power with

Everyone has a distinct and unique perspective on life, and in order to feel valued people need the experience of having their perspective heard and respected. This key restorative theme is not, of course, the preserve of restorative justice. It underpins human rights and equal opportunities legislation, libertarian humanistic psychology, democracy and social justice. Despite this it would seem that the right of *young* people in particular to be heard, and to be taken seriously, continues to need legislating for and campaigning for. It was only in 1992 that the United Nations Convention on the Rights of the Child came into force in the UK.

Article 12 of the Convention states:

> Children have the right to say what they think should happen, when adults are making decisions that affect them, and to have their opinions taken into account.

UNICEF UK has felt the need to point out that this Article (amongst others) is one which impacts on all five strands of the *Every Child Matters* agenda (Department for Education and Skills 2003) – being healthy; staying safe; enjoying and achieving; making a positive contribution and achieving economic well-being. Policy documents like 'Youth Matters' (Department for Education and Skills 2006c) and 'Care Matters' (Department for Education and Skills, 2006a) stress the importance of taking the views of young people into consideration. In the autumn of 2008 Communities Minister Hazel Blears appointed Youth Advisors in order that the voice of young people could be heard more on community matters.

In other words, the need to remind people of the importance of the perspective of young people remains an issue in our society. There is often a discrepancy between young people's right, and indeed need, to be heard, as expressed in legislation and policy, and their experience of day-to-day reality. Not for nothing are there charities set up explicitly to give young people a voice – 'Voice' for example, a charity specifically for young people in public care.[8]

Giving young people a voice does not mean, however, that their voice then becomes the dominant one. The significance of a restorative approach is that it creates opportunities for everyone in a residential community to feel heard. It is not a charter prioritizing the views, needs or even demands of one age group over another, and this is particularly important at the very outset of introducing a restorative approach, when defining guidelines for how to behave.

Who makes the rules? Who solves the problems?

Adults living and working with children and young people – whether as natural or as corporate parents, or in a variety of professional capacities, such as teachers or social workers – are constantly balancing the need to create safety, boundaries and some degree of control and discipline, with the child's need for care and nurture, love and support. Too much imposition of boundaries and rules means that young people do not feel listened to and respected, and they may be inclined to resist and ignore the rules. Over-protection and 'mollycoddling' can be just as disempowering and disrespectful, and lack of rules, structures and accountability can be dangerous and confusing. The true balance of structure and care involves respecting each young person's point of view and inviting each to consider what they need in order to feel happy and safe in what is, in effect, their own home.[9] This balance of structure with care is illustrated by a model adapted from an original developed by Wachtel and McCold (2001).

They posit two axes on their grid, with control, discipline and boundary-setting on the vertical axis, and care, support and nurture along the horizontal axis (Figure 2.3).

Environments exercising high levels of control and discipline but with little attention to care, support and nurture they characterize as *punitive*, *authoritarian* and *stigmatizing* (Figure 2.4).

---

8   www.voiceyp.org

9   This proactive side of restorative approaches, and the use of circles for decision-making is discussed in greater details in Chapter 8.

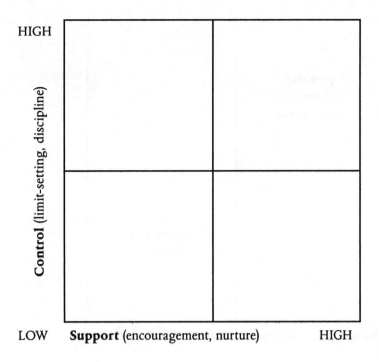

Figure 2.3 Social discipline window (adapted from Wachtel and McCold [2001])

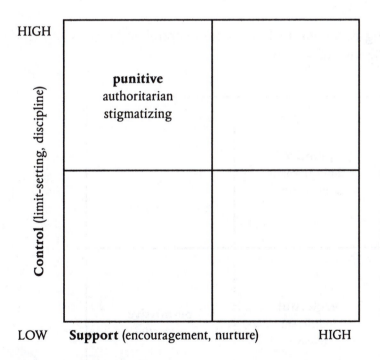

Figure 2.4 Social discipline punitive window (adapted from Wachtel and McCold [2001])

Environments exercising high levels of support and nurture but with few boundaries and little control they characterize as *permissive* and *protective* (Figure 2.5).

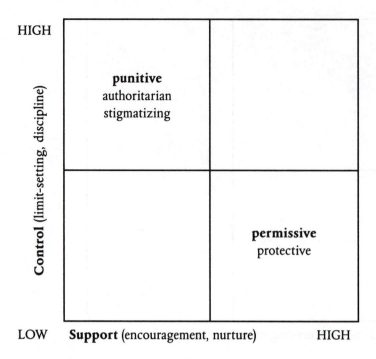

Figure 2.5 Social discipline permissive window (adapted from Wachtel and McCold [2001])

Dismissing environments low on both control and care as *neglectful, indifferent* and *passive* (Figure 2.6) –

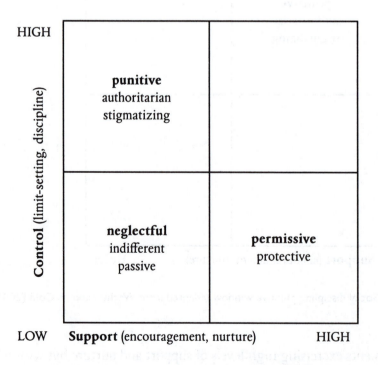

Figure 2.6 Social discipline neglectful window (adapted from Wachtel and McCold [2001])

they turn to their 'middle way' – working with people, in a *restorative, respectful, inclusive* way (Figure 2.7).

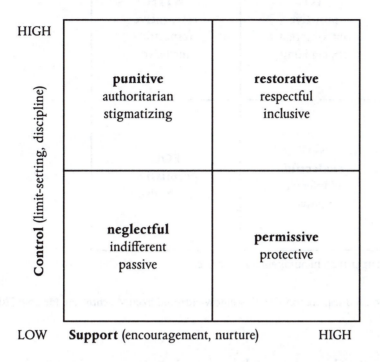

Figure 2.7 Social discipline restorative window (adapted from Wachtel and McCold [2001])

In this 'window' they make the case for an approach that is high on boundary-setting and control but also high on support and nurture. Wachtel and McCold pay tribute to the inspiration behind their elaboration of this model, with reference to commentators and researchers in the field of organizational management and related fields, who use variations of the window to come down in favour of collaborative problem-solving. They then adapt their model, concluding that the authoritarian approach means doing things *to* people, the permissive, over-protective approach means doing things *for* people, the neglectful approach means *not* doing anything at all, whilst the restorative approach means doing things *with* people (Figure 2.8).

Psychologist Claire Cruse has found this model useful in preparing guidelines for residential child care staff in the Derby area:

> As good corporate parents we try to give our children and young people a balance of care, support and nurture with control, discipline and boundary-setting. We aim to get this balance right so that our children and young people are able to make a positive contribution within our home, school and the local community.

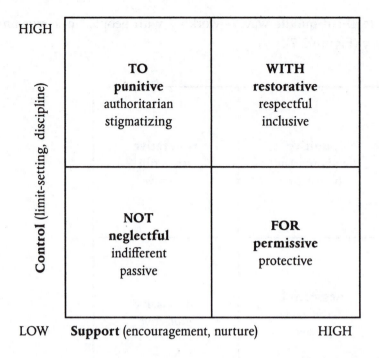

Figure 2.8 Social discipline to/for/with window (adapted from Wachtel and McCold [2001])

The risks of a sanction-based behaviour management system

Many people equate the word 'justice' with the administering of a punishment, and in residential child care contexts a similar expectation prevails, or is believed to prevail. The logic is that if somebody does a bad thing, then a bad thing needs to be done to them. In a sense this is the 'eye for an eye, tooth for a tooth' philosophy, but of course this lesson taught to children by adults can lead to behaviours in care settings and in the community that mimic this approach, which is based on revenge. Arguments between two people can become fights, fights can draw in others and become gang warfare, gang hostility can ignite inter-family and inter-community tensions and in some places in the world terrorism, civil wars, international conflicts and genocide can ensue. We cannot afford to disconnect how we deal with conflict and wrongdoing in schools and at home from the processes used at a local, national and international level. A restorative approach, coupled with interpersonal conflict resolution training, can offer an alternative that may influence the way young people deal with conflicts in later life.

Some people fear that if wrongdoing goes unpunished, then it is likely to be repeated by the offender and others because the wrongdoer has 'got away with it'. Many people argue that there must be a consequence for bad behaviour, and that this threat of punishment ensures compliance. This belief is one of the most dangerous because it can breed selfishness and deceit and possibly achieve the very opposite effect of that intended by the punisher. When a young person is warned that if they do something bad, then unpleasant things will happen to them, then they are being encouraged to think about the impact of their deeds not on others, but on themselves (Figure 2.9).

Figure 2.9 The traditional school of consequences: the threat

This encourages them to think only of themselves, and in fact discourages them to think 'outside' of their own box (Figure 2.10), training them, in effect, to be self-centred and cold-hearted.

Figure 2.10 The traditional school of consequences: encouraging self-centredness

Furthermore, they know that the consequences to themselves will happen only if they get caught, so the obvious strategy is to escape detection through subterfuge and deceit (Figure 2.11).

Figure 2.11 The traditional school of consequences: encouraging deceit

No intelligent person keen to save their skin would admit to wrongdoing if they knew it would lead to punishment. In such an environment any bystanders who report wrongdoing are likely to be branded as 'tell-tales' (or whatever the current or local equivalent term is) and may be ostracized or worse. This 'traditional school of consequences' fails to encourage empathy and compassion for others or develop the link between an action and its impact. It is surely important to encourage people to appreciate that the inevitable consequence of antisocial, thoughtless or unkind behaviour is the negative impact it has, or may have, on others, regardless of whether one is found out or not (Figure 2.12).

Figure 2.12 The restorative school of consequences: encouraging empathy, responsibility and accountability

A restorative response, with its focus not on blame, punishment and alienation but on repair and reconnection, encourages a wrongdoer to take responsibility for the harm they have caused, and gives them an opportunity to repair the harm. Empathy is developed, accountability is encouraged and the outcome can help both wronged and wrongdoer feel better about themselves and the other person.

To my mind having to face up to the impact of one's actions on other people is what true accountability is about – punishment does not usually do this, and as such lets people 'get away' with their wrongdoing, possibly without learning lessons for the future – except to avoid getting caught next time.

In a restorative environment the willingness to be accountable for the impact of one's actions on others is also something that all staff must be willing to model – acknowledging when they make mistakes or cause harm by things they have said or done.

Other key influences shaping the restorative mindset

The link between thoughts and feelings

I first came across the idea that our thinking influences our emotions and that these in turn influence the choices we make in terms of behaviour when I was learning about Protective Behaviours[10] – a highly influential training approach to child safety first introduced into the UK by Australian Di Margetts. I have subsequently learnt more about this notion from my reading about cognitive behavioural therapy, solution-focused approaches and pro-social modelling. I am also aware that recent research into the way the brain works suggests that in fact it is far too simplistic to suggest that thinking always precedes and influences emotions. However, I am not a psychologist, and recognize that there is more to learn and to write about the relationship between all of these approaches, recent understanding about the brain and restorative approaches. Suffice it to say that for pragmatic reasons, based on sound experience and practice, it seems to be useful to encourage people to reflect on their interpretations of a given situation in order to help them understand the degree to which, as a result, they have power and control over these interpretations and their responses, both emotional and behavioural. Cognitive behavioural therapy, solution-focused approaches and pro-social modelling are already widespread practices amongst those working with offenders and with young people engaged in antisocial and disruptive behaviour which may not (yet) fall into the bracket of offending. They are likely to be familiar approaches for care staff, but people will vary in the degree to which they are consciously able to use this awareness in day-to-day interactions.

The additional element for a restorative approach is to provide a mechanism whereby people are invited not only to reflect on their own thoughts, feelings and behaviour but to listen to and understand others' thoughts, feelings and behaviour

---

10　www.protectivebehaviours.co.uk

during a shared incident or time frame. The behaviours of others can be depicted as the tip of an iceberg – what we see or hear (Figure 2.13).

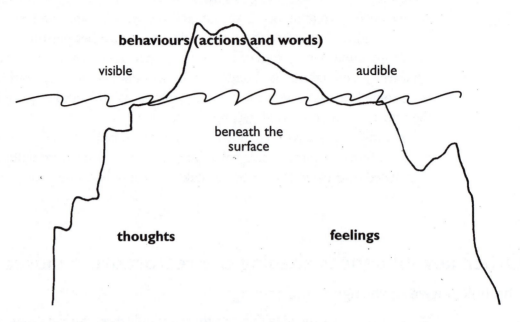

Figure 2.13 Cognitive-behavioural iceberg

The restorative practitioner is mindful not only that whatever is visible and audible is only part of the picture, but that it is likely that this is the information on which most people will be working, and to which they will be responding. Someone with a restorative mindset knows that they may have a role in encouraging people to take time to listen to what is going on beneath the surface, and this is likely to affect the way they themselves respond in such circumstances.

Actively working with these connections in oneself as well as with those around us seems to me to be a crucial part of what I am calling the 'restorative mindset'. In some quarters this would be called 'mindfulness' – staying in touch with what is going on inside. More will be said about this in Chapter 4.

Focusing on needs

The writing and thinking of Marshall Rosenberg has played an important role in forming my construct of the restorative mindset. He has developed a way of thinking and interacting called 'non-violent communication' – which emphasizes the links between our feelings and our needs (Rosenberg 1999). He asserts that in an ideal world human beings seek to meet not only their own needs, but the needs of those around them with whom they interact and whom they care about. It is only when people believe that their own needs and feelings are being ignored that they become less willing to address the needs of others. This is likely to have been the case for many young people in care, but it would be tragic if we assumed that their past experiences prevented them from learning how to care and how to consider others' needs. The starting point, however, is realizing that there are people who care about *them*, and who consider *their* needs. This realisation may pose particular problems for the many young people in public care suffering from attachment difficulties. The restorative framework offers a consistent way for adults to model empathy and respect for people's needs, and as such can begin provide the language and concepts that those with attachment difficulties lack.

Rosenberg has helped me to understand the difference between a need and a demand – a distinction which is crucial when attempting to encourage people to listen to each other and repair any harm that has happened. More will be said about this in subsequent chapters when practice is explained and developed.

The restorative mindset and the inner dialogue

The five restorative themes provide what can become an ongoing internal dialogue, whether in regard to the present or in relation to an incident being related about the past (Table 2.3).

Table 2.3 A restorative inner dialogue

Theme 1	What am I seeing here?…I wonder how others see what I am seeing…
Theme 2a	What interpretations am I making of this? I wonder what is going on in the minds of others here right now?
Theme 2b	What feelings are coming up for me as a result of my interpretations? And what about others here?
Theme 3	How am I being affected? Who else is being affected or even harmed by what is happening here?
Theme 4	What do I need at this moment? And others here? What needs are being expressed, albeit maybe in terms of accusations, insults or demands?
Theme 5	How can those involved become accountable and take responsibility for putting things right? Is it appropriate for me to play an equal role in finding a way forward here, or is it my role to support others here to find a way forward for themselves?

The questions flowing from Theme 5 in Table 2.3 will be returned to in Chapters 3 and 4 as it raises interesting questions about neutrality and/or impartiality about restorative practice, on the part of care staff working in such close proximity to their colleagues and the young residents.

Practical applications of the restorative mindset

Staff in residential homes, units and schools, and foster parents, need a range of flexible strategies for dealing with the day-to-day conflicts and challenges of living and working with young people 24/7. Potentially challenging situations are numerous but include welcoming young people or new staff into the setting; meeting with family members; preparation for, and returning from visits; setting the group rules; getting out of bed in the morning; going to bed at night; behaviour at school; mealtimes and in-between snacks; rules around access and behaviour in the kitchen; television times and what to watch; access to telephones and private calls; conflict with other children in the home, with other 'local' children, and between children and staff; activity negotiation; wanting to go out without staff; control of/access to money, clothes, etc.; behaviour in transport/on journeys; when something in the home has been broken; when there is an accusation of theft; attempted at self-harm; use of drugs and/or alcohol.

In all of these situations the young people will learn from the way in which they see adults handle the situation. The behaviour of the adults will teach the young people key lessons in life for when they are faced with challenging situations – in work settings, socially with friends, and as parents themselves. All of these situations are examples of social pedagogy and pro-social modelling in action – where staff can model, and young people can learn, appropriate social skills and appropriate language in each situation.

Sharing a restorative mindset in relation to all of these situations will enable staff to think in a consistent way about each one, and the following chapters will provide the framework for acting consistently as well.

Conclusion

In order to draw together the strands of this chapter I want to characterize the restorative mindset as one of remaining curious and compassionate, empathic and respectful, but still fair and firm. It is one that has high expectations of people – in that everyone is expected to be accountable for their actions and to take responsibility for putting things right when they go wrong. Above all it is a mindset of trust in the essential goodness of people and their ability to do the right thing *when their own needs are also being met.* Young people in care need this unconditional trust and belief and need to be allowed to make mistakes time and again, because they are likely to have lived lives where their own needs have rarely, if ever, been met. This does not mean being allowed to get away with *any* harmful action; in fact, it is zero tolerance under another guise. But it does mean knowing that after any, and every, mistake there will be a chance to make amends and move on – and that the unconditional acceptance – and even love – of who they are does not stop.

Chapter 3

Restorative Enquiry – Asking the Right Questions

Introduction

This chapter is about restorative language and how the five restorative themes inform not only what we say, but also how we say it, when interacting with other people. It focuses on one type of exchange involving two people which I have called 'restorative enquiry' (Hopkins 2004). Restorative enquiry – the art of asking questions informed by the five restorative themes – informs many of the restorative interactions described in this book. It can provide a framework for:

- day-to-day discussions and negotiations with residents and staff when making decisions and plans

- one-to-one counselling strategy simply to help someone to get something off their chest and move forward

- residents' meetings

- preparation before face-to-face meetings to resolve conflicts or repair harm

- meetings and discussions to ensure all sides feel heard

- record-keeping, ensuring that paperwork reflects the restorative approach as well as hands-on practice.

The chapter begins by explaining the difference between restorative enquiry and restorative dialogue, an explanation which begins to address issues such as impartiality and rank (differentials in power and status) in residential settings. It then acknowledges and anticipates some of the reactions of readers new to this approach and makes a plea for open-mindedness.

The main part of the chapter recapitulates the five key restorative themes and suggests some essential questions informed by these themes. These questions, asked in a particular sequence, comprise what I call 'restorative enquiry'. The chapter offers several versions of restorative enquiry for different circumstances. The brief version can be adapted for spontaneous interactions throughout the day. The longer version is more appropriate when an incident or issue needs more time or someone needs a listening ear.

Restorative enquiry and restorative dialogue

Restorative enquiry differs from what I call a 'restorative dialogue'. The former can be used by someone initiating a restorative exchange when they themselves may not have been directly affected by what has happened. This enquiry mode differs from a restorative dialogue which is used for interpersonal conflict resolution and for achieving mutual understanding, and this will be the focus of Chapter 4.

I believe it is important to distinguish between restorative enquiry and restorative dialogue for various reasons. In the former there are issues of rank (or status) and impartiality. The latter is an attempt to give more equal rank and allows for vulnerability and even accountability on both sides. The implicit assumption when using restorative enquiry is that the enquirer has played no active role in what has happened – the enquirer is assuming the role of the facilitator, the one who asks the questions, and the person responding, however respectful the enquirer, has less power in the exchange. Furthermore the nature of the enquiry is such that the questioner remains detached, not sharing their own thoughts and feelings whilst encouraging disclosure from the person being questioned.

Much is made of the importance of impartiality when facilitating a restorative enquiry or a restorative meeting. It is argued that to facilitate a restorative meeting between two people in conflict, and to prepare for such a meeting by using restorative enquiry with each separately first, the facilitator must not be seen to take sides. However, some people would assert that in a close-knit community such as a residential home it is likely that the facilitator will also be affected by what has happened. So the issue is not whether the facilitator is taking sides, but whether in fact they have a side too – their own – and whether *not* to declare this would be inauthentic.

Of course, for foster parents it is even more challenging to consider whether taking the role of neutral facilitator or impartial listener is appropriate. In my experience as a parent I have found, mediating the conflicts between my two daughters (which I have done for over 15 years, since they were four and six respectively), that there were times when I was able to provide an impartial listening ear and there were times when I was not. My challenge was to realize when either was the case and to be aware of any bias in my own response that was likely to compromise my ability to facilitate.

A plea for open-mindedness

As the previous chapter has explained, being restorative involves a change of mindset – and of course this then influences what we say, and how we say it. Our interactions with others may begin to change – not only at challenging moments, but at every moment. We may find ourselves listening in a different way and responding in a different way. I say 'may' because many people, on discovering more about restorative justice and restorative approaches, realize that they have been using this way of communicating with people already but have not given it a name. They often welcome the framework, and indeed validation, to continue to act in ways that at times challenge mainstream thinking. Others recognize similarities between restorative communication and other approaches they may use or have used – solution-focused approaches (De Shazer 1988), life space interviewing (Redl 1966), pro-social modelling (Cherry 2005) and strategies for developing resilience and attachment (Gilligan 2000, Golding 2008). My plea to you would be to keep an open mind and be willing to look at what is similar about tried and tested strategies you use already and how restorative communication may differ, and perhaps add it to your approach.

There will be yet others for whom thinking and interacting restoratively amounts to that 'paradigm shift' I mentioned. I have talked with enough of these people to know that the 'penny dropping' or the 'lightbulb going on' can be amazing and exciting, but also upsetting – because this realization brings a feeling of regret and even guilt for missed opportunities in the past. 'If only I'd used this approach when my own children were young' is a not uncommon response, or even 'Oh, my God, I've been getting it wrong all these years'.

For those of you who may be tempted to beat yourselves up on reading the next few chapters, I am absolutely sure that you have always done the best you could possibly have done at the time – if you are like me you have never had training in how to be a good parent, corporate or otherwise. I never had training as a teacher in how to manage conflict and anger – my own anger, as well as that of the young people in my care. I was never given any way of encouraging and persuading young people to co-operate other than bribes and threats – and I used to use both of these when my own children were young and when I first started teaching. So – as Stuart Macneillie (the Thames Valley Police officer who first introduced me to restorative justice conferencing back in 1994) used to say – 'Cut yourself a bit of slack'!!

Key restorative themes and questions

Restorative enquiry is underpinned by the core values of restorative justice which, as Chapter 2 suggested, are essentially the values that underpin a commitment to relationships. It is based on the five key restorative themes, themselves in turn informed by certain theories or beliefs.[11] Here are these themes once again:

---

11 Thanks to Caroline Newton and Luke Roberts for giving me some clarity over these key themes.

- **Theme 1**: Unique perspectives

- **Theme 2**: Linking thoughts, feelings and behaviour

- **Theme 3**: Harm, effect, affect and repair

- **Theme 4**: Needs

- **Theme 5**: Accountability; empowerment; collaborative problem-solving.

It can be useful to think of these themes as the various juggling balls one has to remember to keep in the air at all times. In training I introduce the five themes and related skills one at a time, so that people can gradually build up the whole model in stages.

Juggling all five balls of restorative enquiry can actually be very simple once the themes, the skills and the language that goes with them have been internalized. It can be used with anyone – regardless of whether they are suspected of being in the wrong or not, and regardless of their age or status. I am baffled by some models of restorative practice that offer a different set of questions for the so-called 'offender' or 'wrongdoer' and the so-called 'victim'. Apart from the point that I would never apply such labels to young people anyway, there is the simple and rather obvious point that it is rarely clear in the first instance what has happened, especially in educational, residential or domestic settings. Even if we have witnessed with our own eyes an apparently clear-cut case of A hitting B, for example, we do not know what B may have said five minutes beforehand that inflamed or upset A, and so to assume guilt and then use one set of questions to A and another to B could already be escalating the situation and taking sides.

Restorative enquiry – the short version

In a nutshell the five themes give us five key questions (if we think of the second one being in two halves). Table 3.1 illustrates how these questions might look in referring to an incident of a minor nature that has just occurred. Using the dice metaphor, Figure 3.1 may be more useful for some people.

This set of questions is not a script, nor are all five questions necessarily relevant in every intervention or every conversation. Apart from anything else it is possible to engage in restorative enquiry simply to encourage or persuade a young person – or a staff member – to do something.

I am aware that residential staff and foster parents are constantly encouraging, cajoling, persuading and sometimes even telling young people what to do. They will have lots of tried and tested strategies based on what works with each individual young person. Indeed, it is the relationship with each individual that is the key in every case. I do not want to patronize extremely experienced staff or suggest that what has worked in the past needs to be changed. Developing restorative skills does not mean throwing the baby out with the bath water.

Table 3.1 The five key restorative questions

Theme	Question
1. Unique perspectives	What happened?
2. Linking thoughts, feelings and behaviour	What were you thinking? And so how were you feeling?
3. Harm, effect, affect and repair	Who has been affected by what has happened?
4. Needs	What do you need for the harm to be repaired so you can move forward?
5. Accountability; empowerment; collaborative problem-solving	So what needs to happen now? (*If appropriate*: 'and what can you do?')

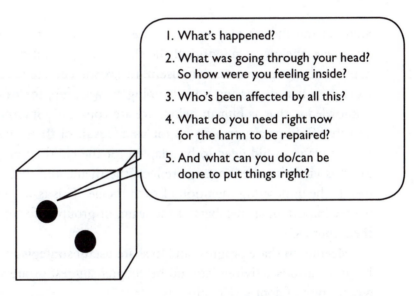

Figure 3.1 Restorative enquiry

However, what it does mean is checking that the tried and tested strategies fit with the restorative ethos of mutual respect, inclusiveness and accountability, and maybe the best people to let you know are the young people themselves. Once they know that people are trying a slightly new approach they could be asked for feedback every now and again. Having a checklist would also be a way of encouraging them to use similar techniques with each other – so that there is a sense in the residential home, unit or school (or at home, in fostering situations) of you all learning together.

Table 3.2 illustrates how the themes might inform questions for on-the-spot problem-solving.

Table 3.2 Restorative problem-solving one-to-one

Theme	Question
1. Unique perspectives	OK – we need to do X soon. What do you suggest we do, and how?
2. Linking thoughts, feelings and behaviour	So what's up for you right now? What are you thinking? How are you feeling? What if you thought of it this way…?
3. Harm, effect, affect and repair	Who's likely to be affected if we do it that way?
4. Needs	What do you need right now? What need of yours would be met if we did it the way you suggest? Is there another way that need could be met?
5. Accountability; empowerment; collaborative problem-solving	So what needs to happen now? (*If appropriate*: 'and what could you do?')

Some of the themes may not need a question in every exchange, but the speaker must nevertheless be mindful of the theme in their interaction. So, for example, it may not always be necessary or useful to ask someone to vocalize their thoughts and feelings (when discussing who is going to wash up, for example!) but we can still acknowledge that as human beings we are constantly interpreting what is going on and that feelings are coming up for us as result of these interpretations. Of course the language would need to be adapted for the children or young people involved, but it is vital that the language reflects the theme and that the adaptation does not distort the underlying intention of each theme. This is where ongoing staff support is very important as members of the team, or group of foster parents, begin to adapt their approach.

Meeting to share progress and to share useful strategies and phrasing can be very helpful. Various activities later in the chapter suggest group activities for developing a repertoire of appropriate phrases.

Theme 1(a): Ask, don't tell

How do you encourage young people to think for themselves on a day-to-day basis? How many decisions do you inadvertently take for them? For an easy life, how many conflicts do you head off at the pass by foreseeing the problems and sorting them first? How about anticipating problems with the young people and asking for their suggestions? Or even – heaven forbid – building in potential conflict and then encouraging people to sort it out for themselves fairly? Or even letting them make mistakes and then think about what went wrong and how they could do things differently next time? (Since this is a potentially inflammatory activity it needs to be tried on a relatively calm day, or with some warning, so that it can be treated as a game.)

ACTIVITY 3.1

- At tea-time provide a plate of cakes with the number of cakes being one or two less than the number of young people present. (Variants would be biscuits, slices of one cake or pie, fruit, etc.)

- Before – or after, once they get better at this – everyone reaches for a cake, discuss how the potentially unfair situation could be resolved to everyone's satisfaction.

- Use language of thoughts, feelings and needs so that it becomes commonplace.

- The quick version, with a possible illustration of the cake scenario in Figure 3.2, has proved surprisingly successful to de-escalate minor issues and conflicts in school and domestic settings.

Figure 3.2 Restorative enquiry – a simple example

However, there is more than meets the eye to each of the questions and I know from experience that unless people have had time to practise and reflect on the more in-depth version of restorative enquiry, as described later in this chapter, and unless they have also taken on the restorative mindset described in Chapter 2, there are pitfalls in the short version. Some schools and residential homes like to issue all staff with a credit-card-sized aide memoire with the key questions on it. My advice would be to ensure that only those with sufficient training hold such a card, or a generic cartoon version such as Figure 3.3.

Figure 3.3 Restorative enquiry – an aide memoire
*This question might be inappropriate if you are certain that the person you are talking to is on the receiving end of unprovoked harm – although it could help them to think of ways of developing coping strategies.

The coaching tip below illustrates how even the first question can go badly wrong if not phrased appropriately.

Coaching tips

'*What happened?*' or '*What's happening here?*' signals genuine curiosity. Try to avoid phrases that suggest blame or invite an antagonistic response, such as:

- 'What are you two up to?'

- 'What's been going on?'

- 'Oh no, not you two again!'

- 'Why did you do that?'

A rule of thumb might be: how would you respond if someone used these responses with you, if you found yourself in a conflict with a colleague or were caught doing something generally frowned on or considered inappropriate? Some people like to precede the question with a comment about what they are seeing or hearing: 'I'm hearing angry voices – what's happened?' or 'I can see two angry faces – what's up?'

The 'why' question is a particularly challenging one and more will be said about how to get round this later in the chapter. For now – how would it be if the 'why' word was banished from staff vocabulary in challenging situations?

Be very careful to avoid:

- taking sides

- expressing disapproval

- sighing with impatience

- making assumptions

- wading in with demands or reprimands.

By observing all these guidelines you are modelling respect for those involved and essentially saying 'I do not know what is going on here, and I appreciate that you will both have a different take on it, which I am interested to hear.'

Of course there are alternatives, depending on the situation, the age of the people involved and whether the question is being asked in the heat of an incident or some time later:

- 'What's up?'

- 'What's going on?'

- 'How do/did you see things?'

- 'Please tell me your side of the story.'

ACTIVITY 3.2
PRACTISING INITIAL RESPONSES TO MINOR INCIDENTS

- Invite staff to consider day-to-day occurrences involving potentially difficult situations, either between themselves and one young person, or between two young people or within a small group (resistance to getting up or going to bed; unwillingness to do chores; unhelpful behaviour at mealtimes; unfavourable report from school about behaviour that day, etc., etc.)[12]

- Discuss what works best in terms of phrasing, delivery and body language.

- Ensure that strategies shared meet the 'restorative test' – are we asking or telling? Are we working with them, encouraging them to take responsibility for coming up with options, as opposed to imposing a solution or 'rescuing' them?

- Invite people to work in groups of two or three and take it in turns to role-play one, two, or more young people and a member of staff (see footnote).

- Suggest the 'young people' start an argument, or have one person do something potentially antisocial or harmful, and then have the adult intervene using a variety of different 'starter phrases' and 'opening questions'.

---

12 It might be useful for training purposes to invite staff ahead of time to identify challenging situations of a day-to-day nature and write these on individual cards – you could have a selection of staff–young person situations and some involving two young people and even groups of young people. Practise each type of intervention separately, and share best practice.

- Keep the activity short and focused – as soon as the 'adult' has used their 'starter phrase or question' suggest the 'young people' give them feedback about whether the wording and the body language, tone, volume and pacing made them more or less likely to calm down, respond and be willing to engage in further conversation.

- Many staff will already be using these kinds of open questions, and it may be worth discussing what can sometimes get in the way of consistently using this non-judgemental approach.

Restorative enquiry – longer version

There are times when staff will be intervening in more serious incidents. Many residential care staff will have had restraint and de-escalation training and will know that sometimes tempers will be too high to be able to engage in rational thought or conversation. The understanding about how human brains work when people are angry is vital in such circumstances. Responding to someone who is 'beside themself', literally unable to think rationally owing to the amygdala, our 'fight and flight' mechanism, having been activated, takes patience, empathy and a fair degree of skill. I must emphasize that restorative enquiry depends on people being able to respond with a fair degree of rationality. People may need time to calm down before engaging.

Having said all this, the way in which staff intervene in the heat of an incident and use their restraint or de-escalation skills will also set the tone for the restorative steps taken later. If young people have picked up messages of disapproval or disappointment, experienced side-taking, or felt disrespected, even in their anger, they will be less likely to engage when they have calmed down.

Of course, even when they have calmed down, the people questioned may be reluctant to reply for a variety of reasons:

- fear of repercussions

- strong emotions still bubbling below the surface

- lack of articulacy

- confusion over what did actually happen

- embarrassment

- needing to save face.

What follows is a series of activities to help people develop their restorative enquiry skills following a more serious incident when people have had time to calm down. (These activities may be familiar to staff who have had training in counselling, life-story techniques and solution-focused questioning and I encourage such staff to identify where these approaches complement each other, and where they differ.) I shall link each stage of restorative enquiry to a key restorative theme.

Theme 1(b): Developing skills to encourage people to share their experience and perspective

It can be helpful to think of the listener's role as that of encouraging a storyteller to tell their story. The intention should be to enable the speaker to recount their experience and to clarify in their own mind what has happened, first as a sequence of events. It may be useful for the listener to think of themselves as helping the speaker to construct what is known as a 'storyboard' – almost like a cartoon or film sequence of events in their heads.

Most people already use a lot of these short interjections, nonverbal gestures and even little 'noises' to encourage people to open up and say more. These are called 'minimal encouragers'. Minimal encouragers include brief verbal prompts, all with a rising, encouraging intonation. The wrong intonation – threatening, disapproving, surprised – can all close someone down. The accompanying body language and facial expressions, open and non-threatening, are also important. Rosenberg (1999) has a great phrase:

'Words can be windows or walls.'

I would like to add that this is also the case for our nonverbal communication – it can help keep the window open or bring down the wall.

ACTIVITY 3.3

Key skill: Minimal encouragers

- Invite people to think of minimal encouragers they already use and write them on some flipchart paper for all to see and to refer to, including verbal and nonverbal examples, e.g:
  - 'Mmm-mm?'
  - 'Go on?'
  - 'Tell me more?'
  - 'And then?'
  - 'Uh-huh?'
  - 'What happened then?'
  - nodding
  - encouraging hand gesture
  - silence whilst smiling slightly.
- In pairs, suggest that one person describes their first day in a new job to their partner, who responds only with the minimal encouragers that are on the flipchart paper.
- After a few minutes re-convene as a group and share the experience – maybe swap over and try again.
- Reflect on the temptation to say more than is on the flipchart. As the person facilitating this activity becomes more familiar with the whole restorative

enquiry framework they will be able to help staff recognise that they have only been given one part of one ball to juggle for this activity (to use the earlier juggler metaphor). Some other balls will come in later. Some things people want to say are not part of restorative enquiry at all – and in time they will develop what I call 'restorative antennae' for unrestorative language.

• Figure 3.4 may help to illustrate the idea of a cartoon unfolding.

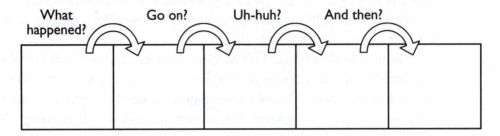

Figure 3.4 Minimal encouragers

Sometimes, in training, people suggest words they have used as encouragers, that to my mind come with a risk – words like 'OK', 'right', 'I see' and 'I understand'. The restorative listener must at all times be perceived as impartial[13] and these examples might suggest a degree of support for what is being heard. There is skill in listening to someone's perspective on their experience with empathy and yet without implying that you are on their side, or approve of what they are saying.

If as a listener you are not getting a clear picture of what has actually happened in each frame, then slow down the questions, and ask for more clarity. This requires another technique called 'echoing' – picking up on the speaker's last phrase or word, rather like an echo, and encouraging further elaboration or clarity. This is a technique that can be very useful in helping a speaker clarify their story whilst also encouraging reflection on some of their own interpretations. It can help the listener gain some clarity if the speaker rushes a bit of the story (maybe wanting to avoid certain bits perhaps, or being muddled themselves) and those 'frames' of the carton become rather unclear. Judgemental or exaggerated descriptions of behaviours can similarly be separated into the description, and the interpretation of those behaviours, in ways that do not threaten the speaker but help them to see the difference, and maybe even re-consider their interpretation. The success of the echo however lies in the ability of the listener to remain genuinely curious and never to imply that the speaker's perspective is inappropriate or erroneous.

The 'echo' technique often has the effect of encouraging the speaker to open up a bit more and go a bit deeper. They may offer aspects of their experience that the listener will suggest are returned to ('Thanks for that – I'll come back to that later if

---

13 Or multi-partial – the stance of openness and acceptance of all sides' perspectives without favouring any one side.

I may') or simply give a more detailed picture of their experience. It can be useful to think of minimal encouragers as tools that move the storytelling on, whilst the echo encourages a pause, and a chance to go deeper or to fill in certain gaps.

ACTIVITY 3.4

Key skill: Echoing

- Invite people to work in pairs.

- Suggest one person talks about a recent challenging incident or a situation at home or at work that involved strong emotions.

- Their partner listens and encourages the speaker, using minimal encouragers in the first instance.

- Then invite the listener to notice which words contain some emotional resonance – a judgemental adjective or adverb, for example, or a colourfully descriptive phrase to describe someone's actions. This word can then be echoed back to the speaker – alone with a rising, questioning intonation or followed by a phrase like – 'Go on? Tell me more?' Or even a more direct invitation for clarity such as – 'What do you mean by…?' (Intonation is crucial here or this question could sound suspicious or threatening.)

- After a few minutes reconvene as a group and share the experience – maybe swap over and try again.

- Figure 3.5 may help to consolidate this activity.

Figure 3.5 Echoing

My own experience has taught me that the 'What happened?' question, together with minimal encouragers and echoing to draw out the story, can almost be enough in themselves to help people feel heard and respected.

Key skill: self-restraint

It is valuable to stop at this point and reflect on what a restorative practitioner is *not* doing or saying, because it may well be the absence of other responses that can be the key to enabling a person to respond in a positive, productive way. Chapter 2 pointed out that in difficult situations people need an opportunity to put their side of the story and feel heard, and that if this opportunity is given people can often find ways forward for themselves, and feel better about themselves. Whatever the situation, then, the restorative practitioner must remain as calm as possible and avoid:

- showing judgement
- offering unasked-for advice
- issuing reprimands
- displaying expressions of surprise/shock/anger/disapproval
- taking sides
- assuming they know what has gone on previously.

The restraint this calls for can be very demanding in the heat of the moment and may challenge deeply held beliefs about the role of adults caring for children or young people. However, I always find inspiration from Faber and Mazlish (1980) in their classic book about communicating with children, *How to Talk so Kids will Listen and Listen so Kids will Talk* – surely a 'must-read' for all parents and carers.[14]

> When I'm upset or hurting, the last thing I want to hear is advice, philosophy, psychology, or the other fellow's point of view. That kind of talk only makes me feel worse than before… But let someone really listen…and give me a chance to talk more about what's troubling me and I begin to feel less upset, less confused, more able to cope with my feelings and my problem. (p.8)

Key skill: Clarifying the narrative thread and the time line

It is important to allow time for the full story to emerge. Remember that any incident is simply a chunk of someone's whole life, a small window, and things do not happen in a vacuum. Even if something happens completely out of the blue, the way people react will depend on what has happened before – either just before or over a period of time, if not their whole life.

---

14   And its recent sequel *How to Talk so Teens will Listen and Listen so Teens will Talk.*

When asked 'What's happened?' the speaker may start at a point that is most critical to them, or at a point that glosses over incidents that reflect less well on themselves, or perhaps omit past history simply because they do not consider it relevant. The facilitator needs a way of providing a structure for the narrative thread to emerge, to help the speaker and the listener clarify what has happened, but without asking leading questions that rule out unforeseen or unexpected influences being mentioned.

We suggest the facilitator thinks in terms of three 'time zones' (although there may be refinements of these, depending on the circumstances) – the presenting incident, what happened earlier, and what has happened since.

I have already referred to the idea of thinking of someone's story in terms of a storyboard – maybe a sequence of cartoons. When the listener asks 'What's happened?' the narrative may begin at any point. With minimal encouragers and the use of echoing, and maybe some judicious summarizing, the narrative moves forward (Figure 3.6).

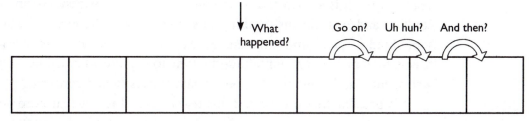

Figure 3.6 The time line – what happened at the time?

At a given point there will be a sense that the speaker has said as much as they want to say about the presenting incident. At this point the listener can invite them to talk about what happened earlier (Figure 3.7).

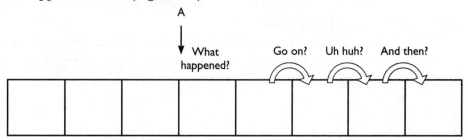

Figure 3.7 The time line – what happened earlier?

What is meant by 'earlier'? A few minutes before? Earlier that day? Maybe the day or even the week before?

Suggested questions for taking people back

- Can I take you back a bit – how were things earlier?

- How were things that morning?

- Anything happened earlier this week? Last week?

- How have things been between you and X in the past?

This type of question has proved very useful in my experience of mediating between young people in school contexts. So often the fiercest conflicts have been between people who had been friends. Something has happened to alienate them and the hurt and grief at the loss of the connection has fuelled even stronger emotions than if the two had never been friends. The questioning allows the story to be told and the gaps filled so that speaker and listener get a sense of the bigger picture.

I am not necessarily suggesting that the facilitator visits all these 'earlier' sub-zones – minutes before, hours before, days before, weeks before and even months or years before. It is a matter for common sense – but it is more common than not for conflicts and/or incidents resulting in someone being harmed in some way to have some kind of preceding rationale, at least on one person's side. There is always a reason for a behaviour, and taking the time to explore what led up to it will be time well spent – and demonstrates, once again, curiosity and concern.

It is possible that these questions reveal several issues that need addressing and the restorative enquirer may need to take the time to embed several mini-'restorative enquiry' sets of questions into the main framework. Alternatively there may be the need to address the most serious issue, but flag up that there is more to discuss at a later date. Clearly, if what is being discussed raises alarm bells for the restorative enquirer, in terms of child protection issues or mental health issues, for example, then the restorative enquirer may need to explain that there is a limit to what can be discussed at this stage, and that other people may need to be involved to address the issues being raised.

Finally it can sometimes be useful, if some time has elapsed since the incident or the events being talked about, to ask what has happened *since* the incident or event (Figure 3.8).

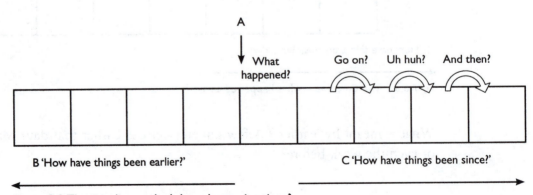

Figure 3.8 The time line – what's been happening since?

During this period all sorts of things could have happened, spiralling out from the original action – affecting more people, maybe leading to secondary incidents or harm – and it can be insightful for both listener and speaker to appreciate just how extensive the impact of a single incident can be, and just how many people can become involved and affected. The question of affect and impact will be revisited later, but simply reflecting on the sequence of events can help to develop this awareness.

ACTIVITY 3.5

Key skill: Maintaining a narrative thread and knowing which 'time zone' the story is in

It may be useful for the person facilitating this activity to model what is to be practised first, referring to some of the diagrams in this chapter.

- Invite people to work in pairs and take a letter for themselves – A or B.

- Ask A to think of a recent day that included a challenging situation and to recount this to their partner.

- Encourage B to use minimal encouragers and echoing (and also a little summarizing of sections, if appropriate, to check for understanding) until A comes to a natural pause, having explained the challenging event (Figure 3.6).

- Suggest that at this point B uses an appropriate phrase to take A back to earlier – in the day perhaps, or even before that, as appropriate – and so help them gain an understanding about what may have led up to the incident, and possibly their own responses (Figure 3.7).

- Once again, minimal encouragers and echoing can help A fill in the gaps of this sequence of events.

- When this part of the story has been recounted it may be appropriate for B to ask what has happened since the situation described, up to the present if appropriate (Figure 3.8).

- Reconvene in a group and invite each person, in the round, to share their experiences of listening or being listened to in this way.

So much for the detail of what has happened, but what about the invisible experience – a person's thoughts and feelings during the unfolding of events? The next section will concentrate on the skill of drawing out the 'inner landscape' of thoughts and feelings. I will then return to the notion of the narrative thread and integrate the time line with the ups and downs of the inner journey.

Theme 2: Developing skills to draw out the link between thoughts, feelings and behaviour

What people think and feel as events unfold is hidden from view – this is the invisible part of what is happening, and yet it is a vital part of any story because it influences the behaviour of everyone involved. Appreciating that there is a link between thoughts, feelings and behaviour constitutes the second key restorative theme.

This theme has links with cognitive psychology and shares the notion that the story we tell ourselves about what we perceive – our interpretation or thoughts moment by moment – gives rise to the emotions we experience. This insight can help people consider whether telling themselves different stories in similar circumstances might lead to different emotions and therefore different responses. In her book about developing pro-social behaviour, *Transforming Behaviour* (Cherry 2005) Sally Cherry uses the analogy of an iceberg and, drawing on cognitive therapy principles, suggests that what we think and feel are the invisible elements of our experience, beneath the surface, and that it is our outward behaviour that is above the surface (see Chapter 2, Figure 2.13).

Similarly, we ourselves only see and hear others' behaviour. Unless their thoughts and feelings are articulated accurately and truthfully, these remain beneath the surface. This iceberg metaphor is also used by Kim Golding (2008) in her book for foster carers, *Nurturing Attachments*:

> the hidden iceberg consists of the child's internal experience, all the feelings, thoughts and beliefs that underlie the child's outward behaviour.' (p.104)

So many misunderstandings and conflicts arise because the hidden elements are never surfaced, or considered, or those present make assumptions about why others acted the way they did. In other words, we either ignore the hidden aspects or we assume we know what is hidden – what others are thinking and feeling – and therefore assume we know the reasons for their actions. The sad fact is that we are sometimes cut off even from our own interpretations and feelings and find ourselves simply responding in the heat of the moment.

Restorative enquiry integrates aspects of cognitive psychology, and its applications in pro-social modelling and solution-focused work, with strategies for developing empathy for others and understanding others' motivations. Encouraging people to reflect on their own thoughts and feelings can help them reach greater understanding of why they themselves behaved, or reacted, in the way they did. Giving them a chance to reflect on, and then hear for themselves, what others' thoughts and feelings were in what appeared to be the 'same' situation can help people to find ways forward in what may have appeared to be intractable clashes of interests.

Key skill: Asking about thinking

The first half of the question, the 'thinking' question, concerns the interpretation a person is putting on an event, and just as with the 'What happened?' question, there are different ways of phrasing it. In training we suggest using the question:

- 'What were you thinking at this point?'

Alternatives might include:

- What were you thinking as this was happening?

- What was in your thoughts at this moment?

- What were you telling yourself when you saw that?

- What was going through your head when you heard that?

Or, in the present tense, for ongoing situations:

- So what goes through your mind when this happens?

- What do you tell yourself as this happens?

What this question is *not* about is inviting an opinion. This can be a potentially in-flammatory thing to do and does not move a situation forward. It can bring someone back to the present and invite judgement, when in fact what it should be about is taking someone back to the past and remembering what was going on for them at the time. In training I have interrupted and corrected people when they use phrases like:

- 'What did/do you think about that?'

- 'So what were/are your thoughts on this?'

If, in response to a properly worded 'thinking' question, a reply is expressed as an opinion, it could be worth clarifying whether this was what the person was telling themselves at the time –

- 'So, at that point, you were thinking (telling yourself) that he was out of order? Or is this your opinion now?'

It is important to understand the point of the question in order to phrase it correctly. Remember that we are, all the time, making sense of the world around us, and it is this internal commentary which then influences the emotions that arise in us. These emotions influence the choices we make about how we behave. Emotional maturity is achieved when we are able to make the links between our thoughts, our emotions and our actions and realize that we have choices around how we make sense of things – and that sometimes we jump to conclusions based on too little information. Many conflicts arise because of this.

ACTIVITY 3.6

It takes practice to reframe the 'thinking' question and differentiate it from questions inviting opinions.

- Invite people to work in threes, with one person being A, another B and a third C.

- Ask A to recount an event from the previous day, using some of the skills already practised, such as minimal encouragers, echoing, and encouraging a narrative thread.

- At appropriate points B gently interrupts ('Could I stop you there...') and invites A to reflect on what they were thinking at that moment – practising a variety of different ways to do this. C observes and notes down the phrases used.

- After a few minutes stop the activity, invite C to read back the phrases B used and suggest A gives feedback, after each one, on how helpful this was in encouraging B to relive the moment and recall their 'self-talk'.

- Swap around and gradually develop a list of useful phrases.

- Reconvene as a group and draw up a useful list of 'thinking' questions – and as a group develop antennae for the difference between questions inviting opinions and judgement, and questions inviting 'self-talk' or inner dialogue.

Key skill: Asking about feelings

The 'thinking' question informs how people feel and so, in restorative enquiry, the thinking question always precedes the 'feeling' question, which goes something like:

- And so what were you feeling inside (*implied*: as a result of this thought)?

Variants might include:

- How did you feel inside?

- What feelings came up for you?

Avoiding blame

Try to avoid inviting the speaker to blame others, or the situation, for their emotions:

- 'So how did that (i.e. the event) make you feel?'

- 'How did John make you feel?'

The belief underpinning the link between the thinking and the feeling is that the *interpretation* of events is what influences the resulting emotion, and not the events themselves or the people involved – since these are open to numerous interpretations. For example, person A might observe person B turn off the television as A enters the room. A then interprets B's action as a wilful attempt to stop A watching their favourite programme – and so reacts with an angry outburst. It may in fact be the case that B is pleased to see A and wants to hear about his day rather than watch the television, wonders why A reacted the way he did, and feels hurt.

There are probably scores of examples of when one person has interpreted another's actions in a way that has engendered anger, only to discover it was a misunderstanding. Similarly, staff probably have many examples of how an action by a young person on one day 'makes' them feel angry and then on another day – because of the mood the member of staff is in – the action is like water off a duck's back. The point here is that people do not 'make' us feel anything – it is our own interpretation that gives rise to the emotion.

It might be argued that this emphasis on the ownership by each person of their own emotional reactions implies that, in the case of harm, the negative affects experienced by the person harmed are not the 'fault' of the person causing the harm. It would be specious to argue that the emotional experience of someone on the receiving end of bullying, assault, theft, or even a single insult or hurtful remark, was unrelated to the harmful deed perpetrated by the wrongdoer. However, as Victim Support is keen to point out in its training – not every person reacts the same way to what might appear to be a similar incident, and so it is important for both sides to take the time to understand and listen to the 'spin' each is putting on the other's actions and how this spin is affecting them emotionally. It is common for the wrongdoer to have grossly underestimated the impact of their deeds on those they have harmed, and to have failed to consider how their actions may have set in motion a set of interpretations that have left the other person feeling fearful, disempowered, confused and locked in a very stressful state.

In an ideal world we would all be in complete control of our actions, our thoughts and our emotions and be able to shrug off all attacks on our person, physical and verbal. I have a friend who was once mugged and left unconscious, and claimed to be completely unaffected once the bruises had healed and I know others who have been deeply traumatized for months if not years by such an occurrence, to give just one example. But the fact is, we are human. If someone does or says something intentionally harmful, or even without harmful intention, then a conversation needs to take place – on both sides there may be a need to take some responsibility for the ripples ensuing from the event. On the one hand there may be a need for greater consideration, on the other the need for more resilience; both may need more empathy for each other and greater awareness of each other's needs in certain situations, and both are likely to benefit from an exploration of how to handle a similar situation next time. This is the opportunity that restorative enquiry and, following that, a restorative meeting, provides.

People sometimes respond to a question about thinking by explaining how they were feeling. My advice to people when they are first learning these questions is that if you get a 'feeling' answer to a 'thinking' question, leave it at that, unless you sense that the speaker would like to say more. In which case it might be useful to use the echo strategy, e.g. 'So you felt angry. Tell me more?'

This can often encourage further expression or elaboration of emotion. Sometimes beginners in restorative practice, on getting a 'feeling' answer to a 'thinking' question, insist on the thoughts being recalled, concerned that if this does not happen they have somehow 'got it wrong'. It will be a matter of judgement whether it is useful to go back and encourage the speaker to remember the thought that prompted the emotional reaction.

Feelings versus opinions

Where it is useful to take more time is when a 'thinking' response is given to a 'feeling' question. It is unfortunate in the English language that we have various ways of using the word 'feel'. 'I feel that…' is one way people express opinions, and 'I feel as if…' can also be used to introduce a judgement.

For example, the listener might ask – 'So what were you feeling when he did that?' and get the reply, 'I feel that he was out of order…' or 'I feel as if he doesn't care at all about what he said.'

If the listener senses that the emotion has yet to be expressed, and that the speaker needs help to do this, a useful question in this situation might be 'So, how does that thought make you feel inside?'

Another way in which the 'feel' word is often used is in the form of a simile or metaphor, which can in fact be a very effective way of describing an emotional state:

Speaker: 'I feel as if the whole world is against me.'

Listener: 'So what does that feel like – inside?'

If after one or two prompts the speaker is unable to find words for an emotion, it might be useful to use another tactic: 'It sounds like you might be feeling…?' This response is different from making an implicit judgement ('That sounds tough.') A response that begins 'That sounds…' is risky, since it could be interpreted as the listener expressing a judgement and, as such, threatens the impartiality that is at the heart of restorative practice.

In restorative enquiry the thinking and feeling questions may be asked not just once, but at various stages during a person's story.

The following two activities can be used to help people practise ways to ask about thinking and feeling.

ACTIVITY 3.7

- Invite people to work in threes, with one person being A, another B and a third C.

- Ask A to recount an event from the previous day, using some of the skills already practised, such as minimal encouragers, echoing, and encouraging a narrative thread.

- At appropriate points B gently interrupts ('Could I stop you there…') and invites A to reflect on what they were thinking at that moment – using a variety of different ways to do this, as already practised. They then immediately follow up each 'thinking' question with a 'feeling' question. C observes and notes down the phrases used.

- After a few minutes stop the activity, invite C to read back the 'feeling questions' B used, and suggest that A gives feedback, after each one, on how helpful this was in encouraging B to relive the moment and recall the emotion that followed the thought.

- Swap around and gradually develop a list of useful phrases.

- Reconvene as a group and draw up a useful list of 'feeling' questions – and as a group develop antennae for the difference between questions inviting opinions and blame, and questions inviting emotions.

ACTIVITY 3.8

THE THOUGHTS AND FEELINGS GRAPH

The activity is adapted from an excellent manual on conflict called *Ways and Means* (Kingston Friends Workshop Group 1996) which we use to help people understand how and when to ask 'thinking' and 'feeling' questions.

- Invite people to work in pairs (A and B) and suggest that the activity works best if both agree to honour confidentiality and keep the detail of the conversations between themselves.
- Distribute blanks sheets of A4 paper.
- Invite A to act as listener, and, on the sheet, in landscape format, to draw a graph with a vertical axis denoting feelings on a scale from 0 (the worst that B could ever feel) to 10 (the best that B could ever feel) and a horizontal axis denoting the passing of time (Figure 3.9).

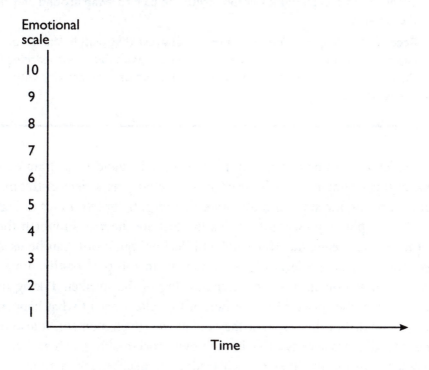

Figure 3.9 The thoughts and feelings graph

- If possible, demonstrate what is going to happen by inviting someone to talk through a recent day of their choice, and act as listener, recording their emotional 'graph' on a piece of flipchart paper, checking where they are emotionally as the day progresses.

- A starts by inviting B to tell them about a recent memorable day, from the moment of waking up. A draws out B's story using minimal encouragers and empathic body language and begins to chart the graph. A will need to ask B questions like – 'So where are you on the graph at this point?' B will assess where on the scale of 1–10 they were at each stage of their day and guide A to mark points in the appropriate places. A will join the points up as the story unfolds, creating a visual record of B's emotional ups and downs during the day (or of the specific incident about which they are talking, which could be longer than a day, or shorter).

- A then invites B to go back and explain what they were thinking and feeling at key points from the beginning of the graph – points of change, for example. A draws a thought-bubble at each point on the graph and writes in a few key words, prompted by B. A then draws a small heart linked to the thought and invites a 'feeling' word related to the thought.

- Because the second part of the activity requires a fair degree of emotional literacy, and a vocabulary of feelings, it can sometimes be useful to have a list of emotion words handy for reference (invite the group to draw up a flipchart of positive emotions and a list of more negative emotions, perhaps?) – or even a set of picture cards illustrating various emotional states. This can certainly be helpful when having such conversations with young people whose emotional vocabulary is not well developed for various reasons.

- When A has completed B's graph, invite the pair to swap around and repeat the activity.

- Reconvene in a group and, in the round, suggest that people share not their day, as this would be confidential between the pairs, but their learning from the activity, and maybe ways in which staff could use the activity with the young people.

The following example may help readers to understand what I am explaining, and indeed this example could be used in the activity as a demonstration – with one person reading the story and the other drawing the graph. Refer to Figure 3.10.

This graphic representation helps to illustrate the way in which the two halves of the second theme, the 'thinking' and 'feeling' questions, can be used to go back over the story at the level of detail and fill in the part of the story that will be invisible to any outsider – the internal reality of the speaker. Taking time over this can also help the speaker him- or herself to make sense of what happened and why they responded in the way that they did at any given moment. It also helps them to understand themselves as a role in their own story-making, and as their own internal commentator, and the links to their feelings and subsequent actions.

This graphic representation can actually be used in one-to-one situations to help someone talk through an experience, and then sit back from it and reflect on how things could have turned out differently, or how similar situations could be handled another time. In school settings staff have developed the activity for one-to-one work with people struggling in certain situations with their emotions and subsequent

Listener – *So when did you wake up, and how were you feeling?*

Speaker – *About 8am. I was OK.*

Listener – *So where shall I put the first point – 5?*

Speaker – *Yeah – about 5.*

Listener – *Draws first point (A). And then what happened?*

Speaker – *Nothing much – had my breakfast – a fry-up, felt a bit better, but still basically a 5. (Point B)*

Listener – *And then?*

Speaker – *Well…then the post came and I had a letter from my aunt. So I suppose I went up to about a 7. (Point C) But it was bad news – my cousin was ill and that made me very worried so I went down to a 3 (Point D) and basically stayed grumpy all morning 'cos I suppose I was worried. (Point E).*

Listener – *And then?*

Speaker – *At lunchtime I was watching the telly and heard that Liverpool had got through to the finals and that was fantastic – 8 (Point F) and then Mark came in and said that Liverpool were rubbish – I got really mad – started yelling at him, and he yelled back.*

Listener – *So it sounds as if you went right down…?*

Speaker – *Yeah – maybe a 2. (Point G)*

Listener – *And then?*

Speaker – *It kind of just blew over. Dan one of the staff, came in, said Mark didn't know what he was talking about, Mark just laughed and said he'd been winding me up but didn't really mean it – and he left – and to be honest I just forgot about it and ended up just feeling really good about the team. Oh, and then my auntie rang up to say my cousin was better so I felt much happier. Yeah – ended up on an 8…(Point H)*

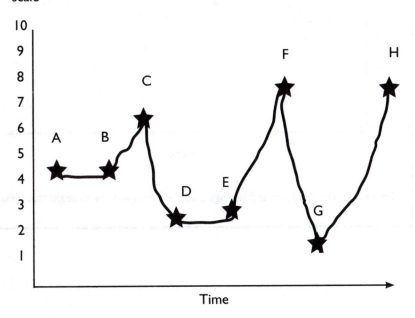

Figure 3.10 The thoughts and feelings graph – points of change

Represented graphically in this way it is clear that there are certain points in the story when feelings improved or deteriorated, and these would be points to focus on.

Figure 3.11 illustrates how the graph then becomes enriched by reflecting on the thoughts and the feelings during the day.

Listener – So you woke up about 8am – what were your thoughts at that point?

Speaker – I was pleased it was the weekend and I didn't have to get up in a hurry.

Listener – So, thinking that – how were you feeling?

Speaker – Good – I felt good.

Listener – And then you mentioned having breakfast.

Speaker – Yeah – well, on Saturdays we always have a fry-up – which I like.

Listener – So thinking about the fry-up made you feel good?

Speaker – Yeah, I s'pose.

Listener – And then you said you realized you had a letter from your aunt?

Speaker – Oh yes – and she often sends me money, so I was pleased.

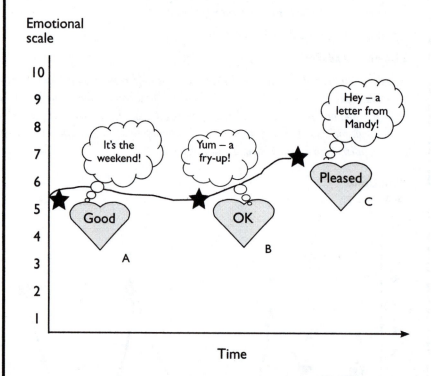

Figure 3.11 The thoughts and feelings graph – identifying the thought that influenced the feeling

behaviour, using it to help them identify the potential 'hotspots' and how they can make changes to their thinking, feeling and behaviour at any given moment.

The 'hands-on' nature of the activity can be satisfying and the visual representation of the speaker's inner world can help them gain a greater understanding of what can sometimes be experienced as random chaos. It is also a very real demonstration of empathy on the part of the listener – they are showing by their graph, and the careful checking to see if they are drawing it correctly, that they are interested and care.

It can help to encourage reflection on what kind of situations can lead to emotions dipping below what for that person is the norm – whether certain situations generate particular trains of thought, and hence certain emotions. People could then consider whether it is the situation itself that evokes a reaction, or whether it is the story that is being told about the situation, and how that could be changed.

The thoughts and feelings graph can help people understand how and when to draw out thoughts and feelings. It can also be a useful activity in itself to use with young people or with staff in supervision. In his new *Victim Empathy* manual Pete Wallis has made use of the thoughts and feelings graph to encourage young offenders to put themselves in others' shoes and imagine what *their* graphs would have looked like during an offending incident, just before and afterwards (Wallis and Tudor 2009).

Even when the graph is not actually drawn it has helped people to keep the metaphor in mind as they use the 'thinking' and 'feeling' questions and have their antennae out for the ups and downs of emotion that may need drawing out.

Thoughts, feelings and the narrative thread

Having introduced the element of thoughts and feelings I want to return to the narrative thread and the sense of a time line, using the graph metaphor. The listener may spend some time encouraging the speaker to tell their story in their own way and in their own time, perhaps drawing out the thoughts and feelings as illustrated in Figure 3.12.

However, at some point the speaker will have said all they want to say about that particular part of the story and it is time to go back to the 'earlier' time zone with a series of tentative questions.

Once again it may be pertinent to identify 'hotspots' which seem to have emotional resonance, and invite the speaker to reflect on what they had told themselves at that point and what they felt as a result (Figure 3.13).
The same applies if it is relevant to explore what has happened since the incident – there may be certain points which were of particular importance to the speaker.

Keeping in mind the metaphor of a storyboard or cartoon, together with the graph metaphor, may help people understand the importance of being thorough and being patient when encouraging people to tell their story. Figure 3.14 is an attempt to show graphically the full restorative enquiry process when used for more serious situations, or at times when the process must not be rushed.

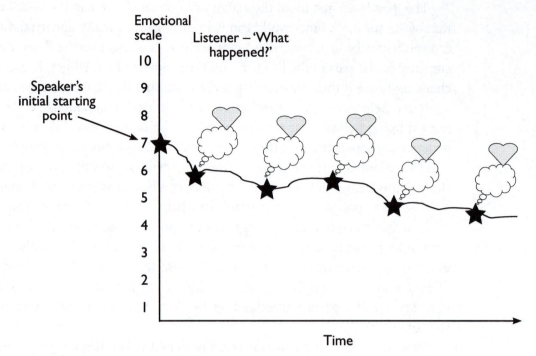

Figure 3.12 The thoughts and feelings graph and the time line

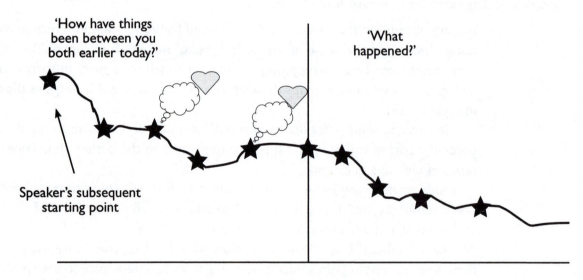

Figure 3.13 The thoughts and feelings graph and the time line – earlier?

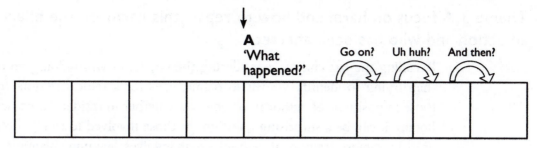

B 'Now – can I take you back?' (Explore thoughts and feelings.*) :

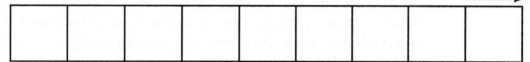

C 'How have things been earlier?'

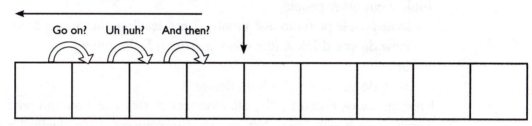

D 'And again – if I could just take you back…' (Explore thoughts and feelings.*) :

E 'How have things been since?'

F 'And so, going back…' (Explore thoughts and feelings.*) :

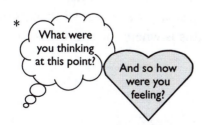

Figure 3.14 Restorative Enquiry – the whole process

Theme 3: A focus on harm and how to repair this harm; on the effect of an action and who has been affected

Recalling the last chapter, considering the impact of wrongdoing on others, rather than trying to identify who is to blame, calls for a radical rethink from many of those in positions of authority or power – whether in residential homes or in foster homes. It can be a surprising question for those involved to think about, if they are used to a more traditional response that involves 'naming, blaming and possibly shaming'.

The question 'Who has been affected by what has happened?' invites someone in the thick of the situation to think about its impact not only on themselves and the other person, but also on those around them. In a residential setting this is quite a significant wake-up call, since tensions, conflicts and wrongdoing will inevitably have ripple effects throughout the home, on young people and staff alike. It is a question that also helps the questioner assess whether the speaker is ready or able to think about other people.

Some people prefer to ask a more direct, leading question such as

'How do you think X (the other person) is feeling now?'

Or

'How do you think this has affected X?'

I remain unconvinced by the effectiveness of this question and tend not to use it myself. I am hoping that after speaking to someone individually I will be able to encourage everyone affected to meet face-to-face. The most effective way of encouraging empathy is for someone to hear how their actions have impacted on others *from those people themselves*, in their own words and conveyed with the emotion those people are feeling.

My reservation about the 'How do you think X feels/felt?' type of question is that it invites, from an angry or hurt person, a response such as 'I don't care' (often phrased in a much stronger way), which may serve to escalate the hostility or compound the harm. I also think that only asking this question misses the point, which I believe to be an opportunity for the speaker to stand back and look at the wider impact of the situation on their community – in this case the other residents and staff of the residential home.

Another important point to remember with the 'affect' question is for the facilitator to keep the question open and not ask leading or pointed questions. It is possible that at this early stage in the process the speaker is unable to show empathy, either for themselves or others. It is not appropriate for the facilitator to make suggestions, leave telling silences, look meaningfully at anyone or react if there is no response. A 'nil' response is simply information – this is where the speaker is 'at' emotionally at this stage of the process.

Theme 4: An appreciation of individual needs and also that there is much similarity between the needs on all sides

Restorative enquiry, when it is conducted one-to-one, is often in preparation for a meeting when people can come together to find ways to repair harm, or find ways forward in difficult situations. In such contexts it is not useful to encourage the speaker to take too rigid a position on what they believe needs to happen or should be done to repair the harm. Instead the emphasis needs to be on what they personally need in order to move on.

The question 'What do you need so that the harm can be repaired?' (or variations of this that are language-appropriate) comes from our understanding of what people need when harm has happened. As explained in Chapter 2, whether someone has been harmed or has caused harm, the needs are very similar (Table 2.1). As a result it is important to show empathy by taking an interest in everyone's needs, regardless of their role in the conflict or incident.

Behaviour can always be construed as what we do to get our needs met in specific situations (Rosenberg 1999). Inappropriate behaviours are, therefore, by extension, inappropriate ways to get our needs met. Rosenberg writes, for example:

'Violence is a tragic expression of an unmet need.'

I would adapt this in relation to anger and suggest that anger is an inappropriate and ineffective expression of an unmet need. Inviting people to express what their needs are can help them to think about more appropriate ways to get their needs met. Rosenberg, in his development of non-violent communication, has helped to clarify the concept of need. He identifies a limited number of human needs, expressed as abstract nouns, that we all share in common – needs for love, support, respect, belonging, acknowledgement, clarity – to name a few. The idea underpinning the emphasis on underlying needs is that, once people can express these clearly, it becomes easier to explore alternative ways of getting the needs met.

ACTIVITY 3.9

It is strongly recommended that the person facilitating this activity has read *Non-violent Communication* by Marshall Rosenberg (1999) – and even better, attended some training on this excellent way to communicate in everyday situations as well as challenging ones.

- Invite people to work in small groups and review what they identified that they needed from each other to work at their best together.

- Review the list and see if these have been expressed in terms of other people's actions or as an abstract noun.

- Practise identifying underlying needs beneath requests or demands using this list'.
  E.g. 'I need people to listen to me'.

Question – What need would be met if people did this?'
Answer – Respect? Support? Understanding? Etc.

- Now think of examples of what people can sometimes say when they are making demands of each other or of another person – and one person say it to their partner:
  'I need you to tidy up your room.'
  'I need him to help me with the washing up.'

- The partner practises responding either with a question or a suggestion:
  Question – 'What need of yours would be met if this happened?'
  Suggestion – 'So its sounds as if you might be needing...' (followed by an abstract noun like – support; consideration etc.)

The important point is that when the needs are expressed as personal needs, and not demands, they are more easily heard and accepted. More often than not people in conflict, or in the aftermath of harm, share common needs, and it is in identifying these that reconnection begins to happen. It takes practice to translate demands into needs, but unless that is done, empathy is unlikely to develop and outcomes and agreements may feel imposed and punitive, especially for those who have caused harm.

Theme 5: Ownership of problem-solving and decision-making by those directly involved

The fifth theme of restorative practice – ownership and empowerment – is most relevant at the end of restorative meetings. However, it also has its place at the end of a one-to-one conversation if it is thought of as individual action-planning – the 'what next' part of the conversation. After identifying what the needs are, the listener can help the speaker think through the next steps, what they can do to begin to get their needs met, when they will do these things and how. A variation on the question that could be useful at this stage might be:

'What could happen now to move things forward and meet those needs you have just expressed? What could you do?'

This restorative theme presents its own challenges for those adults who are more familiar with offering suggestions and advice to young people. The challenge is to stay in the role of facilitator and encourage the speakers to think for themselves. This is the point of empowerment, and is an extremely important part of an adult's role. In his book *Restorative Justice – the Empowerment Model* Charles Barton (2003) asserts that the quality of the restorative experience depends on the extent to which participants felt empowered at every stage of the process.

As long as we solve young people's problems for them and tell them what to do, either with the benevolent approach of the 'rescuer' or in the less benevolent role of the authority figure, we fail to prepare them for a time when they will be on their own and will have to make their own decisions. Furthermore, the act of doing things *for* or *to* people can imply, maybe even unconsciously, that we neither respect nor trust them to make appropriate decisions for themselves. In addition, the decisions that people make for themselves spring from a host of factors that could well be invisible to an outsider. Sometimes, from an outsider's perspective, the way forward is evident and the answers to a problem obvious. However, if they are not obvious to those whose situation it is, then the chances are that there are some hidden elements influencing their choices. It may or may not be possible to surface them. The best way to show respect for another human being is to respect their choices (providing they do not obviously harm themselves or another person), even if we do not personally agree with them at the time.

Pulling together the threads

It can be seen from the previous description of the various stages of restorative enquiry that the process requires intuition, spontaneity, empathy, sensitivity and judgement and defies being captured and fixed as a script. No two people might conduct a restorative enquiry with the same person in quite the same way, and different people might make different judgements about when and how to invite reflection on the thoughts and feelings underpinning certain stages of the story, for example.

This is not to say that it is a chaotic or an unstructured process, however. As this chapter has described, everyone needs to understand the rationale for each question and appreciate what variations are appropriate and which are inappropriate. Learning to use restorative enquiry effectively takes a lot of practice. The longer version of restorative enquiry is underpinned by exactly the same themes and basic questions as the shorter version – but with a lot more to think about at each stage.

Using restorative approaches with young people with attachment disorders

It is useful to consider whether restorative approaches can be used with young people who have attachment difficulties – possibly the majority of young people in care. Will they be able to develop empathy and make links between their thoughts and feelings? In fact their difficult experiences and their lack of empathy are precisely the reason why these restorative conversations need to be used with such young people consistently and regularly. With such conversations the adults model and therefore teach empathy – empathy for self and for others.

In her book for foster carers *Nurturing Attachments* (2008) Kim Golding writes:

> Parenting needs to be focused on understanding the feelings and beliefs that the child is having and communicating this understanding via empathy. Empathy will help the child to understand and ultimately manage her own feelings and beliefs and true behavioural change will follow. (p.103)

Kim does not refer to restorative practice in her book and indeed may not be familiar with the model, but she endorses the importance of the role of the adult in showing empathy by the language they use, and her definition of empathy echoes the key restorative themes:

> Being able to empathically listen to another person is essential if we are to build a relationship with him. To empathize with someone you need to listen deeply, paying attention to the words and also to the thoughts, feelings, beliefs and perceptions underlying the words. If we understand and accept what a person is expressing, and can help him to experience this understanding, he will feel connected with us. This deepens the relationship and provides a platform for further communication. (p.102)

Educational psychologists in Hertfordshire, a county leading the way in training all of its care staff in restorative approaches, argue that the five restorative questions provide a consistent empathic framework that care staff teams can adopt and use on a daily basis, to the point where the young people themselves can learn the language and use it amongst themselves. They point out that this consistent framework and the constant repetition of the same themes helps those children and young people with attachment difficulties to learn connections they may have failed to learn earlier in life.[15]

Case study

A young boy had recently returned from school whilst staff were having a hand-over meeting and started behaving in a way that demanded attention. He repeatedly tried to come into the office and was sent away and asked to come back when staff were not busy. He then began to annoy other young people, making loud noises and interrupting their conversations. A member of staff was called to ask him to stop, and this time he was reprimanded and asked to behave. Eventually he came back into the room where staff were trying to talk and began rolling noisily around on the sofa. Staff tried using an ignoring tactic until the boy's noise drowned out their discussion. Eventually one of the staff team recalled the training she had recently had in restorative approaches and remembered the first restorative question. She went over to the boy, crouched down and quietly asked the boy, 'What's happened?'

The boy realized that at last someone was genuinely interested and was prepared to listen to his story. He explained that he was going to be expected to read a piece of work out loud in class next day and he didn't want to go to school because he was afraid of being laughed at.

Using the sequence of questions outlined above, the member of staff was able to support the boy to find, for himself, a way of coping next day at school.

---

15 Having run an awareness raising day for Hertfordshire's Educational Psychology team in 2008 I asked them whether attachment difficulties may mean that children in care would not respond to restorative language. They gave me the answer outlined in this paragraph.

There is undoubtedly more research to be done on the contribution a restorative approach can make to the social and emotional development of those with attachment difficulties. However, at this early stage the signs are that the approach is worth trying and persevering with.

Conclusion

This chapter has introduced restorative enquiry in terms of five key restorative themes operationalized by five questions that draw out these themes. (An aide memoire bringing together the whole process can be found in Appendix A.) The questions, or variations of them, are widely used in the field of restorative practice. The chapter has illustrated the challenges of using each question with care and emphasized that what is said, how it is said, and also what is not said, are all vital.

Some people like to think of these questions as a script, but the chapter has also illustrated that it is impossible to mandate exactly what will be appropriate in each circumstance. Furthermore, skills like minimal encouragers, echoes and judicious repetition of questions about thoughts and feelings must be left to the judgement and skill of the restorative enquirer.

One-to-one conversations using restorative enquiry have many applications – they can help de-escalate minor incidents and head off a more serious incident at the pass, they can serve as preparatory meetings before bringing various individuals together, and they can provide a framework for mentoring or counselling. The key themes can inform any discussion between two individuals and, as the next chapter will show, in difficult situations restorative enquiry can provide an effective framework for conflict resolution.

Chapter 4

Restorative Dialogue – Sorting Things Out Together

Restorative enquiry was first developed for use by a supposedly impartial listener. However, it can be difficult, if not impossible, to remain impartial in the context of residential care, or as a foster parent, owing to the close proximity in which residents and carers live. When situations arise in a home the ripples of harm can affect everyone, even those who were not present at the time. Adults may feel frustrated, disappointed and possibly torn between the neutral role of a listener and the more active, partisan role of a friend, supporter or colleague of others affected by what has happened. At such times they need the skills of restorative dialogue – a more equal, two-way process, allowing both, or all sides to engage in a conversation that involves everyone sharing their perspectives, thoughts, feelings and needs. Such a dialogue is more likely to result in a mutually acceptable outcome (Figure 4.1).

1. What happened from my side was…
2. What was going through my head at the time was…and so I was feeling…
3. I think…has been affected by all this.
4. What I need to put it right is…
5. OK, so what I can do is… Do you agree?

1. What happened from my side was…
2. What was going through my head at the time was…and so I was feeling…
3. I think…has been affected by all this.
4. What I need to put it right is…
5. OK, so what I can do is… Do you agree?

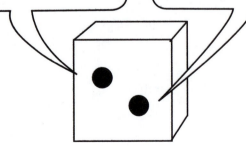

Figure 4.1 Restorative conversations

Furthermore, restorative dialogue is not only something for adults to use with young people. It is also for adults to use among themselves, since young people need good role models where conversation and conflict resolution are concerned. How the adults talk to each other, discussing daily issues, debating around the meal table, negotiating who will do what, and how – all these are examples of social pedagogy in action.

Restorative dialogue has an inner and an outer form. The inner form is part of the restorative mindset – a silent conversation with oneself that runs prior to, or simultaneously with, what we are saying out loud (Table 4.1).

The outer form has two variants – 'I' messaging (pages 93–98) and 'Your turn, my turn' (pages 98–100).

The 'affected' listener

We are often reminded that active listening requires us to be impartial. In fact, especially in close-knit communities and families, it can be challenging to be impartial or even act impartially (which are two different things). If we care about the young people in our care and about our colleagues or foster partner (if we are lucky to be sharing this role), then when things go wrong, we are affected. We may make judgements, take sides, feel angry, disappointed, worried, confused – or all of these at once – and it will be virtually impossible to hide these responses – they tend to leak out in our tone, body language and facial expressions.

I believe, from my experience as a parent and professionally, that it is nevertheless still possible to respond in restorative ways and even to facilitate restorative discussions and meetings. However, in order to do so it is important for the listener to stay in touch with their own inner dialogue at all times so that they are able to react moment by moment to what is going on, and not make matters worse by reacting in an un-premeditated way. The five restorative themes provide a framework for this inner work.

A key restorative value is that of empowerment, and the power and status of an adult in a situation involving young people must not be underestimated. I find the ideas of Arnold Mindell (1997) useful here. He talks of people having rank by virtue of numerous factors – contextual (e.g. age, experience, position, gender), psychological (e.g. degree of confidence) and spiritual (e.g. experience of inner personal development work and a heightened self-awareness). Rank brings privilege, and with awareness and sensitivity people can recognize the privilege that their rank gives them and use this with compassion and respect. By virtue of their rank, adults can, on the other hand, inadvertently influence the choices young people make, simply by a comment or a nonverbal reaction, let alone the more overt influence exerted by opinions, advice, strong emotion and disapproval.

Restorative inner dialogue

It can be helpful to keep the five key restorative themes in mind in difficult situations. Table 2.3 in Chapter 2 offered some suggestions for what we may be telling ourselves. The same figure is reprinted here (Table 4.1) for ease of reference in the light of the coaching tips that follow.

Table 4.1 A restorative inner dialogue

Theme 1	What am I seeing here?…I wonder how others see what I am seeing…
Theme 2a	What interpretations am I making of this? I wonder what is going on in the minds of others here right now?
Theme 2b	What feelings are coming up for me as a result of my interpretations? And what about others here?
Theme 3	How am I being affected? Who else is being affected or even harmed by what is happening here?
Theme 4	What do I need at this moment? And others here? What needs are being expressed, albeit maybe in terms of accusations, insults or demands?
Theme 5	How can those involved become accountable and take responsibility for putting things right? Is it appropriate for me to play an equal role in finding a way forward here, or is it my role to support others here to find a way forward for themselves?

Coaching tips

Theme 1

Asking ourselves 'What is happening here?' seems quite innocuous, but judgemental description is all too easy. We can ask ourselves the first 'what happened' question in a slightly different way:

What am I seeing and hearing?

Marshall Rosenberg's *Non-violent Communication* (1999) is helpful in clarifying the difference between what one can see and hear (the indisputable evidence that everyone present might be able to agree on) and the interpretations or judgements we make of these observations. He would differentiate between a neutral description of a situation, e.g.

I can see Mary's plate, and the food that was on it, lying on the floor.

And the implicit judgement and criticism of:

*Mary has **chucked** her meal **all** over the floor, for the **umpteenth time**.*

Theme 2

The 'thinking' question helps us to realize that we are likely to be making some kind of interpretation, despite knowing that we do not yet know the full story:

What is my interpretation of what is happening?

This is a different sort of contemplation from 'What do I think *about* this?'

Judgements may well be surfacing, and these will be emerging in connection with the interpretation we are making. There is skill in standing back mentally and asking ourselves if there could be different interpretations made of what we are seeing and hearing. Better still would be to remain in an open-minded state of 'not knowing'.

We also need to check in with our emotional responses and ask ourselves the 'feeling' question:

How is my interpretation influencing how I am feeling at the moment?

Theme 3

Being fully mindful in the situation will help us to focus on who has been, or is being harmed, rather than who has done, or is doing what. It will also help us to stay in touch with how the incident is affecting or even harming us. Although it may sound like heresy to suggest it, there may even be a case at times for the facilitator in these very close quarters of residential settings to acknowledge that they are also affected. This does not necessarily bar them from facilitating a restorative process, and it could be argued that *not* to disclose personal affect is misleading and confusing to those around, who can see with their own eyes that the facilitator is affected.

Theme 4

We must ensure that we are looking after ourselves, and that we are conscious of our own needs in the situation. Clarity on this can give us some space to ensure that our response is a considered one. If we respond in such a way as to meet our own needs, we must be aware that this is our intention – and maybe even be clear about this to those around us.

What do I need right now?

Marshall Rosenberg's insights on the finite number of universal human needs can inform us and develop our self-understanding. If we are holding the space for others to find ways forward and address their own needs, it may be that we ourselves put our own needs on hold until later. On the other hand it is very likely that our intervention is in part motivated by our own needs for safety, harmony, mutual respect and resolution. In fact these needs can be so uppermost in our minds that we can be tempted to manipulate the process we are facilitating. It is possible that those in conflict or between whom harm has happened need different things from ourselves. To what extent are we even able to permit people to meet their own needs if they are in conflict with our own?

Finally, based on all these questions to myself I will make a decision about what to do next – my own agreement with myself, made with awareness and empathy for myself.

What am I going to do now to meet my need and identify the needs of anyone else involved?

These questions become second nature with practice, and follow on one from the other in rapid succession.

Here is a real example, an incident I experienced several years ago when running a workshop on conflict management with some young people in the livingroom of their residential home. At one point one of the boys, who was about 14 years old, decided he would climb up on top of a high bookcase in the corner of the living-room. This was an unusual thing to do, and I knew that my response had to model the work we had been doing. My inner dialogue went along the following lines:

Case study

Theme 1: What can I see and hear?
I can see John lying at the top of the bookcase and I can hear him saying he will not come down.

Theme 2a: What is my interpretation of what is happening?
John needs something that he is not getting and has climbed the bookcase – maybe to get that need met – I am not yet sure. He is looking curious, and I think he is wondering what I am going to do next. My priority is to ensure he is safe before we engage in further dialogue.

Theme 2b: How is my interpretation influencing how I am feeling at the moment?
I'm feeling curious as well as anxious for John's safety.

Theme 3: Who do I think may have been affected and will be affected?
John, the other young people, me and my co-facilitator – and John will be badly affected if he falls.

Theme 4: What do I need right now?
I need cooperation and consideration – and reassurance about John's safety. I also need inspiration!

Theme 5: What am I going to do now to meet my need and identify the needs of anyone else involved?
I'm going to tell John what I see, share my thoughts and feelings and ask if he'd be willing to come down from the bookcase and explain what was going on for him.

This internal dialogue, based on the five questions, helped me to become aware of my own internal state and helped me stay in the moment, balancing my own needs with those of other people involved. In the example above I decided to share my own observations with John, using an 'I' message, before asking for his side. The next section explains what an 'I' message is and what I actually said to John.

'I' messages

My variation of the 'I' message – a format that many others have described and adapted (Bentley *et al.* 1998, Fine and Macbeth 1992, Rosenberg 1999, Whitehouse and Pudney 1998) – is an attempt to identify the five restorative themes at work in this highly effective communication strategy. It has developed from the early days, when I first came across it as a community mediator, and since learning more about conflict resolution, anger management and non-violent communication. In my experience each of the five elements is useful – but none of the elements are set in concrete and it takes a while to become comfortable with using what at first sounds formulaic and unnatural.

What I would say, however, is that the more the language of the five themes is used between adults and then between adults, and young people, the more likely is it that the young people themselves start to use the language – and of course the concepts behind the language – for themselves and between themselves (Table 4.2).

Table 4.2 'I' message, incorporating the five restorative themes

Theme	Reminder to self	'I' message
1	Ensure that my description is neutral and likely to be recognized.	When I see…or hear…
2	Acknowledge there may be deeply held beliefs – which others may not share – informing what I think.	I felt…because I think/believe… (or …because what was running through my head was…)
3	Keep this neutral – it is your problem, not theirs, or they would be acting differently!	…and so, because I am affected by this…
4	Try and find a noun that sums up the need – not a request. E.g., 'I need you to…'	…what I need is…
5	Make the request – or offer to hear their own side.	…so would you be willing to…?

Note the slight variation in Theme 5 – this is still action planning, but putting a suggestion forward as a request that the other person is free to refuse. The speaker must be open to the possibility that the request may not be granted and another strategy might be suggested (perhaps one that meets the other person's need?), and some negotiation may be required. An 'I' message is not a clever way to get people to do what *you* want, but an invitation to them to help you feel better, and also the beginning of a discussion to sort out what their needs are as well.

What I ended up saying to John went something like this:

When I see you up on that bookcase I am wondering what's up for you, and I'm feeling worried because you might fall off and get hurt. It may be my problem, but I need your help — would you be willing to climb down, and then let me know what's up?

It worked — he got down, and we did talk.

I am not advocating this kind of lengthy introduction to every enquiry, but it does have advantages as well as disadvantages. By running through the five themes with John I was mentally checking in with myself, and ensuring that my response was not a knee-jerk one. By saying the words slowly and calmly I was slowing things down and, in the example, giving John and myself time to think. I am modelling a non-confrontational, respectful model that avoids assumptions, reprimands, blame or disapproval, and I hope I appealed to John's better nature — 'I need your help.'

The disadvantage may be that it is rather a 'sledgehammer' approach when a small 'nutcracker' might have been sufficient — some humour perhaps: 'What's the view like from up there?' or empathy: 'Whoops — what's up? Sounds like we may need to change tack.' My recommendation is to be aware of all five themes and use the ones that best fit the circumstances.

ACTIVITY 4.1

PRACTISING 'I' MESSAGES

(It is strongly recommended that the person facilitating this activity has read *Non-violent Communication* [Rosenberg 1999] or has some familiarity with other versions of 'I' messaging.)

- Suggest everyone sits in an open circle.

- Perhaps have a flipchart with the five themes and some space to build up the framework of the 'I' message gradually. Some people like to have a pen and a notepad to try out some ideas.

- Invite people to think of a time when they felt angry, frustrated or vexed.

- Explain that the activity is not compulsory but people might like to take the opportunity to practise having a conversation with someone with whom there has been a problem that they have either failed to address, or have tried and it has back-fired.

- It will help if the facilitator of this activity also takes part and gives the first example. The activity takes the form of several 'sentence completion' rounds, in which people gradually build up the 'I' message formula given above.

- The first round involves completing the sentence 'When I saw/heard... I felt...'

Each person in the circle, if they are willing, completes the sentence in relation to their own chosen situation. (The facilitator's role consists in checking with everyone that the description given is neutral, short and without tell-tale exaggeration or colourful description giving away the strength of feeling.) For example:

*When I saw wet towels **chucked all over** the bathroom floor **for the umpteenth time**, I felt angry.*

The words in bold may invite denial and resistance. 'When I see wet towels on the floor' is a more neutral description (as long as there *are* wet towels on the floor for all to see, of course).

- The second round involves repeating this first sentence and adding 'because', so that now people have to think about what is going on inside their heads that is causing them to feel what they feel. (It can be quite hard to face up to deeply held beliefs about how people or things should be, when these beliefs or concerns are not shared.) For example:

When I saw wet towels on the bathroom floor again I felt angry, because I like the bathroom to be tidy and I know that they will start to smell.

- The third round involves repeating the first two parts, and admitting the situation is getting to you, using the neutral term 'affecting' and identifying the unmet need. For example:

*When I saw wet towels on the bathroom floor again I felt angry, because I like the bathroom to be tidy and I know that they will start to smell. This is affecting me, and **I need understanding and cooperation**.*

- The fourth round 'takes it from the top' and adds a request, which may even be an invitation to hear the other person's side:

When I saw wet towels on the bathroom floor again I felt angry, because I like the bathroom to be tidy and I know that they will start to smell. This is affecting me, and I need understanding and cooperation. Would you be willing to pick them up and hang them on the rail – or maybe tell me if there is anything I can do to make this easier for you?

If people have not met this formula before, there may be some hilarity and disbelief that what sounds so artificial can actually make any difference at all. And yet others swear by it and have, with practice, moved away from stilted formulas and made the sequence sound more natural and closer to their usual way of speaking.

When an 'I' message is not enough or appropriate

'I' messages do not always have an immediate positive effect – they may inadvertently trigger a strong response – either because we have somehow touched a nerve or because the other person is so used to different sorts of responses that they themselves respond with an attack anyway. And in fact sometimes we can find ourselves on the receiving end of an angry exchange before we have even had a chance to explain our own perspective.

At this point we have various choices:

- respond with some immediate empathy – e.g. 'You sound angry', and then immediately, running your own internal dialogue to keep in touch with what is going on for you, use the restorative enquiry process as described in Chapter 3

- use a reverse 'I' message (see below)

- acknowledge that we are in the midst of the conflict ourselves and use a strategy that I will refer to as 'Your turn, my turn' (see page 98)

- use a mixture of all three as appropriate.

Reverse 'I' messages

Sometimes the person you are addressing is still far too angry to engage in dialogue and the main task will be to de-escalate the conflict and try to calm the other person down. I am aware that there are some excellent 'restraint training' packages available for care staff and that these involve verbal de-escalation skills as well. It will be worth reviewing these techniques and strategies in terms of consistency with restorative values and principles.

The reverse 'I' message, adapted from practice used by Marshall Rosenberg, involves reaching out empathically to the other person to try to help them frame what they are saying in a way that makes it easier to address their need. As restorative practitioners we are always trying to help people identify their unmet needs and find ways to address them.

So when people are beside themselves with anger and hurling abuse at you it can help them, and indeed yourself, to try and translate what they are saying in a way that

- tries to understand the thinking behind the emotions

- acknowledges the strength of the emotions

- attempts to identify the needs

- seeks to clarify the request being made.

Essentially the reverse 'I' message incorporates elements of the 'I' message but is used more tentatively because the speaker is only guessing, respectfully trying to make sense of what is being said, without putting words into the speaker's mouth for fear of angering them all over again (Table 4.3).

It is quite difficult to explain this without some live examples. In training we invite people to step into the shoes of an angry teenager and hurl abuse at their partner, who has to try and capture the essence as explained above, using the five themes as appropriate; for example:

Table 4.3 Reverse 'I' message, incorporating the five restorative themes

Theme	Reverse 'I' message
1	So what you are saying is – When you saw…(or heard…)
2	You felt…because you think/believe… (or else Because what was running through your head was…)
3	And so, because you are affected by this
4	What you need is…
5	And you'd like me (or X) to… Have I got that right?

*That's it. That is IT. I've had enough of that f****** b******. He does my head in – like really…p***** me off. Why can't he just p*** off and leave me alone? If he says that stuff one more time I'm going to kick his f****** head in.*

This could be reframed into something like:

So when you hear Paul saying that stuff (Theme 1) *you feel very angry* (Theme 2b) *because you find it offensive* (Theme 2a) *and it's getting to you* (Theme 3). *You need time alone and…sounds like you need some respect?* (Theme 4) *You want him to stop saying those things and leave you alone?* (Theme 5)

The first time I ever used this reverse message in a residential care home, the impact surprised even me. I was running a weekly conflict management group for some of the young residents.[16] At the beginning of the evening, just as my colleague and I arrived, a young girl in her mid teens came rushing down the stairs, dressed up for a night out. Seeing us there, she stopped in her tracks and began shouting angrily at me:

'I'm not coming to your f****** class. It's a load of b******* and I'm off into town, so you can both f*** o**.'

I could quite see her point, although I was sorry she was not finding it useful – so I responded:

'You sound very angry – you were looking forward to going out, and when you saw me here you thought I might make you stay in, and join the group – which you do not want to do – am I right?'

---

16 An ill-conceived project, I now admit in retrospect, as my co-trainer and I would have been better off training the staff to run this for the young people. They had the relationship and, once they had learned the skills themselves, could have modelled and encouraged them in the young people – but this was many, many years ago and hindsight is a glorious thing.

The girl looked amazed, immediately calmed down and offered, spontaneously, to join us for half an hour. I hadn't even dreamt of suggesting this but she trotted into the room like a lamb, joined in our discussions, and after half an hour left to go into town, as agreed.

Your turn, my turn

Most of the literature on conflict management concurs in that, when in conflict, what people need is a chance to tell their side of the story and feel heard; a chance to express their feelings and have these acknowledged and valued; an opportunity to understand what is happening and why; for the conflict to be over and to feel safe again. The most effective strategies to use to meet these needs are: listen to the other person's perspective as well as explaining your own; ensure that everyone has a chance to express their feelings; identify, where possible, common ground and work together to find a mutually acceptable way forward (Stone *et al.* 1999, Cornelius and Faire 1993; non-violent communication).

Table 4.4 Your turn, my turn

Theme	Your turn, my turn
1	OK – you tell me what's happened as far as you are concerned, and then I'll tell you how I saw it.
2	So what was going through your mind at that point? … OK – can I tell you what I was thinking? … And so how were you feeling at that point? … Well, I was feeling…
3	How has this affected you? Anyone else? … Let me tell you how it affected me…and maybe it's also affected …
4	So what do you need right now to put this right/to feel better about this – or so we can make things up? … OK – well, what I need is…
5	So what can we do to make sure we get our needs met, sort this out and move on? … OK – here are my ideas too… Now what can we agree on?

An 'I' message is a way to give this to someone in one go by way of an invitation for some further discussion. A reverse 'I' message is a way of translating a verbal barrage into a frame that sheds some light on the feelings and needs of the speaker and helps them to feel understood. 'Your turn, my turn' develops these two strategies into a two-way conversation. If all young people, indeed all people young and old, could adapt this framework for having a restorative dialogue whenever they found themselves in disagreement with someone else, there would be no need for a facilitator (Table 4.4).

This type of dialogue sounds very unnatural at first, but in effect it is the 'self-help' version of the type of restorative meetings that will be described in later chapters, involving two or more people. (Readers may prefer to read these later chapters first and then return to this one.)

ACTIVITY 4.2

- Invite a staff team to work in pairs, choosing a partner with whom they have recently shared a shift and giving themselves a letter A or B.

- Sharing a single piece of paper, invite them to draw a graph like that in the 'Thoughts and feelings graph' activity in Chapter 3. (Familiarity with that activity will help this one.)

- Invite them to talk over an incident or activity that they were both involved in, not necessarily involving conflict between them but one they would both have witnessed. (This could be as simple as an evening making and eating tea with the young people.) Specify the time scale along the bottom of the graph (e.g. 6.00pm–6.30pm–7.00pm).

- First, A invites B to talk through the incident, marking the ups and downs of B's emotions as for the previous activity, and then takes B back to various stages of the graph, asking 'So what were you thinking at this point and how were you feeling?' and marking in the thoughts and related feelings, using, if liked, the thought-bubble and heart diagrams.

- Next, B invites A to talk through the same incident, overlaying A's graph in a different colour over B's own – and again, taking A back to reflect on their thoughts and feelings at key times.

- Both people can then, using the graph as a reference point, take the conversation further if appropriate, so that at certain lower points on either of their graphs they can reflect on what each needed at such moments and whether they had their needs met, either then or later.

- Finally, invite a closing go-round reflecting on the experience of this more visual way of having a 'Your turn, my turn' type of conversation and whether it might be useful in working with young people in the future.

Case study

We had a situation which involved repairing a damaged relationship between a member of staff who sustained an injury and was subsequently off work, and a 12-year-old girl whose aggression and violent behaviour had caused the injury during an episode of 'positive handling'.

The member of staff was off work with a hand injury all over Christmas and the impact on her family was massive. So, as you can imagine, she was holding a lot of anger and frustration and wanted to tell the young person exactly who had been affected and how much. However, the girl was intent on attacking and blaming the staff for their actions rather than accepting the reasons why they had to do it, owing to her behaviours at the time. It was a situation fraught with further problems and continued poor relationships.

It was commented how good this young girl was at hairdressing, and it was suggested that we purchase a hairdresser's 'training head' for her to practise with. The (injured) member of staff knew exactly where to obtain one of these items. By this means both parties were able to engage in a conversation, each having the opportunity to talk and express her feelings and listen to the other without having to give ground, 'lose face' or become angry. So the conversation started along the lines, 'The manager has asked me to talk to you about where we can find a training head.' As there was no adverse reaction or anger, it allowed the member of staff to express 'I also need to explain some of my feelings about what happened between us, and I would like you to tell me how you are feeling too.' Within 15 minutes both had the chance to say how they were feeling, there was accountability for all that had happened, and a really fragile and damaged relationship had begun to be repaired. They are still spending one-to-one time together to continue the process, and the relationship is very much improved, which three weeks ago seemed to be practically impossible.

(Example from a residential home in Walsall.)

Social and emotional literacy and social pedagogy

This type of emotionally literate language is being encouraged by the new Social and Emotional Literacy (SEAL) curriculum in schools in England and Wales since autumn 2007. It is also an aspect of the social pedagogy that care staff are being encouraged to model in their interactions with young people. It makes sense for 'corporate parents' to work in partnership with educational professionals and be aware of each others' agendas and aspirations for the young people.

The five key themes for the SEAL curriculum, a mandatory part of the National Curriculum in England and Wales in both secondary and primary schools since the autumn of 2007, are:

- self-awareness

- managing feeling

- motivation

- empathy

- social skills.

Each of these themes is elaborated further in the Department for Children, Schools and Families (DCSF) guidelines.

Self-awareness is defined in terms of:

- being able to understand what I need to work at my best

- knowing what I am thinking and how that relates to how I am feeling

- being able to take responsibility for my actions (i.e. my choices).

These three aspects are embedded in the restorative approach and operationalized through the five key restorative themes and questions.

'Managing feelings' is defined by the DCSF as:

- being able to identify and recognize a range of feelings and express them in ways that do not hurt myself or other people

- knowing that thoughts, feelings and behaviour are linked

- understanding that changing the way I think about people and events changes how I feel about them.

Again, these three aspects are modelled by adults responding in restorative ways to conflict and challenging behaviour when they follow the restorative framework of questions or use restorative dialogue to express their own experience of a situation.

Motivation is defined in terms of:

- setting goals and thinking of the long-term consequences to myself and others

- making choices about how activities and tasks can be tackled

- helping to shape my own classroom ethos and environment.

All of these aspects can be found in the restorative response to conflict and challenge and they can also be developed in proactive community-building activities that will be discussed further in Chapter 7. These proactive aspects of a restorative approach are as important as the reactive elements.

Empathy is defined in terms of:

- understanding and respecting another person's point of view and how they might be feeling

- knowing that all people have feelings, while recognizing that they might experience and show them in different ways or in different circumstances

- knowing that my actions affect other people for better or worse.

Restorative dialogue and interventions are all predicated on the development of empathy and understanding between those involved. Both proactive and reactive interactions based on the five key themes can provide a framework for adults to model, and young people to learn, emotionally literate ways of engaging with each other.

Social skills are defined as:

- being able to live and work as part of a community (in class/school/at home)

- valuing friendships and relationships with people in my community

- working well in a group, cooperating to achieve a joint outcome

- being able to resolve conflicts

- solving problems by thinking of all the options, identifying advantages and disadvantages and evaluating outcomes in due course.

These elements are in essence what a restorative approach aims to achieve in both school and residential contexts, by providing the language and framework for a range of flexible interactions between members of these communities.

Social pedagogy is a relatively new concept for many social workers and residential staff in the UK, although as a discipline it has an established tradition in continental Europe where it is used in terms of a coherent approach to child development and used across children's services. Social pedagogues would consider themselves interested and involved in all aspects of a child's development, with emphasis on the importance of a good relationship between pedagogue and child. Informed by theory and self-knowledge, pedagogues also recognize that day-to-day interactions and activities are as important for personal development as more formal educational settings. Furthermore, whilst valuing their one-to-one relationships with children and young people, pedagogues also recognize the importance of young people's pro-social relationships with each other, and can be skilled group facilitators. Last but not least, a social pedagogue recognizes the contribution of all those with the interests of the child at heart – the various professional agencies involved, as well as the child's friends and family – and places importance on collaborative working (Petrie *et al.* 2006).

In Europe the training to become a social pedagogue is at university level and involves theoretical studies in behavioural and social sciences, as well as training in group work facilitation, conflict management and creative skills.

It may be early days in the development of theory and practice around social and emotional literacy (SEAL) in school contexts and social pedagogy in residential contexts, but in both contexts it would seem imperative that staff strive to work together and ensure consistency of approach.

Conclusion

In a residential or family setting where restorative language and ideas are being used, young people and adults do find themselves gradually learning some of the language, and using it for themselves to avoid major conflicts occurring. Even if the framework is not quite as 'word perfect', the five key themes can become second nature and start to inform the dialogues people have. It is perfectly possible to have a prolonged conversation which mixes pure restorative enquiry, 'Your turn, my turn' and both versions of the 'I' message, as appropriate. The key is keeping the inner dialogue going:

- What sense am I making of this?

- How am I feeling?

- What do I need?

- What might the other person be thinking, feeling and needing?

- So what shall I do or say next?

Unfortunately there are times when feelings are running too high, or when those involved are unable to have such a dialogue, without the support of a third party – an impartial restorative facilitator. The next few chapters explain this role.

Chapter 5

Small Restorative Meetings

This chapter will discuss how to facilitate a meeting between people who would benefit from a conversation which, for a variety of reasons they may not be able to have on their own. These meetings can be used to:

- resolve tensions, conflicts and misunderstandings between young people, between adults, and between adults and young people

- address an issue where one person's behaviour is causing another some distress on an ongoing basis (e.g. minor bullying; low-level harassment)

- move forward and seek to repair the harm when one person has consciously done something that has caused this minor harm to another person, materially, physically or emotionally.

This chapter will describe a simple generic format for approaching any of these situations, since it can sometimes be difficult at the outset to know what type of situation it is. I have found that this is more useful for people than providing different models of practice depending on the situation. Even when a situation seems clear-cut, involving an apparently unequivocal case of wrongdoing for example, it is so often the case that when people start to talk it emerges that the apparently innocent second party did or said something that triggered the incident. That is not to imply blame, but to encourage both sides to think in terms of their own contribution and recognize that it is a situation from which both sides can learn. A restorative intervention of any length is informed by the same five key restorative themes of restorative enquiry and restorative dialogue.

The main focus of the chapter is on meetings in which a facilitator supports two people to have a conversation. As such this format can be useful in residential units, and also in foster settings when a conflict flares up, needing the help of a third party within the family. The meeting structure can be used for larger numbers of people as well, informally and formally. Chapter 6 discusses the issues raised when facilitating meetings involving more than two participants.

The chapter begins by offering a quick process that can be used informally and spontaneously when something flares up unexpectedly. It will also consider how to prepare for issues of a more serious nature when individual conversations with those involved need to be had first, before a face-to-face meeting. Such meetings involve careful preparation. Sometimes extra time needs to be spent overcoming resistance, and this will also be discussed. Finally the chapter will look at record-keeping.

Informal face-to-face restorative interventions

These brief, often spontaneous interventions are sometimes called mini-conferences, or corridor conferences (to epitomize the spontaneity of an incident that might flare up in a school or residential home corridor or hallway, for example). On the streets, when used by the police when they come across a relatively minor dispute between young people, this instant intervention is being called a 'Restorative Youth Disposal' or 'street RJ'.

In its simplest form, when something flares up quickly in the kitchen, say, or in the livingroom, and needs a swift restorative response, these themes can be embodied in the five questions, asked to each of the people concerned, and can take a matter of minutes (Table 5.1).

Table 5.1 Restorative enquiry – short form

Theme	Question
1	What happened?
2a	What were you thinking?
2b	And so what were you feeling?
3	Who do you think has been affected by this?
4	What do you need to feel better about this?
5	So what needs to happen? (What could you do to make things better?*) *Not always appropriate.

The key to this brief intervention model is the tone, pace, body language and genuineness of the facilitator and their ability to limit what they say, as far as possible, to these five simple questions (Figure 5.1).

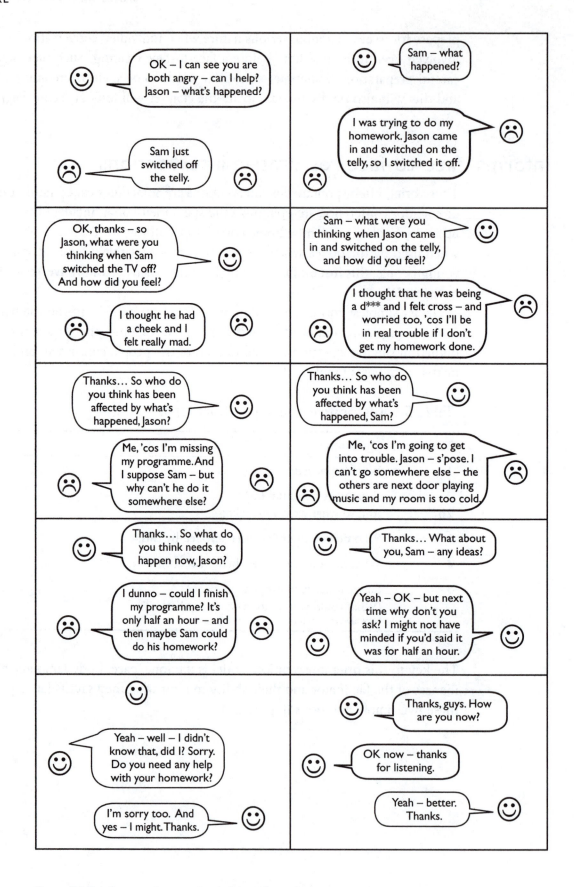

Figure 5.1 Brief restorative meeting (mini-conferencing)

Case study

Two boys, 11 and 12 years old respectively, fell out over TV. Food went up walls, plates and other crockery broken. The boys had to be separated to avoid bloodshed. Both felt they were 'victims'.

A member of staff worked separately with them initially, then got them together. They were then encouraged to listen to each other to hear what was making the other mad/upset today. Halfway through this they put their arms around each other and one started saying, 'I'm sorry, I'll do your washing up for you.' 'No,' said the other, 'I'll do it.' 'Okay,' said the first one, 'then I'll clear up the mess in the dining room.'

(Residential home; Hertfordshire)

More formal meetings

There will be times when a lengthier meeting may be needed, especially after a more serious incident or in the event of some on-going problem, such as bullying. The two people may need a cooling-off period. There may be initial reluctance to meet, and this is where careful preparation comes in.

There may be some risk assessment necessary to identify whether a face-to-face meeting between the two people is the appropriate way forward – especially when bullying has been reported. The facilitator will need to use the long restorative enquiry format described in Chapter 3, with both people separately and privately, first. All the skills described in Chapter 3 may be needed – the minimal encouragers, the echo, the time line, the thoughts and feelings questions asked at various critical points, together with occasional empathic summaries of what is being said.

It is very important that it is the same person who talks to each person privately and also facilitates the meeting. The preparatory meetings help to build trust and rapport and help the facilitator to prepare as well. The facilitator will use essentially the same sequence of questions with each participant as they used in the preliminary individual restorative enquiry, so that each knows what to expect, if not from the other participant, then at least from the facilitator.

It might be useful to think of the individual preparation phase as the micro version of the five restorative themes and the face-to-face meeting as the macro version (Figure 5.2).

Overcoming resistance

The initial meetings using restorative enquiry may also involve some encouragement from the facilitator, since the people involved in the incident may have fears, may still be very angry, and may see no point in meeting with the other person.

Ultimately it is their decision, and whatever this is needs to be respected, but there may well be undesirable consequences if a face-to-face meeting does not take

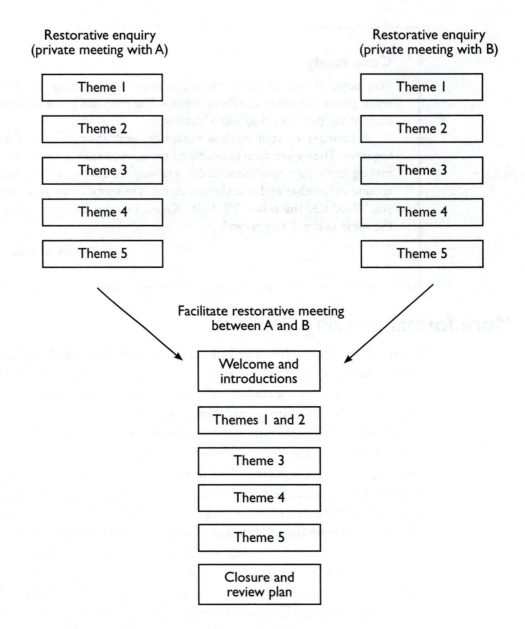

Figure 5.2 The five restorative themes integrated into the preparation and the meeting

place. Depending on the seriousness of the incident, unwillingness to meet may mean that senior staff have no option but to go down a more disciplinary route, either internally or, worse, by calling in external agencies such as the police.

There are some extremely important principles that need to be adhered to in such circumstances. If the resistance to having a restorative meeting comes from the person who perceives themselves to have been harmed (victimized), it is vital that they do not feel any pressure to engage simply in order to avoid criminalizing the other person. This could result in feelings of further victimization. Of course it may well be true that without their consent to a restorative process the matter needs to be dealt with by the police. However, everyone must feel that their wishes are respected, and if they prefer the criminal justice route, this is their right. This is a tricky call for a restorative practitioner, who may be convinced that a face-to-face meeting would actually be far more beneficial, not just for the wrongdoer, but also for the person wronged. There is a fine line between encouragement and persuasion, and the key lies in listening empathically to the way each side is expressing their needs. It may be useful to share case studies of occasions where a member of staff felt much better for taking part, despite the seriousness of the incident.

Case study

A young person flicked his lighter close to a worker's hair, catching it on fire and causing a burn to his head. The worker left the home very upset and angry, saying that he would never return to work there again.

A member of the ROLAC[17] team facilitated a formal restorative meeting during which this worker was able to express to the young person how angry he had been at the time and how sad he now felt about what had happened.

The young person appeared to express genuine regret about his actions and made a sincere apology which was accepted by the worker, who felt that this was the main thing he required for the harm to be repaired. The worker has since returned to work in the home.

(Residential home, Bedfordshire)

Recalling Chapter 3, our needs, expressed as nouns or noun phrases, are actually relatively few, and they are not to be confused with position statements that may be expressed at moments of anger or fear. Initial responses to abuse or attack from another person may leave the injured party expressing what they need in terms of:

- I need them punished.

- I need him to go – it's him, or me.

- I'm going to kill her.

- I'm going to get my mates to do him over.

These initial angry responses may soften if the speaker is simply given time to calm down, if any judgemental response is avoided.

Another technique is to tease out what need would be met by such an option, and usually all of these angry 'position statements', demands or threats can be understood as responses to hurt, unmet need and fear. What people want is for the other person to acknowledge what they have done, put it right and not do it again.

---

17 ROLAC is an initiative called 'Reducing Offending in Looked-After Children.'

Exploring anger and fear

One option, when working with a resistant or reluctant person, could be to use a visual metaphor to help get to the bottom of their anger and identify their needs in the situation. In my organization we have adapted an activity I first met on a course run by an excellent organization called LEAP Confronting Conflict (based in London) based on the training manual *Playing with Fire* (Fine and Macbeth 1992). We share this with participants on our courses and they attest to having adapted it as a one-to-one exercise with individuals, not only when dealing with resistance to meeting but at other times too. In fact it can be seen as a metaphor for the whole mediation experience as well, in the sense that it visualizes how the experience can get to the bottom of what has been going on by drawing out participants' deepest feelings, fears and needs.

ACTIVITY 5.1

- Invite people to work alone initially, and provide sheets of paper and pens.
- Begin by dividing a large sheet of white paper on a flipchart into two, and drawing the shape of an onion in the top half, writing the word 'anger' on the outer layer (Figure 5.3).

Figure 5.3 Anger onion (anger)

- Invite people to copy this onto their own sheet of paper and in the bottom half of the sheet complete a sentence beginning something like: 'I feel/felt angry when...'
- At this point suggest that beneath anger there are often feelings of hurt, and write the word 'hurt' in the next layer of the onion (Figure 5.4).

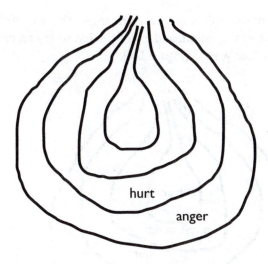

Figure 5.4 Anger onion (hurt)

- Invite people to consider in what ways they may have felt hurt by what the other person is doing or has done and then to write the next sentence: 'I felt hurt because...'

- Next, suggest peeling off yet another layer and identifying what their unmet needs are, or were, in the situation (e.g. needs for respect; consideration; support; acknowledgement). Write the words 'unmet needs' at this level in the onion (Figure 5.5).

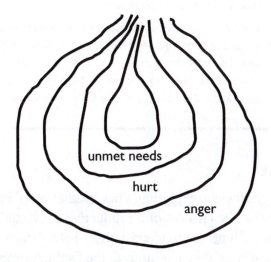

Figure 5.5 Anger onion (unmet needs)

- Invite people to complete a third sentence: 'What I need/needed (but haven't been getting/didn't get) was...'

Remind people about the difference between needs expressed as demands or obligations – 'I need her to/I need to' – and needs expressed as abstract nouns encapsulating universal prerequisites for personal safety and growth.

- At the heart of the onion, and beneath anger, there is often fear. Write this in at the heart of the onion, and invite people to try to complete the final sentence: 'My fear was…' (Figure 5.6).

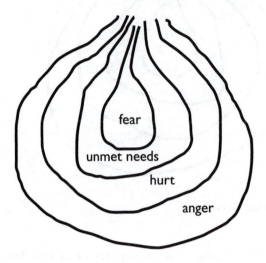

Figure 5.6 Anger onion (fear)

- Some people would argue that if people can identify the fear at the centre of their onion, they are probably able to dive even deeper and find the fundamental needs beneath that – a need for safety, for example, and a degree of control and power in their lives.

- A final stage could be a discussion in pairs about what people have learnt from their own personal onions (the details of which are personal and confidential), and the uses this activity could be put to with young people; also about the insights it can give people to help them understand their own anger, as well as that of the young people they may work with.

Safety and empowerment

Safety needs might include exploring what 'ground rules' both sides will need to feel safe and to increase the chances of a productive conversation – and it is always respectful to invite each person to identify these before the meeting. If either person is a bit unclear about what they might need, the facilitator can make suggestions along the lines of 'In the past some people have found it useful to agree to…'

- Allow each person to speak without interruption.

- Be respectful and avoid insults and abusive language or behaviour.

- Be truthful.

- Respect confidentiality and keep what is shared of a personal nature in the room.

Safety might also be explored in terms of when and where the face-to-face meeting takes place and the seating arrangements. The more each person knows in advance about what to expect, the safer they will feel, and so it is worth talking about all of these issues.

Being consulted about where and when to meet, and where to sit, is also a way of sharing control of the meeting. One person might want to meet as soon as possible to sort things out, whereas the other would prefer to wait until the next day, in order to calm down, for example. Postponement in the confined environment of a residential home might have advantages and disadvantages, and these would need to be explored, again with both sides.

Location

The choice of location for the face-to-face meeting requires consideration. Not every home has the luxury of choice, but every available room or venue may have different associations for each of the individuals involved, and these might impact on their engagement in the meeting or even their willingness to engage at all. Even if there are very few options it is nevertheless important to explore each side's feelings and needs in respect of the meeting room.

If an office or staff room is used this might not be most appropriate for the young people, whereas a living space might not always be private. A room that has windows may be overlooked, telephones and mobile phones in the room would need switching off to avoid disruptions (and negotiations about mobile phones in particular are best done in advance in relation to each person's need for safety and respect), and a notice on the door would need to be organized in advance. The wording of the notice might need agreeing since, on the one hand it is designed to prevent disruption, but on the other hand it signals that something different and important is going on, and might invite unwanted curiosity either at the time or later.

Pre-meeting negotiations

One initial individual conversation with each person, using restorative enquiry, is often all that is needed before proceeding with the face-to-face meeting. However, as the above discussion indicates, there can sometimes be a bit of shuttling back and forwards between people to ensure that both sides are happy with the preliminary preparations and the logistics of the meeting, and this requires patience on all sides. As Charles Barton has said (Barton 2003), the success of the face-to-face meeting depends in large measure on the extent to which all parties feel empowered at every step of the process.

The shuttle process may even extend to the meeting itself and involve written communication between all sides, or some degree of going between each side conveying perspectives, needs and feelings if initial reluctance to meet face-to-face continues.

Logistics

Having had preparatory meetings with all sides using restorative enquiry, and having agreed with all sides where and when to meet, the facilitator also needs to give some thought to practicalities. There is a checklist in Appendix C covering things to think about both for these smaller meetings and for more formal conferences. Common sense is needed to decide which are possible and relevant for each sort of meeting. I make a few comments below about some of the issues:

- seating arrangements
- refreshments
- tissues
- note-taking and record-keeping
- meeting and greeting.

Seating arrangements

What seats are best for those involved? How can differences in age or status be minimized by the choice of seats? What would the impact be if people were seated around a table? Does this create a barrier or a sense of safety? What do those involved prefer? (I must admit that I am a passionate advocate of an open 'circle' of three chairs, equidistant from each other – three points on an equilateral triangle, in effect – and have found tables an unnecessary impediment to healing and re-connection.) Even if one began with a table, could it be moved as the meeting progresses and rapport is established? Where in the room will the seats be placed and how far apart? Who should be nearest the door? (Homes may well already have protocols about meetings involving young people – are these appropriate for restorative meetings and if not, what new protocols are needed?)

Refreshments

Are refreshments best served afterwards as a way of 'breaking bread' together at the end of the meeting to symbolize healing and the re-establishment of relationships? What drinks are best – if hot drinks are served, might these get in the way of the discussion, or be a risk if feelings got high? What receptacles might be used, for the same reason? Glass or china might get smashed or thrown.

Tissues

Tissues are a useful item to have nearby and visible, but not to be offered unless asked for, as an unasked-for tissue can give the message that tears are unacceptable and need to be suppressed, or pose a problem for the facilitator. (They might do, but it isn't the facilitator's role to approve or disapprove.)

Note-taking and record-keeping

This is a bigger issue which I discuss in greater length on page 139. However, suffice it to say in this section that if written records need to be made in the meeting, the facilitator should ensure that the appropriate forms, some blank paper and pens are all on hand. Rough notes, if taken, need to be shredded and disposed of after the meeting.

Meeting and greeting

It is important to think about how, where and when the facilitator will meet and greet both participants. If they are still unhappy in each other's company, then the preparatory meeting may have included a discussion about who comes into the meeting first to sit down, where they will wait prior to the meeting and whether the facilitator needs an assistant to stay with the person left outside while the first person comes in and settles down. Failure to consider these points might lead to some unnecessary setbacks at the outset, such as hostile remarks or body language, last-minute changes of heart, or perception of bias on the part of the facilitator towards one or other party.

The initial greeting at the door, or wherever contact is first made, is also an important opportunity for the facilitator to demonstrate respect for both sides, displaying a positive and encouraging manner, remaining warm and empathic, whilst also appearing impartial to both sides and neutral towards the outcome. The inner dialogue discussed in Chapter 3 will be vital before, during and after this meeting.

Facilitating the face-to-face meeting

The five key restorative themes define the shape of the restorative meeting, together with an opening stage and a closing stage. The opening stage includes a warm welcome and a brief explanation (more of a reminder, as it should have been discussed in the preparatory meeting with each person) of what is to happen, what to expect from the facilitator and what needs to be agreed by way of ground rules for everyone present. The closing stage includes a check with each person about how they are at the end of the meeting, when they want to review how the agreement is working and, finally, some shared refreshments to consolidate the reconciliation or reconnection.

It might be useful to consider the meeting in the form of a flow chart, with six discrete stages, although at times the facilitator may need to backtrack and repeat a stage if multiple issues emerge that need dealing with one by one (Figure 5.7).

What follows is a more detailed explanation about what each stage entails and I hope this is helpful to individuals reading this book. For group training purposes I would also recommend my own peer mediation and training manual (Hopkins 2007) which, although originally designed for young people, has a very useful skills development section with lots of useful activities for developing the micro skills of facilitation, and then gradually consolidating competence and understanding by

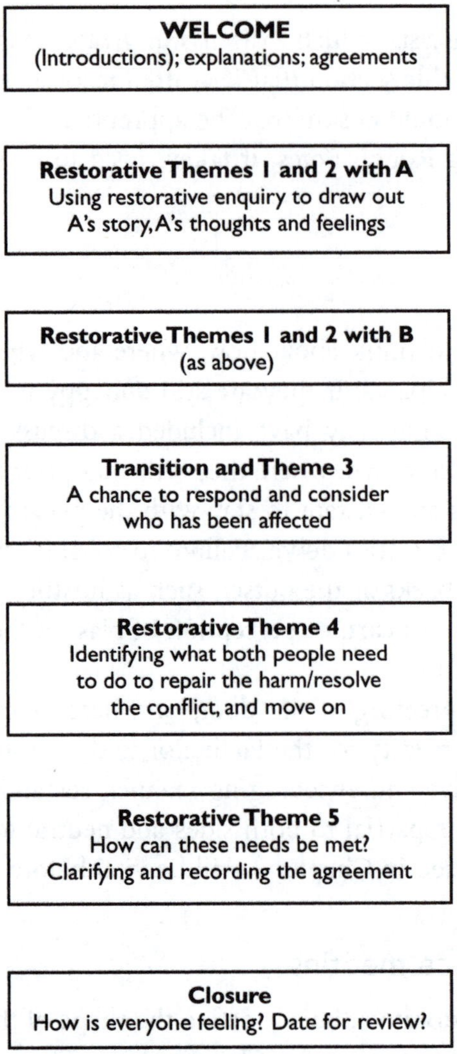

```
┌─────────────────────────────────────────┐
│              WELCOME                     │
│  (Introductions); explanations; agreements │
└─────────────────────────────────────────┘

┌─────────────────────────────────────────┐
│     Restorative Themes 1 and 2 with A    │
│     Using restorative enquiry to draw out │
│     A's story, A's thoughts and feelings │
└─────────────────────────────────────────┘

┌─────────────────────────────────────────┐
│     Restorative Themes 1 and 2 with B    │
│              (as above)                  │
└─────────────────────────────────────────┘

┌─────────────────────────────────────────┐
│         Transition and Theme 3          │
│       A chance to respond and consider   │
│         who has been affected            │
└─────────────────────────────────────────┘

┌─────────────────────────────────────────┐
│           Restorative Theme 4           │
│     Identifying what both people need    │
│    to do to repair the harm/resolve     │
│       the conflict, and move on          │
└─────────────────────────────────────────┘

┌─────────────────────────────────────────┐
│           Restorative Theme 5           │
│       How can these needs be met?        │
│   Clarifying and recording the agreement │
└─────────────────────────────────────────┘

┌─────────────────────────────────────────┐
│               Closure                   │
│  How is everyone feeling? Date for review? │
└─────────────────────────────────────────┘
```

Figure 5.7 The restorative meeting framework

practising first Stage 1 in a role-play scenario, then Stages 1 and 2 together, then Stages 1 to 3, and so on. This helps to develop confidence as well, since at each new stage what had, at first practice, seemed daunting becomes, when it is integrated into the next step, so much easier.

Stage 1: the welcome

The welcome begins from the moment the facilitator engages with the first person and encompasses not only what is said but the way it is said, and the body language as well. Before each person enters the room it might be useful to check whether each is still willing to participate, and thank them for coming.

The facilitator is modelling warmth, empathy, positivity, impartiality with regard to both participants and neutrality with regard to the outcome. Whatever the outcome, the facilitator needs to convey optimism and commitment to the process

– without this positivity the meeting could be doomed from the outset. Clearly the positivity must not be so excessive that the participants are put off – they are likely to be coming with very mixed feelings, and an over-enthusiastic facilitator might strike a discordant note.

It is likely that introductions are unnecessary when there are only two people involved but it is well to clarify how each wants to be addressed, and also to remind people who the facilitator is and what role they are playing that day, if it differs from other roles they play in the participants' life.

A simple welcome might include:

- a greeting, and introductions if appropriate

- thanks for coming and an acknowledgement that the decision to engage in the meeting may have been brave and hard to make

- a reminder of the purpose of the meeting, for example:

    'You have agreed to come to this meeting to talk about what has happened/is happening between you and explore what you both need so that you can move on and feel better.'

- an explanation of the process, for example:

    'You will both have a chance to explain, in turn, what has happened/been happening from your perspective, the sense you have made of these events and the feelings that have arisen as a result. After listening to each other there will be a chance to hear what you both need to move on and then discuss how these needs can be met, and what can be done to put things right.'

- an explanation of your role as facilitator, for example:

    'I am not here to take sides, nor to resolve the issues for you or suggest ways forward. My role is to help you talk together and find ways forward for yourselves, and to support you in coming to a mutually acceptable agreement.'

- a reminder of the 'ground rules' you discussed with each person separately, and a quick check that there is agreement to them, for example:

    'As we agreed, each person needs the chance to speak without interruption; to feel safe and respected; to expect honesty from each other and to feel confident that what is said in the room stays in the room. Are we all still agreed?'

It is important at this stage, from a child protection perspective, to explain that you will also honour this 'confidentiality clause' unless you fear for the safety of either person, in which case you will need to discuss what is said with your manager or child protection officer; assure both people that, should such a matter arise, you will discuss this with them first.

Although I have given an example of the kind of words I might use, I cannot stress enough that each facilitator will find their own words and style for this welcome. The following box may serve as an aide memoire.

- Greeting and introductions.

- Thanks and acknowledgement.

- The purpose of the meeting.

- An explanation of the process.

- Role of facilitator.

- A reminder of the 'ground rules'.

In training, or when first starting out, it will be very useful to get some feedback from colleagues, or even participants in a meeting, as to how your welcome comes across. You might like to ask for feedback on the following pointers in Table 5.2.

Table 5.2 Welcome checklist

Do you appear warm and welcoming?	☐
Is your tone of voice calming?	☐
Do you speak slowly and clearly?	☐
Do you inspire confidence in the process?	☐
Do you balance eye contact between both people?	☐
Do you manage to avoid sitting in a way that suggests bias to one or other person?	☐
Do you sound natural?	☐
Do you use language appropriate to both people?	☐
Is it clear that you are not taking sides?	☐
Is it clear that you are not making judgements about either person?	☐
Do your explanations about the purpose and the process demonstrate your neutrality towards the outcome?	☐

Stage 2: restorative themes 1–2

This is the stage when each person gets the opportunity to tell their side of the story. The facilitator is guided in this stage by the first two themes of the restorative enquiry framework (Table 5.3).

Table 5.3 Restorative enquiry – longer version: first two themes

Theme	Question	Key skills
1. Unique stories	What happened?	• Minimal encouragers • Echo • Time line
2. Thoughts and feelings	What were you thinking? And so how were you feeling?	Judge when to ask these questions in relation to key events during the story.

Who starts?

Much is written about who should be invited to speak first in the restorative justice literature. In my experience, facilitating meetings involving only two participants, the answer is – it depends. In a case of clear-cut harm it can be useful for the person who has done wrong to speak first, so that the one wronged knows that the person has admitted to the deed. On the other hand, if there is still some level of denial and a failure to appreciate the full extent of the harm caused, it might be useful for the wrongdoer to listen first to the person they have affected.

When the meeting is between people who are each blaming the other, then who is invited to speak first may be a matter of judgement or even negotiation during the preparation stage. Sometimes a rule of thumb is, whoever reported the incident first. Another criterion may be which person you think has more patience to wait through the other's story. Pragmatism is the key – but the thing to avoid is a secondary conflict in the room about who should start, so make sure you are prepared, and have prepared the participants for the 'order of play'. Chapter 7 goes into greater detail about circle process, which differs from this more facilitated meeting – and at times, with a small group rather than two people, this less formal style might be more appropriate.

Stage 3: transition

When both people have had a chance to tell their side of the story, return to the first speaker and ask if there is anything else they want to say, having heard what the second speaker has said. This is an important time – the first speaker may have omitted a certain part of what happened for various reasons, including:

- they had forgotten about it

- it was not relevant to them

- there were parts of what happened that they would prefer to omit because they feel ashamed, embarrassed, or worried about incriminating others.

At this stage as well, things that have been said may trigger the need for a response – possibly an early expression of remorse, possibly some denial of the other person's version of events, possibly a need to say more about an aspect the participants had not dwelt on first time round.

In my experience this can be a slight pause in the process, when participants can sometimes have a brief conversation – it is for the facilitator to judge if this exchange is moving things forward or not. An early apology can be acknowledged ('Thanks for that – we'll come back to that later'); more details can be accepted.

It is important not to rush this phase – if feelings are still running high then it may not be appropriate to push on into the next stage. Instead the facilitator must check that people are still willing to be there and still willing to try and repair the harm that has happened.

If there are still signs of anger it may be worth either asking each participant in turn if there is still something they need to add, or even having a pause and speaking to each person privately to check out whether there is something unsaid that they need help in saying.

Finally – when both participants have signalled that they have said all they want to say at this stage, each is asked who, in the light of all that has been said, do they think has been affected by what has happened (Table 5.4).

Table 5.4 Restorative enquiry – longer version: third theme

Theme	Question	Key skills
3. Effect, affect and harm	Who has been affected by what has happened?	Ensuring the question is open, not leading, and with no pressure to name anyone.

This question can be mishandled if the facilitator has their own agenda – wanting or expecting certain answers from the speakers. This is why it is important that the facilitator is constantly checking in with themselves and ensuring that their own judgements or needs are not influencing the process. If a speaker says they do not know, and names neither themselves nor anyone else, then I do not think it is the facilitator's role to put words into their mouth. If at this stage a speaker appeared unable or unwilling to consider the issue of who had been affected, I would consider whether it was wise to continue. On the other hand, it is an unusual question and for many young people a new idea – and so I would use my judgement about whether a 'nil' response necessarily signalled a refusal to empathize with the other. It is also possible that until both speakers realize that both sets of needs are going to be listened to and explored, they may resist acknowledging the impact of their actions.

Stage 4: needs

Refer back to the discussion about needs in Chapter 3 (page 83) to guide you in this stage of the process. To enable people to move from going 'head to head' to being 'heart to heart' we have to help them identify the needs beneath what they may initially frame as demands.

Remember the activity looking at what we need when we are harmed or have caused others harm in Chapter 2 (page 39) – and be aware that both sides are likely to have similar needs. A young person who has sworn at an adult when asked to get out of bed may acknowledge that the adult needs respect and consideration, if the adult accepts that the young person also needs the same, and simply reacted badly to being woken with loud knocking and a brusque reminder that they were 'late *again*'. Together they can work out a strategy for another time in which they can both demonstrate respect and consideration. This may need revisiting more than once – neither side may be able to change ingrained habits overnight – but at least the way forward has been agreed jointly.

'Cards on the table'

Although I never facilitate a restorative meeting around a table, I want to use this metaphor as a way of reminding people to invite both sides (or all sides, in a larger group) to *identify* their needs before discussing how to *meet* these needs. In other words, 'put all your cards on the table'. The facilitator may want to list their needs, maybe even to write them on a piece of paper for all to see. In my experience a facilitator can get in a muddle at this point if they invite an immediate response from the other side after each expressed need. This stage can be a challenge for the facilitator, eager perhaps for things to move forward and be resolved. At no point should a facilitator make suggestions about what the participants need. The facilitator's role is limited to helping the participants articulate their needs – translating demands and requests into needs, but not changing what they need or making suggestions unrelated to these needs (Figure 5.8).

As Table 5.5 shows, identifying needs and then addressing how each will be met are two separate stages.

Table 5.5 Restorative enquiry – longer version: last two themes

Theme	Question	Key skills
4. Needs	What do you need for the harm to be repaired so you can move on?	Listening for the needs beneath the demands.
5. Accountability, empowerment and collaborative problem-solving	So what needs to happen now? (*If appropriate*: And what can you do?)	Keeping out of the discussion. Knowing when to come back in. Supporting people to draw up their own agreement and ensuring it is SMART.

Stage 5: ownership of problem-solving

Once participants have thought about what they need, they can be invited to find a way forward that they can all agree to. At this stage the facilitator should encourage people to talk together. They may need reminding to address each of the needs

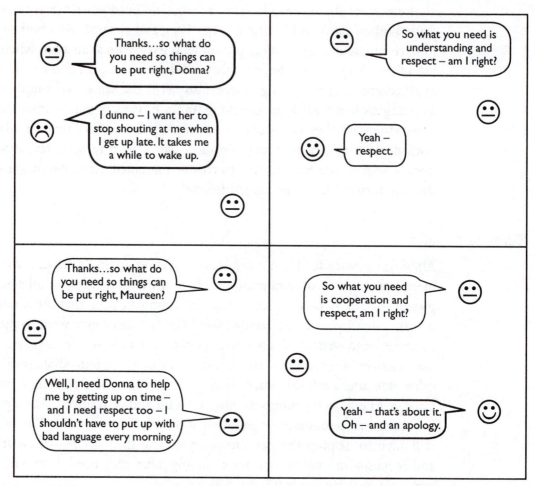

Figure 5.8 Teasing out the underlying needs

mentioned, but the less the facilitator says, the better at this stage. I try to sit back, with my head down slightly, so that people are not tempted to talk to me, but talk to each other.

If the conversation begins to get heated at this stage the facilitator can gently remind people of the purpose of the meeting, check that they are still willing to try and find a way forward, and maybe remind them of the progress they have made.

Once agreement has been reached in general terms the facilitator may need to help both sides ensure that their agreement meets the SMART test, i.e., it is:

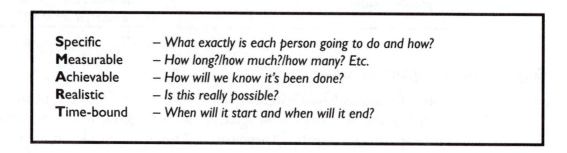

These specific details can be sorted out in the drawing up of a written agreement that both people can sign and have a photocopy to keep.

If the agreement is simply an apology or an exchange of apologies, then a written contract may not be necessary, but it is probably useful to have a record of the meeting in any case. I would suggest that the people involved in the meeting are involved in filling in this record to ensure that they agree with the way it is recorded and the way the outcome is described. Suggested ways to record such meetings are in the next section of this chapter.

This attention to detail can also ensure that both people are now able to negotiate and talk together amicably. Tensions at this stage would suggest that all has not yet been resolved.

Record-keeping

Residential units will already have protocols for recording incidents. Different places will manage the challenge of balancing confidentiality, so that participants in meetings feel safe to speak freely, with statutory obligations to record incidents. The *Best Practice Guidance for Restorative Practitioners* (Home Office 2004) simply states that a practitioner must 'maintain confidentiality, subject to the requirements of the law' (p.19), and as a footnote reminds practitioners of the Data Protection Act 1998.

In Hertfordshire one home's incident book was redesigned to take into account restorative principles, and in Derbyshire a 'significant event' form has elements of the restorative key themes in it. Two suggested formats, adapted from these forms, can be found at the back of the book (Appendix D and Appendix E). Each setting will need to develop its own variation and these basic forms can be adapted to suit the context.

During the meeting itself a very simple form could be used (Appendix F) which can be hand written in front of the participants, who can, literally, dictate the words to the facilitator so that everyone is clear that what is written is what was agreed. Everyone can have a copy of this to keep and a copy could be attached to the more formal record.

Conclusion

This chapter has brought the language and themes introduced in earlier chapters together into a simple, flexible framework that lends itself to a variety of contexts in a residential home, school, or even a foster family setting (Appendix B).

The themes, the language and the framework can be used informally and spontaneously, and the chapter offers this instant format – 'street or corridor conferencing' as it is sometimes called. It has also described a slightly more formal meeting involving two people. The next chapter considers the extra issues involved in more serious cases, which may involve people from outside the home, either as participants or because of their role within a multi-agency partnership.

Chapter 6

Conferencing

Introduction

This chapter focuses on the restorative meeting referred to as a 'conference'. These are the types of meetings which many people associate with restorative justice. The formal conference model is often appropriate when the behaviour of one person (or more than one) has caused another person (or people) significant harm – whether emotional, material or physical. They may involve just the facilitator, the person harmed and the person responsible for the harm,[18] but these formal conferences often include others who have been affected – either by virtue of their relationship to the main parties, or because they belong to the community in which the incident occurred. Depending on the seriousness of the incident these conferences may be facilitated by a member of staff from within the residential home, a member of staff from another home (for the sake of increased impartiality); a member of the local Youth Offending Team's restorative justice service, a trained police officer or, in areas with a strong multi-agency network, an appropriate facilitator from another agency. Multi-agency procedures and protocols are discussed in Chapter 8.

The chapter begins by describing how a member of staff already experienced in the restorative processes discussed in earlier chapters can prepare for and facilitate a restorative conference. The model described here uses a framework virtually identical to that used in interpersonal conflict and less serious issues, described in Chapter 5, with certain key differences which will be explained. The chapter also considers some basic preliminary questions, such as:

- whether to hold a conference at all

---

18 I am unwilling to use the words 'offender' and 'victim' as these are totalizing labels that can be unhelpful and demeaning. They can become self-fulfilling prophecies, blocking alternative choices. They also oversimplify what can sometimes be a complicated situation, since those who do wrong, cause harm or even 'offend' in the sense that they break the law, can also find themselves victimized – and so to label people one or the other can obscure issues that may need addressing on all sides.

- whether to use the conference format, as opposed to other types of restorative response

- who to involve

- how to prepare each participant

- how to prepare the conference venue

- record-keeping

- on-going support and review.

First steps

When a harmful incident has occurred there is likely to be a need for some cooling-down time. This might be a matter of hours or even days, if, for example, the incident has involved a member of staff who has then gone off shift.

This period of time is not easy to handle in a closed community such as the residential home or the family. People still have to go on interacting, sharing mealtimes, helping with homework, and so on. As a restorative response becomes the accepted norm, though, it may become easier to reassure everyone affected that the time between an incident and a formal intervention is an important part of the way forward. People learn to appreciate that such matters need cooling-down and preparation time – and that talking too much about it, taking sides or fuelling the fires is not going to be helpful for anyone involved.

The cooling-down time can be used to listen to all those affected and gather their different perspectives. All those involved need a chance to talk to someone skilled in non-judgemental active listening. (The longer version of the restorative enquiry in Chapter 3 provides this framework. For ease of reference an aide memoire for this preparatory meeting can be found in Appendix A.)

Initial conversations need to be with those most closely involved – the wrong-doer and those directly harmed. Who to listen to first may be an issue. It may be that the order in which people are approached is a pragmatic one, especially if not everyone can be found at first. It is possible that the first conversation is had with the person harmed because they come to report what has happened – but this may not necessarily be the best time to embark on a full restorative enquiry. They may need to off-load in an emotional way, and then later be taken through the five steps in a calmer fashion. (The skills of reverse 'I' messaging [Chapter 4, page 97] can come in handy at such times.)

Resistance to engaging

It is possible that people will show initial reluctance to engage at all, and therefore be reluctant even to talk. For young people and staff, this is more often the case in the early days of introducing restorative approaches, and less likely once people have learned to trust the process and know from experience, or from their peers, that the outcomes are usually positive. This is not to say that it is an easy option for anyone. For the wrongdoer, going through a court hearing might well be preferable to facing everyone who has been affected by what they have done – especially those people whose respect and relationship they value. However, the opportunity to face up to what they have done and put matters right can have such positive outcomes that, once it simply becomes 'the way we do things around here', young people are more likely to engage. The day-to-day practices described throughout this book should all help to prepare people to be willing to take part in these more formal meetings, should something serious arise.

For the person harmed there may be perceived risks – of being re-victimized by the wrongdoer's denial of responsibility; of facing someone whom they have reason to fear, or maybe even because they are afraid of their own anger. They may see no advantage to themselves in going through such a meeting. It is possible that, in serious cases, the person harmed is determined to report the matter to the police and to press charges. This person must feel free to take whatever steps they believe to be necessary, and although the option of the restorative route can be explained, and its benefits to them outlined, it is ultimately their own decision whether to proceed.

It may be disappointing for staff committed to restorative approaches to know that the wrongdoer is willing to engage but the person harmed is not, or indeed vice versa. There may be scope for using patience and seeing whether the resistance on either side is due to fears and concerns that can be addressed and overcome, but in the end the process must be entered into voluntarily. It can be an act of empowerment on either side to make the decision to take another route, even if it is the traditional criminal justice route – a decision other staff must respect and be seen to respect. This could be a particular issue when the person harmed is a member of staff. They may feel under pressure to go down the restorative route, despite being unwilling or not yet ready, and end up feeling victimized not only by the original incident, but by the lack of respect for their needs on the part of their manager or other staff.

No obligation

Restorative enquiry may simply be offered as an end in itself, with no obligation to take the matter any further. The chance to talk to someone and feel listened to and not judged can be a very positive step. The process involves this emotional catharsis, followed by an opportunity to identify options by focusing on needs for moving on. In my experience, giving someone this much time and attention, and helping them to explore their needs as thoroughly as suggested, can help them to consider whether a face-to-face meeting with the other person may in fact be the best option. I am amazed that some models of restorative conferencing do not involve this story-telling stage in the initial preparation. I can well understand that people may choose not to engage if they have missed out on this opportunity.

Who else to involve?

During the conversations with these main protagonists it will become clearer, if both agree to have a meeting, who else needs to be there. The very smallest of conferences can involve the person who has caused the harm, the person harmed and the facilitator. It is that crucial Theme 3 question – *Who do you think has been affected by what has happened?* – that can help with the decision about whether others need to be there.

Strictly speaking, a conference should involve all those who have been affected, so that everyone can tell their story, identify their needs and be involved in finding a way forward (cf. the original Maori meetings involving the whole community see pages 20–21). Indeed, it is possible that once the community of the home becomes used to using the daily circles, as described in Chapter 7, the more formal facilitated conference described in this chapter is the second choice, because the whole community wants and needs to be present – partly because they have all been affected, partly because there may be some shared accountability and partly because everyone wants to help to put things right and avoid similar incidents happening again.

The facilitator will use some judgement as to whether a community circle would be the better option – but whatever the final decision, the central parties need to be in agreement. If the incident has involved local residents, they may prefer to have a smaller meeting with the person responsible, rather than the whole community of the residential home – an understandably daunting prospect, although also in some cases potentially a very positive one.

The question of who should attend raises another issue. A neighbour or local resident may wish to attend with family members. This immediately raises the issue of balance – for every person present to support the person harmed, there needs to be someone supporting the person responsible for the harm, or else they may feel outnumbered.

Readers may at once see that here is a circle that may, at times, not be squared! If, on the one hand, everyone affected should by rights (or by needs) attend the conference, and yet at the same time there needs to be a balance between the person harmed and his/her community of support, and the harmer and his/her community of support, what happens if one or other 'side' outnumbers the other?

My advice is to talk this through with the key participants separately, and with them agree the fair way forward. If this means that some people who feel affected are unable to attend, are there other ways in which they can get their needs met?

Whether to 'conference'

The decision to address an incident using a formal conference will depend on a number of factors, the most important of which, as discussed earlier, is whether those most affected choose to address the matter in a restorative way or not. Other factors that will influence whether the conference model is the most appropriate include:

- the seriousness of what has happened

- who has been affected

- how many people have been affected

- whether the perceived wrongdoer accepts responsibility for what has happened

- whether outside agencies have been involved already.

In addition to my suggestions, protocols developed jointly by Leeds Youth Offending Service, West Yorkshire Police and Leeds Children and Young People's Social Care (2007), which have been developed in relation to police involvement, raise issues which I think are relevant to home-based conferences as well:

- child's cognitive ability (capacity to know right from wrong)

- impact on child's care plan

- probability of repeat incident

- impact of formal police involvement on the young person

- best interests of both parties

- requirement for evidence of formal investigation (insurance)

- the message sent to other residents

- the skill and expertise of staff/carer to deal with a given situation.

This is where the preparation is key, and may take some time, as the decision about the way forward must be made freely by the individuals involved, but with due attention paid to all the factors mentioned. Fortunately a community with restorative approaches already in place will have several different options available, and the members of that community will be able to make an informed choice about which option is likely to best meet their needs. Should the incident involve people from outside the home, such as visiting staff or local residents, then these options would need explaining.

Chapter 8 discusses the role of other agencies, such as the local Youth Offending Team or the police, when issues arise that need to be dealt with in partnership.

Continuity from preparation to conference and review

Best practice would be for the potential facilitator of whatever restorative process is agreed upon to do all the preparation work, as well as facilitating the actual conference and conducting the review. In this way this person has the overview, and has an opportunity to build trust and rapport with all parties, if necessary convey information and views between parties (at their request, and with their consent, of course), and ensure consistency of preparation. If the meeting is to be a large one, then co-facilitation may be considered, but I would still recommend that all the preparation is done by the same person. In a co-facilitation scenario this would mean either that *both* facilitators conduct *all* the preparative meetings together, or that one of the two does all the preparation.

Preparing the participants

Restorative enquiry

The full restorative enquiry process explained in Chapter 3 is what I would recommend in the preparatory stage (see also Appendix A) – undertaken individually and in private, with each of the people involved. It is unwise to allow anyone to attend the conference who has not been given this opportunity – not only does the process help each person to feel heard, the preparation is also a time for the facilitator to explore their role in the meeting.

One other important reason for meeting with everyone prior to the meeting is to assess whether they may present a danger to themselves or to anyone else. Will they be able to abide by the ground rules, stay in their seats and allow everyone to have their say?

The important point to make is that, unlike some models of restorative practice, I would ask *all* those directly involved the *same* set of questions, and I do not differentiate between the person harmed and the harmer in the way I ask these questions. As was clear from Chapter 2 page 39, both sides are likely to need similar things.

The only difference would be in the opening questions when speaking to someone who was not present but heard later about what had happened. In this circumstance it is not appropriate to ask this person 'What happened?' They cannot answer this question directly – what they know is hearsay. This is not the point. What this person needs to talk about is their own experience of finding out about what had happened, and their thoughts and feelings after that. Thus the focus of their story is their own experience, and what they said and did afterwards, which may have involved interacting with either the person causing the harm or the person harmed, or indeed both. Just to be clear, here are some suggested words to use (Table 6.1).

Table 6.1 Variation on first two questions of restorative enquiry for supporters and those not present during the incident

Theme 1 Unique stories	How did you first find out about this incident?
Theme 2 Thoughts and feelings	What were your thoughts when you found out? How did you feel?

I might change my approach slightly in this situation and pause after the description of how the person first found out about the incident to invite them to reflect immediately on what their thoughts and feelings were, and then invite them to tell me more about what happened next (Table 6.2).

I have written *'What did you do next?'* in brackets, only as a reminder that the focus of this person's story is what happened next for *them*. This is their story. Similarly, when you invite them to talk about how things have been earlier, before the incident, what you are inviting them to do is talk about any events leading up to the incident that they want to talk about in relation to those directly involved, and

Table 6.2 Variation on restorative enquiry for supporters and those not present during the incident

Theme 1 Unique stories	How did you first find out about this incident?
Theme 2 Thoughts and feelings	What were your thoughts when you found out? How did you feel?
Return to Theme 1	Please can you tell me what happened next? (What did you do next?)

their relationship with these people. There may have been other incidents which are relevant – some history of difficulty or perhaps misunderstandings that have directly led up to what has happened.

In addition to the enquiry stage the participants will probably have some questions and concerns about the face-to-face meeting. Using your knowledge of the process, explain the format of the meeting and invite any questions for clarification. Invite participants to think about what they will need in order to be able to participate in the meeting – maybe offer suggestions about the type of ground rules usually agreed and ask if there are any others they need. Make a note of these so that at the actual meeting their needs reflect the shared ground rules explained to everyone.

You cannot promise any particular outcome but you can assure people that they will have a chance to have their say and ask the questions they want to. As the facilitator you have no agenda other than to facilitate a process, and so you cannot promise the harmed person that the wrongdoer *will* apologize or make amends. There has occasionally been misunderstanding in some quarters that the meeting is a mechanism by which wrongdoers are 'made' to face up to their deeds and 'made' to apologize or make some kind of reparation. This is to misunderstand restorative practice. It is not the facilitator's role to 'make' anyone do or say anything, and I would be seriously concerned if I met a restorative practitioner who believed that this were the case. In addition, if any participant applies pressure on either the wrongdoer or the person harmed to do something they are unwilling to do, then it is the facilitator's job to check for voluntariness.

The sense of victimization by the wrongdoer

If, during preparation, there is any sign that the wrongdoer is unwilling to engage during the meeting, or deny their involvement once the meeting begins, then this may be a reason for deciding against it. However, a certain reluctance on the part of the wrongdoer to take full responsibility for their behaviour is to be expected, and indeed often perfectly reasonable. Marg Thorsborne, a trainer and consultant in the field of restorative justice in Australia, says that in school restorative work 'everyone is accountable' and I believe the same may be true in a residential home or school. This belief was borne out by Wendy Thompson, overseeing the roll-out of restorative approaches in all of Walsall's residential children's homes:

I suppose the biggest learning point for me from our work has come from understanding how things we do as residential workers and others working with children, which we perceive as normal, really aggravate children and potentially cause ugly situations. Using RJ has given us some insight into this and how changing some quite small things in consultation with children can make a difference to the child and relationships, e.g. a child got angry and a difficult incident occurred which through RJ we later found out was due to her not wanting to attend a CAMHS (Children and Adolescent Mental Health Service) service appointment at the local CAMHS service centre. This was not because she didn't want the appointment, but she didn't want to sit in traffic and then miss first pickings at teatime! A compromise was sought in that CAMHS agreed they would try to come to us bi-weekly so she got her therapy, and the best of the food at teatime – problem solved, ugly situation prevented.

A small change through partnership working and flexibility assisted in securing happiness – a good result for RJ (and all of us).

In his work with young offenders at Grendon Prison, ex-prison governor Tim Newell recognized that many of the inmates had a strong belief that although they had done wrong they were also victims. Until this was recognized the young men were unwilling to accept responsibility for their own wrongdoing. They needed empathy and understanding before they were ready to offer empathy and understanding to anyone else.

I think this whole issue of wrongdoers feeling victimized is a particularly important issue for youngsters in care. They have almost inevitably been on the receiving end of life experiences that have left them feeling victimized, and they need understanding and compassion for this. At the same time, however, we need them to face up to the impact of their deeds on others and to have the opportunity to put things right. I believe that, deep down, they know that they need this too, in order to develop their self-esteem and sense of self-worth. This is why I like the model of restorative practice we use in my team – it respects and values the stories of wrongdoer and wronged alike, without condoning the deeds of the wrongdoer or suggesting that their previous history of victimization gives them immunity from accountability and responsibility.

Owning the preparation process

Remind everyone that it is their meeting, and so enable them to be part of the planning. Is the venue available acceptable to them? What day or time is most suitable? Even if some of the choices are limited for pragmatic reasons, nevertheless, as Barton (2003) says, this approach is about giving ownership and control back to those to whom the problem belongs, and that begins with the preparation. The facilitator's role at this stage is to balance everyone's needs and ensure that no one party dominates the planning process.

Preparing supporters and other participants for their role

Ideally the only people at the meeting are those who need to be there because they have been personally affected. They need to tell their story and they can speak from the heart about how they have been personally affected. Their stories form part of the ripple effects from the harm caused – which is what makes it hard for the wrongdoers to hear. Listening to everyone's experiences is part of the accountability process. More often, certainly in the case of young people, they may have had no idea of the impact of what they had done, not only on the most immediate 'victims' but on all those around them who have felt frustrated, hurt, angered, outraged... In my experience it is not so useful to have people in the meeting only by virtue of their role – a 'corporate victim', for example, or someone representing an organization. This is why an explanation of each person's role is important before the meeting begins.

Some people will have a double role – in their own right as people affected and also in the role of a supporter for one or other of the key protagonists; so they are there both to tell their own story and to support the person they have come with. This double role should be explained to them at the outset and explained at the beginning of the meeting as well.

Logistics

Since this chapter focuses on the conference process, let us assume that:

- the facilitator has spoken to the key participants, and they have agreed to meet. (This may have taken some to-ing and-fro-ing – it is not always as simple as a restorative enquiry with each person.)

- guided by the key protagonists, everyone else affected has been spoken to and is willing to take part as well.

- the facilitated conference model still seems to be the best way forward in the circumstances.

Now it is time for the facilitator to take stock of what needs to happen next. The next few sections look at the logistics and build on those mentioned in Chapter 5. It might be useful to have a pro forma handy for planning purposes so that nothing is forgotten – the logistics can be quite complicated, especially if people from outside the residential home are involved (see Appendix C).

Where and when to hold the conference

The more people who need to be at the conference, the more challenging decisions about when and where become. The gold standard would be for the time to suit everyone and for the venue to be a neutral one in which everyone feels comfortable. The reality may be different and the facilitator will simply need to be as respectful as possible to all parties and do the best they can.

Again, the more people involved, the longer the meeting will take, and it will be much better if everyone who attends can stay for the duration of the meeting. This needs to be factored into when the meeting takes place. Allow at least an hour for a small meeting involving two participants if it is of a serious nature (it may not take that long), and add an extra 10–15 minutes onto that for every extra person involved. This is a very rough rule of thumb. Also allow for some time at the end of the meeting for a chance for people to practise what it is like being back on speaking terms in an informal way over a cup of tea and biscuits.

Preparing the venue

Whether the conference is taking place in the home or at a neutral venue elsewhere, take time to ensure that everything is conducive to a positive outcome. A checklist is provided in Appendix C and a few comments about some points in it are added below.

Seating plan

There are no hard-and-fast rules about who sits next to whom (to some degree it is common sense) and it may be something to discuss with each participant as well, to identify any potential anxieties people have. It may even be useful to share the seating plans in advance so that everyone knows what to expect.

I usually prefer to have the main protagonists near me when I am facilitating a meeting, perhaps on either side of me of there are only two, with their supporters next (if there is only one of these per person) and then others filling in the gaps. In this way, if we get to a rapprochement between the main two, then there is only me in the way and I can sit back and let them talk easily together.

If the main players come with two supporters each, then it is probably a good idea to sit them either side of 'their' protagonist for moral support – but it is always worth discussing this. The permutations are endless – I suggest the facilitator takes a sheet of blank paper and plays around with seating plans until the best option emerges, bearing in mind any concerns or preferences raised by any of the participants. It will not be a good start to the meeting if someone refuses to sit in a particular place.

Once the seating plan is decided, ensure that very clear instructions are given to people as they enter the meeting room – if people sit down in the 'wrong' place it may get the meeting off to a wobbly start if you have to ask them to stand up and move. And if you leave them where they are, this will then throw the plan out – possibly with disastrous results.

Preparing yourself

Having taken time to prepare all the participants using restorative enquiry, take time to prepare yourself. Try and ensure that all the room preparations are done well in advance so that you have some quiet time to yourself beforehand. The next section is about meeting and greeting everyone. Enlist one or two helpers to do this, so that you are not flustered before you begin.

Find a space where you will not be disturbed, ideally the meeting room, and take some time to switch off – if you are practised in meditation or relaxation skills, now is a good time to use them, if only for a few minutes. If you use positive self-talk or affirmations, these can also be helpful to remind yourself about the positive purpose of the meeting and your skill in ensuring that everyone has a chance to get their needs met.

Close your eyes, and in your head visualize the seating plan and go around the circle, holding each person, whom you have already met, in your head for a few seconds. Try and put yourselves in the shoes of each one, imagining what each may be thinking and feeling as they arrive.

Open your eyes, take a deep breath and go out to greet the participants.

Meeting and greeting the conference participants

Do not underestimate how nervous people are likely to be just before the conference. It is worth thinking through how people are going to arrive and enter the room you have prepared – even if all those involved are based in the home.

It is possible that, as time has passed, some of those involved have already had a chance to talk informally and may not mind waiting together, but if this is not the case then keeping everyone apart until the meeting is a logistical challenge. Decide in advance whom to invite into the room first and then, as you go out to fetch the next people or person, check that those left in the room are all right and explain what you are doing.

This starts to sound a bit like the puzzle about getting a fox and three chickens across a river in a boat that only holds two creatures at one time – but it is not a good idea to leave people alone together, between whom there are still barriers of anger and hurt, either whilst they are waiting outside, or in the room while you go to fetch someone else. Ensure you have extra help on the day to attend to this crucial issue – a plan of action would be sensible.

Your body language will be giving very powerful messages – try to appear relaxed, welcoming, confident and optimistic – and give everyone a respectful, sincere greeting as they enter the room. You may choose to shake hands with each person – but remember that what you do for one must be at least offered for all. Think about whether you usher people into the room before you, or ask them to follow you in – and the messages that each of these gives. If you do usher people before you, how will they know what seat to head for?

Once everyone is seated, the meeting can begin, starting with a warm welcome and the 'domestics' – checking that everyone is comfortable as far as heat, light and fresh air are concerned, and aware of fire exits and toilet facilities. These courtesies will not be lost on any young people involved, even if they know where such facilities are found.

The format of the meeting is virtually identical to the one described in Chapter 5 (see Appendix B). For ease of reference it is reproduced here, with room for notes about what to remember:

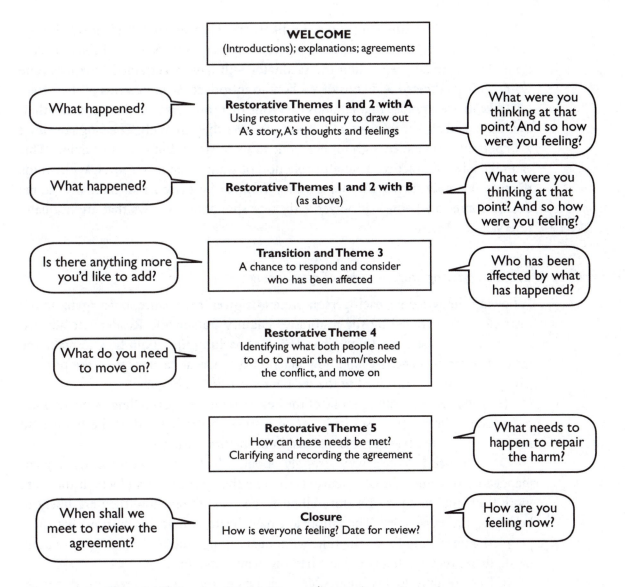

WELCOME
(Introductions); explanations; agreements

What happened?

Restorative Themes 1 and 2 with A
Using restorative enquiry to draw out A's story, A's thoughts and feelings

What were you thinking at that point? And so how were you feeling?

What happened?

Restorative Themes 1 and 2 with B
(as above)

What were you thinking at that point? And so how were you feeling?

Is there anything more you'd like to add?

Transition and Theme 3
A chance to respond and consider who has been affected

Who has been affected by what has happened?

What do you need to move on?

Restorative Theme 4
Identifying what both people need to do to repair the harm/resolve the conflict, and move on

Restorative Theme 5
How can these needs be met? Clarifying and recording the agreement

What needs to happen to repair the harm?

When shall we meet to review the agreement?

Closure
How is everyone feeling? Date for review?

How are you feeling now?

Figure 6.1 The restorative meeting: an aide memoire

The differences are in part due to the extra considerations of the numbers involved, and to the fact that the conference has been convened because of an incident that has caused harm, and that this harm has been admitted by one or more of the people present. This situation impacts on the order of questioning and the emotional journeys that are often associated with this type of conference.

Coaching tips for a conference

The welcome stage

Introductions and explanations

Whereas in the less formal meetings it is likely that everyone involved already knows each other, in the more formal conferences there may well be a need for introductions. In the initial preparation the facilitator will have ascertained how everyone wants to be addressed and considered how to introduce them in terms of their role.

I like to use a phrase that reminds everyone that this person is there to share their own story and also, if relevant, to support whoever they are with. The language used is important – simple enough for everyone to understand, but not patronizing. This can take a bit of practice. Young people do not want to be talked over, with words they do not understand, but nor do they want to be patronized. Similarly, adults do not appreciate being patronized either, or spoken to in ways that are normally reserved for children.

Themes 1 and 2: the storytelling stage – order of questioning

Following the welcome, each person present is given the chance, once again, to tell their story, encouraged by the restorative enquiry framework. Readers are advised to look again at Chapter 3 and Chapter 5 for coaching tips about how to make the most of restorative enquiry, and how much of it to use at each stage of the process. The people directly involved in the incident are asked to begin.

The order of questioning is one of the key issues in the storytelling stage. Chapter 5 discusses whether, in cases of harm, to start with the harmed or the harmer, so readers are referred back to this discussion in the first instance.

One practice I do feel very strongly about, which I have come across recommended by some models of practice, is the one that invites wrongdoers, if there are more than one, to share the storytelling stage – as if somehow they are likely to be telling the same story. The rationale I have heard is that this ensures that these people are not sitting for a long time without speaking, and because they were both, or all, there, they are likely to have had the same experience.

In fact not only is this impossible – remember the very first restorative theme, that we all have a different perspective and experience, even if we are in the same place at the same time – but in fact very often a pair or group of wrongdoers have different views on their level of involvement and responsibility. Splitting the story between them could then create a situation where the two disagree about what happened, who bears the greater responsibility, and so on. This can only serve to antagonize the other participants and introduce unnecessary conflict at the outset.

The running order following on from the main protagonists will depend on who is there, the degree of their involvement and their role. It is very important that the facilitator has thought this through, perhaps marking the running order on the seating plan they will have in front of them. In a small meeting involving the two main protagonists and a supporter each, I would suggest the following order:

1. either the person harmed or the person responsible for causing harm

2. whichever of the two above has still to speak

3. supporter for the person harmed

4. supporter for the person responsible for the harm.

In other words, regardless of whether I began with the person harmed or the person responsible for causing harm, I would always ask the person supporting the latter to go last. The rationale for this is an interesting one. In some cases the person supporting the wrongdoer (and this is particularly true in school settings involving parents or carers) is not fully aware of what the person they are supporting has done. They may even have been told only half-truths (or untruths) by this person. For them, listening to everyone else's story of how they have been affected can be a devastating and upsetting experience. Their reactions and their emotions are a significant part of the process – the full impact of the wrongdoer's deeds may only now be affecting this person for the first time, and it is happening in full view of everyone present and in particular in front of the wrongdoer.

The circle needs to be very well held for this emotional catharsis to feel safe. The supporter may feel angry, let down, ashamed, embarrassed, distressed – or all of these and more besides. What this person now says (and they may direct some of their emotions towards the person they are supporting) may be the very thing that breaks through the wrongdoer's mask of denial, and so again, strong emotions can arise on all sides.

In summary, with respect to order of questioning in this storytelling stage, it is impossible and inappropriate to prescribe a set order. Careful preparation and consultation will help to identify the optimum order – and different facilitators may make different decisions.

Introducing Theme 3

The other difference in these larger meetings is that I would ask each of the supporters the question about who they think has been affected (Theme 3) in this storytelling stage, and reserve the transition stage for the main protagonists. This is partly because I have found that the larger meetings can otherwise drag on far too long, and partly because hearing from everyone who they think has been affected can help the wrongdoer understand better the full impact of their actions, and mean that the transition stage can be a real turning point for them.

Transition and Theme 3

Once everyone has had a chance to say as much as they need about what has happened, the facilitator returns to the main parties. In larger meetings involving harm I would tend to reserve this section for the wrongdoer or wrongdoers – and after them a chance to say more if they want to, and also ask them to reflect, in the light of what they have heard, who they think has been affected.

For the wrongdoer this can be a very difficult moment – a time when feelings of remorse, shame and despair can almost overwhelm them. Given the vulnerability of many young people in care, it is the stage of the process that needs most care. Any signs of remorse can be acknowledged, but lightly – 'Thank you for that' is all that is needed. Any early expression of apology can also be acknowledged: 'Thank you – we will be coming back to that shortly.'

No short cuts

Be aware that apologies may be expressed at any stage of the process by various participants in these conferences – and they can all be acknowledged, but they are not a reason for short-cutting the whole process. Encouraging expressions of remorse and apology, whilst welcome at any time, are not the purpose of the meeting. Instead it is an opportunity for rebuilding relationships and connections, developing empathy and understanding, restoring mutual respect and enabling people to do things differently next time, draw a line underneath what has happened, learn and move on.

To these ends the whole process is important, and early signs of any of these outcomes are welcome, acknowledged and then put to one side as the process continues. Transformative mediators state that the whole purpose of such encounters is to re-establish recognition and to re-empower people, and there may be signs of this happening all along the way.

Theme 4: needs

Much has been written in earlier chapters about the importance of framing the question about needs carefully and possibly helping speakers by reframing if their needs are expressed as demands.

Regarding the order of questioning for this stage, I would recommend going around in the very same order as used for the storytelling stage. Remember, this is *not* a negotiation stage – people are simply 'putting their cards on the table'.

In larger meetings this may be a time when the facilitator needs to jot down a few brief notes, or even use a flipchart so that everyone can see the various needs being listed – in effect, an agenda for the discussion that comes next.

Theme 5: ownership and empowerment

Once all the needs have been expressed, the facilitator can invite the wrongdoer to begin by saying what they would like to do to address some of the needs expressed and repair the harm. After this the meeting works best if the facilitator throws open the discussion to those present and plays as small a part as possible. The facilitator's only role at this stage is to encourage everyone to participate, and to ensure that outcomes are not being agreed upon by everyone except either the wrongdoer or the person wronged. Ultimately these are the people who need to feel comfortable with the outcomes.

When a clear consensus emerges about what the wrongdoer, and possibly others in the group as well, need and are prepared to do, the facilitator can come back into the meeting, as it were, and invite the participants to dictate what needs to be written on the agreement form.

See Appendix F for an informal sheet on which the facilitator can write the words of each participant. (See Chapter 5 for more discussion about this and Appendix D and E for suggested pro formas which can be adapted for larger groups.) The facilitator also needs to be keeping a sharp eye on everyone's body language at this stage. It is perfectly acceptable to say 'John, you look unhappy with what is being said – would you like to say anything?' and to check out what you think you are seeing. Do not be tempted to steamroller people through this vital stage.

Once the agreement has been drawn up and signed by everyone (or just before), a review date is agreed and added to the contract so that people know that they will all be accountable for what they have said they will do, and that support will be available to help them stick to their word.

The final part of the formal meeting is the closing go-round. I have found that at this stage it can be a nice gesture simply to go around the circle, maybe starting with the person harmed, then the harmer, and then around the circle in order, asking 'How are you feeling now?'

Last but not least is the 'breaking of bread' together – the symbolic sharing of tea and biscuits, which gives everyone a chance to practise interacting after the meeting now that the matter is closed. It is a very important stage of the healing process and allows informal exchanges between people. Sometimes hugs are exchanged, or just a shaking of hands and an acknowledgement that things are sorted.

The reflective practitioner

As part of a restorative practitioner's ongoing development I would suggest that someone facilitating restorative meetings on a regular basis keeps a portfolio of these meetings (and I am not referring to contracts here, which I deal with separately), with details of seating plans, order of questioning and key issues that each meeting throws up. These will be invaluable in learning from each meeting, may be useful in supervision meetings, and also, if accreditation is being sought, serve as a record of practice. Furthermore, the record-keeping – perhaps with notes on the outcomes, possibly a brief questionnaire to participants and the review, will serve as data for evaluation. A suggested format is in Appendix G.

Conclusion

Chapters 5 and 6 have described restorative meetings of varying sizes and of various levels of formality. These responses to harm, conflict, disruption, bullying and damage to property focus first and foremost on the people affected – and as such provide a much needed strategy that meets the needs of everyone affected. In this regard it is unique amongst all existing alternatives in residential care settings, many of which are in place either to provide a listening ear and support to the young people, or to give them a lesson of varying severity in an attempt to teach them to do things differently. Restorative responses consider the needs of everyone affected – direct 'victims' but also secondary ones, those inevitably affected by the ripples of harm that spread out and contaminate the closed quarters of a residential establishment or foster family. For residential staff and foster carers especially, this new way to address challenges must surely be a welcome innovation.

The next chapter, about working in circles, is an extension of the restorative meeting framework described in Chapter 5 and 6, and also an exciting precursor – in that the more the circle becomes an organizing mechanism in a residential setting, the fewer formal meetings will be needed to put things right.

Chapter 7

Circles

This chapter could, and maybe even should, be the starting point for any residential home or foster family seeking to develop a restorative approach to life and to work. Everything I have said so far about 'being restorative' comes together in circle gatherings. Sitting together, learning to listen to each other, to respect each other's views and to appreciate how each person's behaviour impacts on everyone else, for good or ill – this is the basis for living in a community. This remains true whether the community comprises the young people and the staff caring for them, or whether it is simply the community of a family – of foster parents and the children in their care.

Most residential homes have something called a 'group meeting', even if this is relatively informal. One manager told me that they did not have meetings as such, since this was the young people's home – but they did chat informally around the supper table. Group meeting or supper-time chat – either of these could be thought of as the basis of the restorative circle as long as they meet various criteria:

- Does everyone get the chance to have their say without interruption?

- Does everyone feel that what they have said is respected and valued, if not necessarily agreed with?

- Does it feel safe to express feelings and needs?

- Do the young people have the same opportunity as the staff to speak and make decisions?

Not every gathering of people around a meal table is a circle meeting, nor needs to be, and there are, and surely must be, times when informal conversation and banter has its place. However, not all mealtime chats are necessarily positive and enjoyable, and some of the conventions of circles might enhance even the most informal of chats around the table. Nevertheless, my suggestion is that circles for planning, decision-making, problem-solving and reviewing the day be held after a meal, as a different 'event' with different 'rules of engagement'.

Circle time and circle process

Some readers may be familiar with a process called 'circle time' – a wonderful activity used in schools and youth clubs, more often with younger children than with young people of secondary age (which is much to be regretted, as it is much needed among this age group as well – not to mention the staff). 'Circle time' involves, as its name suggests, sitting in a circle and engaging in a structured and facilitated set of activities designed to develop belonging, enhance self-esteem, develop trust and respect, enhance communication skills, and encourage cooperation, with an emphasis on fun and shared goals. There is no reason why young people in care cannot be involved in a more structured set of activities of this kind, or why some types of circle time games cannot occasionally be thrown in at the end of a more formal discussion. Younger children may like to start and finish a more formal discussion with some games – and these are wonderful ways of having a laugh together and building a sense of belonging. Young teenagers may be resistant, but it depends on the young people – in my experience, once people get into the games, they actually enjoy themselves.

'Circle process' is my own name for an activity which I believe to be different in some respects from circle time, and yet similar in others. Circle time and circle process share certain values and principles, which I will explain shortly. However, whereas circle time is usually a planned set of activities with a teaching objective, facilitated by someone who would be able to identify at least some of the learning objectives of the session, circle process may at times be quite open-ended. A circle can be convened with no set agenda other than to allow all present to reflect on what they need to talk about at the time; and it can also be convened with a very specific purpose, but not necessarily with a predetermined outcome. Circle time might involve a fair amount of moving around – playing games or working in pairs and small groups before ending once again seated in a circle. Circle process usually requires people to stay seated in the circle, in the places where they first sat down. In both circle time and circle process, sometimes everyone sits on the ground, and sometimes chairs are used. When chairs are used it is ideal if all the chairs are of the same height, because an important part of both circle time and circle process is the notion of equality. Ideally everyone, young and old, is able to make an equal contribution, and their views and ideas are regarded as all equally valid. The best circles are open – with no barriers formed by tables or desks.

Circle time and circle process share certain values and principles, very much those that underpin restorative practice:

- Everyone in the circle is valued equally.

- Everyone is given an equal opportunity to participate, including the facilitator.

- Everyone has the right to pass on a given round if they choose.

- Everyone respects the ground rules, which they will have agreed as a group at the outset (see next section).

Many people using circles like to pass round an object to indicate whose turn it is to talk – this 'talking piece', as it is often called, can be a stick (maybe decorated by the members of the community with objects of their choice), a soft ball or a conch – or a different object could be used each time, depending on who facilitates the circle. For younger children a soft toy is often used. The usual convention is for the talking piece to be passed around the circle in one direction, and as it moves round everyone takes a turn (or may choose to let it pass). It is not usually passed across the circle, so as to encourage patience and an open mind, since others may say first, and maybe even better, what someone later in the circle had wanted to say. The act of waiting one's turn can have the effect of helping people to see things from many different perspectives and come to a collective agreement about something that no one had thought of before.

The first time the community meets in circle they need to decide how they want things to be – what the shared agreement is going to be about, how each wants to live together, and what each needs from everyone else. The section below describes how to use circle process to establish this starting point for restorative work.

Creating the ground rules – what do we all need from each other?

In order to develop an environment in which everyone in a given community can feel safe, valued and included, everyone must have their say in developing an agreed code of conduct – a way of living together that honours the diverse needs of every-one else. All too often new residents, and indeed new staff, are told what the rules are to ensure a harmonious environment, rather than asked what they themselves need for this to be the case. Involving people in rule-making is a significant part of restorative practice.

The activity is a simple one to do, and can be done by the staff separately as a way of identifying a team contract, but it is also important to do as a whole community, so that any contract of behaviour developed is felt by the young people to be inclusive and not only about how *they* behave. Each new resident or member of staff can be asked the same question on arrival. Their needs are unlikely to differ signifi-cantly from those identified already – the important thing is for them to recognize that their views are being sought and respected.

ACTIVITY 7.1

ESTABLISHING HOUSE AGREEMENT ON DEVELOPING AND MAINTAINING GOOD RELATIONSHIPS

Aims

- to establish some shared understanding about what everyone needs to get along

- to encourage empathy and mutual understanding

- to encourage buy-in to an agreed way of working/living together
- to demonstrate a commitment to working democratically.

Resources

- piece of flipchart paper or a large piece of paper on the wall or on a stand
- large marker pens
- sticky dots.

Invite everyone (staff as a team or whole community of adults and young people) to sit round in a circle, preferably informally rather than round a table. Suggest they talk first in pairs and come up with answers to the question:

'What do I need from everyone else to feel safe and happy living here?'

A staff-only circle might ask the question:

'What do I need from everyone else to work at my best here?'

People can either write each idea on a post-it note (a piece of coloured paper with a sticky edge), or else, when everyone is ready, people can make contributions around the circle.

Common responses to the question have included:

- mutual respect
- a listening ear
- acceptance
- honesty
- tolerance
- trust
- inclusion
- empathy
- praise and acknowledgement
- a sense of humour.

If the list is long, then it can be reduced to the essentials by giving everyone three sticky dots and asking them to stick their three dots on what for them are their three most important needs.

It can sometimes be useful to clarify what people mean by each of these needs. One extension activity that works well if people are up for it is 'sentence completion'.

- Choose one word from the list of needs (e.g. respect, support, trust) to be the focus of the activity.
- Explain that the first round will be a chance to give an example of behaviour that fails to meet that need, and model an example. It is important to keep sentences general, naming no names.

'I don't feel...(respected/supported/trusted) when...'

- People can pass on the first round, but check to see if they want another chance by going around again, if need be.

- The second round is on the positive note: behaviours that met the need – again, mentioning no names but talking in general terms – and then another go-round, ending on a positive note:
- *'I do feel…(respected/supported/trusted) when…'*

If this type of formality in group meetings is too structured, then it may still be possible to have informal chats about these shared needs, or else maybe to talk about it first on a one-to-one basis with each young person. However, the intention is eventually to develop a shared understanding that most people need essentially very similar things in order to feel safe and happy in an environment, and that it is within everyone's power to create that environment. The discussion might lead to certain action points, so that everyone is involved in creating the environment they need.

Case study

Bessels Leigh School, in Abingdon, a residential special school for boys between the ages of 11 and 16 with emotional and behavioural difficulties, found itself using such circles daily, at the end of each school day, once they were introduced. Behaviour had been getting worse and the school had found that the traditional system involving sanctions was no longer working.

Staff began by having circles at the end of each school day, inviting everyone to reflect on what had gone well, what had not gone so well, and what they had done to put things right if they had gone wrong. Gradually boys learnt to facilitate these circles themselves. This is the unique feature of restorative circles as opposed to more formally facilitated meetings described earlier in the book: the facilitator participates too, because he or she is a member of the community.

After a year they found themselves introducing circles also at the beginning of the school day to help reflect on the previous day's educational experience and plan for the coming day. The circles are also used to celebrate success and achievement. In addition they now have fortnightly staff circles, including domestic and secretarial staff, who have also been trained in restorative skills, so that every member of staff is using similar language and approaches.

Developing resilience with empathy

Circles become the bedrock of the residential experience, used to reflect on and plan things in the future, and also to reflect on the previous day. Their daily use means that everyone in the community is constantly reminded that everything they do has an impact on everyone else – for good and bad. However, there is also the issue of how much others are in fact responsible for what we feel – bearing in mind that it is largely how we interpret what we see and hear that controls how we feel, and then how we react. I believe there is a continuum around how we choose to interpret what we see and hear around us – from sensitivity verging on paranoia at one end, to total denial of any feeling of pain at the other. Unfortunately the previous life experiences of the young people in care may have pushed them further in one of these directions than is helpful or safe.

In order to be able to cope with day-to-day interactions with others, we gradually learn how to protect ourselves from minor criticisms and unpleasant exchanges – developing a thick enough skin to be able to shake things off and keep going. This ability is about developing resilience and the ability to bounce back and carry on. However, a life, even a short life, of too much hurt and pain can lead to the development of such a thick skin that, to outward appearances, nothing is getting through. Despite this tough exterior being to some degree just a facade, nevertheless, for such people, admitting feelings of hurt and pain is just too risky. This kind of extreme level of resilience is counterproductive, because not only are emotions locked in, they are also locked out – and the overly thick skin can also mean that other people's feelings are not considered. Circles held on a regular basis are the beginning of rebalancing the young people's levels of resilience and empathy for themselves and for one another.

The paranoia-'tough nut' continuum can be played out in exchanges where one person can end up blaming another for what they are feeling:

'It's not my fault you are hurt – you are just far too touchy.'

'It was just a joke – can't you take a joke?'

It can also be played out when someone is genuinely sorry for something they said or did and tries to apologize or make amends, but the other will not even admit they felt hurt, and refuses to engage. This can leave the person who wants to make amends still feeling bad about what happened, and these feelings of discomfort and guilt can then get recycled back into aggression:

'Well, stuff you, then – I only wanted to apologize!'

The relative formality and consistency of the restorative framework creates space for people to explore where they are on the continuum, without risking being blamed for over-sensitivity or accused of lack of it. It can be in the regular circles that everyone starts to learn the language of the five themes elaborated earlier in the book. The circle is in fact the 'seedbed' for developing the ethos of the home or the family and for providing a safe space to develop the language of restoration.

What follows are some examples of the type of circles that can be held – variants on the daily get-together where people just 'check in' with each other and reflect on how things have been.

The circle meetings can also involve visitors and members of the multi-agency support teams, as in the following example from Walsall.

> ## Case study
> The main repeat behaviour by the children is aggression either to staff or peers. We now have involvement with the police local beat teams and Community Support Officers and have a dedicated team who are developing excellent relationships with the young people. They visit the home on a regular basis, hopefully during our circle meetings or just after to follow up or deal with any issues raised. Our circle meetings are much improved especially around listening skills. The young people are more aware of allowing each other time to speak before making comments or replying. We have benefited by nominating a supporter for one of our younger children who struggles with the social and verbal skills required to be able to speak up without getting angry. His 'mentor' is able to offer him advice, give him the option of time to think or just be there sitting alongside him for support.
>
> Walsall Residential Home

Daily circles

These are the short daily gatherings that everyone has, maybe just before or after tea, for about 20 minutes, before evening activities. There may be two sorts of daily circle – one for staff, perhaps at handover time, and another for residents and staff. Inevitably, not everyone will be present at any one meeting – staff are on different shifts and young people's lives are such that there will be some days when they are elsewhere. However, the regular meetings, with a consistent framework, provide a regular mechanism for airing thoughts, feelings and needs. If it can't be done one day, the opportunity will arise the next. Nothing is left undealt with for long – and indeed, nothing can be avoided for long!

The regular circles are for everyone in the building at the time, if at all possible – so in this way agency staff, domestic and administrative staff, everyone, become involved in the restorative way of thinking and speaking, and also feel included and valued as part of the community.

The format of the daily circle reflects the five main restorative themes, although it may not necessarily involve all five questions. It may be as simple as:

Round 1: *What's your day been like today?* (Theme 1)

Round 2: *How are you feeling right now?* (Theme 2b)

Round 3: *What do you need from us here to have a good evening/good day tomorrow?* (Theme 3)

Round 4: *What can you do to help anyone else here tonight?* (Theme 5)
Variations on the opening question might include prompts such as –

• *What's gone well/not so well?*

- *What have you done today that you enjoyed?*

- *What did you do today that you are proud of?*

The main point is that whatever questions you ask need to be the same all the way round the circle – although clearly the nature of the response will vary. The other point is that the versions above, although they may ring the changes, may be too hard for some to answer or may create an environment where more difficult things get brushed under the carpet.

Variations on the 'feelings' question might include, for example, the following.

- On a scale from 1–10, with 10 being the best I've ever felt, right now I'm a number...

- If I was a weather, right now I'd be sunny/rainy/stormy/windy (!!!), etc.

- I feel like *that* card there. (A pack of 'mood' cards has been scattered on the floor in the middle of the circle.)

- I'm feeling like that 'blob person' there. (The person points to a character on a poster.[19])

Sometimes the circle can be convened in the knowledge that something has happened earlier in the day that needs addressing by everyone. It is also possible that somebody approaches the circle facilitator before the meeting and asks if a particular issue could be brought up.

What then follows could be a variation on the daily circle – or be seen as an addition to the daily circle if the situation is urgent. My suggestion is that if the daily circle needs to address more serious issues, and these are known about in advance, the opening go-round still involves a more general 'check-in' along the lines of 'How are you and what's your day been like?' People can be told that there is something else to be discussed, but it is important that everyone's need to feel heard is met – otherwise there could be a risk that on many days only particular issues get discussed, and only certain people's issues are given priority. Remember the 'check-in', then, when considering the variants that follow.

Problem-solving circles – ask, don't tell

Circles can be used to think about a problem that is facing everyone in the community – or maybe just a small group. Rather than the adults coming up with the solution and telling the residents what is to happen, the problem becomes an opportunity to learn how to solve problems, how to negotiate and how to share responsibility when things get complicated. The format of the meeting uses the same five themes to inform the same five questions that are used in other restorative processes.

---

19 Posters and cards to develop emotional vocabulary can be purchased from suppliers such as Incentiveplus.co.uk – and of course, young people could be encouraged to draw their own.

The facilitator begins by acknowledging everyone present and thanking them for coming. It is unlikely that there is anyone unknown in the circle, but if staff or young people do come and go, or if an agency member of staff is on duty that day, then introductions would be in order, going round (maybe using a talking piece) at the outset. Next, the facilitator explains the reason for the circle in language appropriate for everyone sitting in the circle – some variation of:

> We are sitting here to talk about what to do about X, for each of us to explain how we see things, how we are affected by what is happening or may happen, and to think about what we each need to move on from this. Then we will try and come to an agreement about what we can all do to resolve this problem.

It might be appropriate to remind people of certain guidelines:

- Please remember that it is only the person holding the talking piece who has the right to talk.

- Try not to talk for too long – let everyone have their say.

- Allow your neighbour, when they have the talking piece, to finish what they want to say and pass in on to you before you start to speak.

- Remember that you have the right to pass, but if you do, you will need to wait until the ball has passed right around the circle and gets back to you, before you can speak again.

- Please respect what everyone has to say, even if you do not agree with it, and keep your expressions and gestures respectful.

You may want to broach the subject of confidentiality, if it is an issue, but always remember to let people know your legal responsibility to pass on any concerns you have for their welfare, should you have any. This can be discussed if and when it arises, with those concerned.

Following this welcome stage, you are ready to begin the first four rounds of the circle. Each round begins with a question which the facilitator asks of themselves and models the length or the answer (see below for examples of good practice).

Round 1: 'The way I see it, the problem is…'

People may need to be reminded of a key rule in this work: it is not people who are the problem – *it's the problem that's the problem*!

It may take practice to frame an issue in terms of a problem that is out there and detached from the individuals affected, but on a day-to-day basis staff can set a good example by using this technique rather than blaming individuals – even in jest. For example, note the difference between a problem framed as 'Danny':

> 'We were all late for school because we waited for Danny, and 'cos he was so slow getting ready, we missed the bus' –

and the problem described in a more neutral way:

'We are all ready to leave the house at different times, but the bus usually arrives at the stop at the same time' –

or:

'We all take a different amount of time to get ready and the bus is almost always on time' –

or even:

'We want to leave the house in time to catch the bus.'

Beware of the temptation to substitute the word 'somebody' for a name:

'We all missed the bus because *somebody* – naming no names' (but staring at the culprit) 'was late again.'

It is so common to want to name names and blame people – we do live in rather a blame culture and it is an excellent life skill to be able to identify a problem to be overcome without feeling the need to blame someone else, and in so doing divest ourselves of any responsibility to resolve the issue. A willingness to address a shared problem, whoever may technically be at fault, is a sign of resilience and maturity – as well as reducing the likelihood of recrimination and squabbles.

It may not be necessary to arrive at a consensus about how to describe the problem in the first place – indeed, people may identify different issues about what seemed like a single problem. However, it can sometimes be easier to have a shared goal, or goals, to address. If and when consensus arises, the problem or problems could be written on a sheet of paper or card and placed in the middle of the circle. Sometimes the time spent on identifying the problem in a neutral way is half the battle – options become clear if we simply take away the need to blame one person and see it as a joint problem to solve together. A problem shared is a problem halved – or quartered – or divided into many little pieces!

By the way, although this is called 'Round 1', achieving clarity on what problems are being discussed may take several go-rounds.

Round 2: 'What I'm thinking is... and I'm feeling...'

Although the talking piece gives only the holder the right to talk, the facilitator retains the right to remind the speaker of the ground rule of naming no names and blaming no one, should it happen. The 'thinking' part of this question is, of course, not inviting judgement or opinion, and may take practice to frame in terms of 'what runs through my head at such and such a moment'. The facilitator and staff could help by modelling this type of sentence:

'When I heard that people had missed the bus, I thought about what the people at school would say when you arrived late, and I felt anxious.'

'When I heard you come back and begin shouting at Danny, I wondered what had slowed him down and felt curious, and concerned.'

Round 3: 'I'm affected because…and I also think…is being affected, because…'

This statement is relatively self-explanatory, but may invite some reflection on the ripple effect of problems in the home, and even the possibility that the person whom everyone was blaming is being affected in different ways. Again, if empathy is not everyone's long suit, then those less affected, or more able to express empathy, may be able to model this by thinking about the wider ripples of who has been affected or could be.

Round 4: 'What I need for things to be OK is…'

This way of framing the question will seem strange to many people until they become more used to thinking about needs in the way I have described in earlier chapters. As I have explained, making demands of others can lead to barriers and blocks in conversation, but sharing our needs can lead to a softer, more amenable exchange if everyone tries to sort out how they can help each other meet their needs.

It might be useful to write some of the needs on cards and put them into the middle of the circle. In the past I have used a set of large cards called 'Strengths in Teams' (produced by St Luke's Innovative Resources) available from Incentive Plus.[20] They identify all sorts of wonderful qualities that people and teams need to pull together. These words can be a source of inspiration when problem-solving and help extend people's vocabulary.

Round 5: 'So what needs to happen to solve this problem is…and what I can do to help is…'

This is another round that may need several 'revolutions'. The 'needs' or 'strength' cards may help – and can even be used as prompts to encourage solutions and ideas. Any final agreements can be written on a large piece of paper or card and signed by everyone, if that is appropriate and relevant to the issue being discussed. The actual words used are not as important as the fact that the rounds help to bear in mind each of the key themes, and can be adapted depending on the matter being discussed.

Table 7.1 sums up this kind of circle and serves as an aide memoire.

Table 7.1 General problem-solving: planning or reviewing

Theme 1	Go-round 1	The way I see it, the problem is…
Theme 2	Go-round 2	What I'm thinking is…and I'm feeling… *or* How am I being affected by this problem?

---

20 www.incentiveplus.co.uk

Theme 3	Go-round 3	I'm affected because…and I also think…is being affected because…
Theme 4	Go-round 4	What I need for things to be OK is…
Theme 5	Go-round 5	So what needs to happen to solve this problem is…and what I can do to help is…

Repairing the harm after an incident

Following an incident which has affected everyone in the home or the family (and it may be argued that this is the large majority of incidents when the community is small), a circle can be convened to address the harm caused. The format of the meeting uses the same five themes to inform essentially the same five questions used in other restorative processes. It becomes a matter of common sense which questions are most appropriate for each circle, and the language must be accessible to all present (Table 7.2).

Table 7.2 Circle following an incident affecting everyone

Theme 1	Go-round 1	What happened for me was…
Theme 2	Go-round 2	When this happened I was thinking…and feeling…
Theme 3	Go-round 3	I've been affected because…and I also think…has been affected because…
Theme 4	Go-round 4	What I need for things to be OK is…
Theme 5	Go-round 5	So what needs to happen to solve this problem is…and what I can do personally is…

Circles for celebration

Daily circles can build in special moments of celebration, but it is also nice to dedicate one circle regularly to celebrate an aspect of life in the community, or even the life of one person in that community. It is rare for some people ever to hear nice things about themselves, and as a result they may not even have the capacity to take nice things in. These circles will need sensitive handling, but they can be a very valuable part of everyone's role in building a sense of belonging, care and love.

Festivals

Opportunities for celebration can arise from external events, and people can become quite inventive in thinking about how the circle go-rounds can reflect an event – different cultural festivals spring to mind – regardless of whether the people in the community actually represent that particular culture. So, for example, the usual questions can be shared, but perhaps the talking piece changes for the day, or else a special drink or snack representing that festival can be passed around. Maybe one or two games or circle activities can be thrown in for good festive measure. When people get into the swing of this, sometimes the young people themselves can be asked to facilitate the circle and can think of extra bits to make it festive in a relevant way – using music, perhaps? People could be asked to wear a particular colour or even go for 'carnival' and wear something the wrong way round or back-to-front – just to turn the world upside-down for a change!

Birthdays

The birthdays of residents and staff clearly provide opportunities for special activities beyond the circle, but it is also nice if the daily circle on that day honours that person – maybe they can facilitate the circle if the day has not involved anything unpleasant to address. Maybe they can choose a question to pass round, or else a game to be played, or a piece of music at the beginning? If appropriate, the circle that day could be used to celebrate the person as an individual, as described in the next section. (I want to describe this type of circle separately, because I do not want it to become only associated with birthdays.)

Celebrating individuals

How often do we tell somebody what we like, or admire, or appreciate about them?

How often do we hear such things from other people? We live in a culture where people tend to refrain from saying nice things about themselves for fear of being thought arrogant or boastful, and only say nice things about others when they retire or leave, or at their funeral.

There is a possibility that if we live and work in environments where it is just not done to say nice things to each other, or worse, in an environment where people 'slag each other off' or use humour and put-downs as a way of communicating, the ability to say nice things is lost, or even never learnt in the first place. Furthermore, if we live in environments where the culture of the 'put-down' is rife, or we are used to being told we are useless, bad, incompetent, stupid, or worse, then our self-esteem drops to such an extent that if someone does say something nice, we wonder what their agenda is – what it is they want. It is heard as false, manipulative and insincere. The possibility that the remark is genuinely what the other person thinks of us – or what may seem even more unlikely, actually a reflection of something in us – is beyond our wildest dreams.

In order to help young people develop resilience we need to help them develop self-esteem and an unshakeable sense of self-worth and self-belief. This is a hard task, given what they have experienced, and are still likely to experience, in their lives. Nevertheless, we have to make a start and everything so far in this book will contribute to this endeavour. Being listened to, having their views acknowledged and valued, being included in decision-making, being able to put things right when mistakes are made – all of these help to build an individual's sense of worth.

Circles of celebration are a more overt way of doing this. They focus on one particular individual. Ahead of time, everyone else is invited to think of at least one thing that they value or appreciate about that person, for example:

- their dress sense

- their sense of humour

- their talent at art, music, computer games, etc.

- their consideration

- a kind thing they said or did recently

- their friendship.

The thing can be a quality, a character trait or a specific deed that was appreciated.

The circle can begin in the usual way with a check-in, and then the facilitator explains that the purpose that day is to celebrate X, and let them know how much everyone appreciates them. It is probably a good idea to have the person seated next to the facilitator because it can sometimes be quite emotional to hear what people have to say.

The next go-round is a sentence completion:

One thing I value/appreciate/like about you, X, is...

Someone could act as a scribe and write each contribution onto a large piece of paper that can be awarded to X at the end.

These circles need a bit of planning to ensure that no one is going to sabotage them with an unexpected negative comment but usually, if circles are being run daily to pick up on everyday problems, this should be rare. Instead they can become amazingly emotional and moving occasions where the individual is deeply touched by what is said, and those giving the affirmations feel very good as well.

Incidentally, part of the 'bargain' of giving someone affirmation is that they accept it – and this can take practice. Think about how often someone passes us a compliment and we brush it off:

'Oh – this old thing – I bought it from Oxfam!'

'Oh, it wasn't just me – in fact I hardly did anything.'

'Clever? Not really – just lucky, probably.'

I have found that if people are asked to listen to a piece of affirmation and say nothing but 'Thank you' it seems to enable them to take it in better. Somehow the sabotaging 'self-talk' does not kick in and there is more chance that the person allows themselves the possibility of imagining that the affirmation may be valid. Furthermore there is a rather magic moment between the giver of the compliment and the receiver when the receiver looks at them and simply says 'thank you'. It is akin to giving and receiving a gift. If I give someone a gift and they shrug it off, say they didn't want it, even throw it back n my face, I feel hurt and maybe even angry (anger onion stuff!) or embarrassed. But if they accept the gift, smile and say 'thank you' and seem genuinely pleased, then I also feel good – and am more likely to give them other gifts in the future. We want people to learn to become givers and receivers of positive affirming messages – to look out for and appreciate others' qualities and also learn to appreciate their own.

It is interesting that we tend to notice qualities in others that we also value in ourselves. So if I notice and appreciate warmth and kindness in others, it is probably true that I aspire to these qualities myself (and am told by others that I give these back). If I admire someone's artistic skills or their football skills, the chances are these are important to me – ones I am striving to develop. If I compliment someone on their clothes I am also suggesting that I share their taste in fashion or colour – so giving people compliments in these domains strengthens the bonds between us because we are signalling a shared interest or affinity with these aspects of their character or person.

If these circles are going to form a regular part of life, then it is important to write up a timetable so that over the year everyone – young residents and staff – gets 'their' day. Life can sometimes get in the way – incidents flare up, staff come and go, and so do young people – but someone needs to keep a check on whose turn it is, and also whether they are able to take it when it is due. If someone is going through a particularly hard time they may not be up to such attention. It will be a matter of judgement, and possibly being inventive about how to manage an affirmation circle for someone with such low self-esteem that it is difficult for them to listen to too much 'niceness' in one go.

In the early days of doing these circles people may need help thinking of things to say about someone, and a set of cards in the centre of the circle with pictures and/ or words may help.

ACTIVITY 7.2

- Invite everyone to sit in a circle, and open with a check-in go-round.

- Ask for help to spread a set of 'strengths' or 'qualities' cards on the floor in the circle. If the circle is large and people find it difficult to read upside-down (if you are using cards with words), then suggest that a 'path' is left around the outside of the cards to allow for an initial stroll around the circle, so that everyone can see all the cards.

- Going around the circle, invite each in turn to pick up a card that for them describes a strength or quality of the individual being celebrated. The cards can be given to the person or stuck with Blutak on a wall. (Some suppliers of these cards also make stickers, so the cards could be stuck onto a individualized poster.)

- The next person has a go, and so on round the circle.

- At the end these strengths and qualities can be written onto a big poster, or even a small piece of A4 for the person to keep. It may be that some of the more artistic members of the community offer to help to do this.

Celebrating the community or the team

In addition to these very special, individualized circles, there may also be a place for an occasional circle that allows everyone to celebrate everyone else – and eventually this kind of circle can spin out into day-to-day life, so that giving and receiving compliments, gratitude and affirmations becomes embedded into the culture and 'put-downs' are mere history.

The cards I referred to earlier can be useful for these kinds of circles as they help initially to give people ideas and the vocabulary to use for qualities and strengths. Cards can also be made by the young people themselves, coloured in and laminated for regular use.

ACTIVITY 7.3

- Invite everyone to sit in a circle, and open with a check-in go-round.

- Ask for help to spread a set of 'strength' or 'qualities' cards on the floor in the circle. If the circle is large and people find it difficult to read upside down (if you are using cards with words) then suggest a 'path' is left around the outside of the cards to allow for an initial stroll around the circle so everyone can see all the cards.

- Going around the circle, invite each in turn to pick up a card that for them describes a strength that everyone in the community or team shares, and that makes the place special. They then replace it.

- The next person has a go and so on round the circle.

This type of activity can also be used to celebrate everyone as an individual in the teams and groups. (I have sets of cards for use with younger individuals, with older people and with teams or groups.) As an individual celebration in the larger group the activity would work like this.

ACTIVITY 7.4

- Invite everyone to sit in a circle, and open with a check-in go-round.

- Ask for help to spread a set of 'strengths' or 'qualities' cards on the floor inside the circle. If the circle is large and people find it difficult to read upside-down (if you are using cards with words), then suggest a 'path' is left around the outside of the cards to allow for an initial stroll around the circle, so that everyone can see all the cards.

- Going around the circle, invite each in turn to pick up a card that for them describes a strength that the person on their left has. That person accepts the card, says thank you, and puts it back on the floor in case anyone else wants to choose it.

- The next person has a go, and so on round the circle.

- A more private form of this activity is to go round the circle and suggest that people work in pairs (do not simply say 'Choose a partner' as this is highly risky and could leave a person alone between two pairs if both their neighbours turn away from them), quietly taking it in turns to indicate the card for a quality that they think their partner has – or else leave it to them to say something they have valued or appreciated in their colleague recently. This is a more sophisticated version, in some respects, but of course paves the way for such exchanges to become the norm anyway.

Conclusion

This chapter, although I have placed it later on in the book, is nevertheless key to starting the restorative journey. I would go so far as to say that, without regular circle meetings, all the reactive restorative conversations will not necessarily bring about the culture change you are after. It would be like building your restorative framework on sand.

As I have explained, people need to learn new ways of thinking and new language – and the circle becomes the seedbed for all of this. Even without formal training for facilitating restorative meetings everyone can, by taking part in daily circles, learn how to:

- pose and answer the five main restorative questions

- think about and describe what has happened to them in clearer ways

- listen without interruption or judgement

- understand the impact of people's self-talk on their emotions, and the impact of these emotions on their subsequent choices of action

- develop empathy and resilience

- identify the difference between expressing needs and making demands

- work together to find ways forward when there are decisions to make, problems to solve or harm to repair

- develop a greater sense of belonging.

In the next chapter I am going to look at how to implement a community-wide restorative approach, and what barriers there are to overcome. This chapter on circles has its rightful place at the beginning of this process.

Chapter 8

Working in Partnership

Introduction

This book has shown that working restoratively with children and young people is not simply about reducing offending. Giving young people the language and strategies for making, maintaining and repairing relationships means providing them, in some cases for the first time, with skills that could help them in their personal lives and in the world of work. The respect and empowerment implicit in a restorative approach needs to be consistent across all the agencies and institutions with whom they interact, and indeed is implicit, and often explicit, in much of the new legislation and policies emanating from the government. A consistent restorative approach operationalizes much of the rhetoric of the new legislation.

This chapter considers the role of the various agencies and partners responsible for the education and welfare of children and their families in the delivery of a consistent restorative approach. This is a rapidly evolving field, both at the level of practice and at the level of policy development and new legislation. Over the course of 2009, and beyond, what is described in this chapter may change, but I will endeavour to provide as up-to-date a picture as possible.

Not only is the field rapidly evolving, it is also evolving in different parts of the UK in different ways and at different speeds. This chapter does not claim to be accurate for every local authority, or for each of England, Scotland, Wales and Northern Ireland. However, it considers what is evolving in terms of best practice, and suggests ways forward to create a truly multi-agency restorative approach for the benefit of the young people, their families and the professionals who support them. By offering examples of good practice from around the UK, the chapter offers some benchmarks for other areas that have less well developed protocols and strategies.

The chapter begins by hinting at what a local authority committed to becoming restorative may be working towards – an undoubtedly utopian objective at present, but one that is considerably closer than 15 years ago when this vision (and this particular visionary) was dismissed as eccentric and unrealistic. With reference to the plethora of new initiatives in the field of child and family welfare, it suggests how a local authority can become a more restorative corporate parent, even working within current frameworks, policies and legislation, indicating that these may be changing in even more advantageous ways for all concerned.

Key players in this regard, some of which will be mentioned in this chapter, include the police; the local Youth Offending Team (YOT); social services; Children and Adolescent Mental Health Service (CAMHS); local authority Behaviour Support Teams and education providers such as local schools, pupil referral units and out-of-school provision. As the director of an organization providing training and consultancy to all of these sectors I can attest to growing interest and an increased demand for awareness raising, as well as hands-on skills development. It would appear that we may be approaching a tipping point in public awareness, and even acceptance, of more restorative ways of working.

The provision of formal restorative opportunities by other agencies will be of particular interest to foster parents, who may otherwise be unlikely to facilitate a conference in the more formal sense. Should the child in their care commit an offence or become involved in antisocial behaviour, then being able to identify how to give them access to a restorative conference and support them through it will be very valuable.[21]

Of course, young people in care may also find themselves on the receiving end of antisocial and harmful behaviours, and again it can be useful for carers and foster parents to know how to ensure that their charge has access as a victim to a restorative process – since evidence suggests that such a process will help them deal with the experience better. They are more likely to be satisfied at the end than with more traditional approaches that leave them with many unanswered questions and feelings of fear and inadequacy – feelings that could lead to post-traumatic states and depression.

A restorative local authority

There is a whole new book to be written about what constitutes a restorative local authority and what this might mean for the workforce within a local authority. In fact this type of question is being considered by an increasing number of local authorities, and even whole counties. Figure 8.1 is adapted from a model first developed by Mark Finnis and Paul Moran when they were at the Sefton Centre for Restorative Practices, and is inspiring more and more areas to set up multi-agency steering groups to start planning for a joined-up restorative approach.

---

21 The situation regarding responses to antisocial or offending behaviours and the role of the YOT and the police is changing and developing in the light of recent policy and legislative changes. Readers are advised to check with their own local YOT and their police liaison officers what the current situation is in their own area.

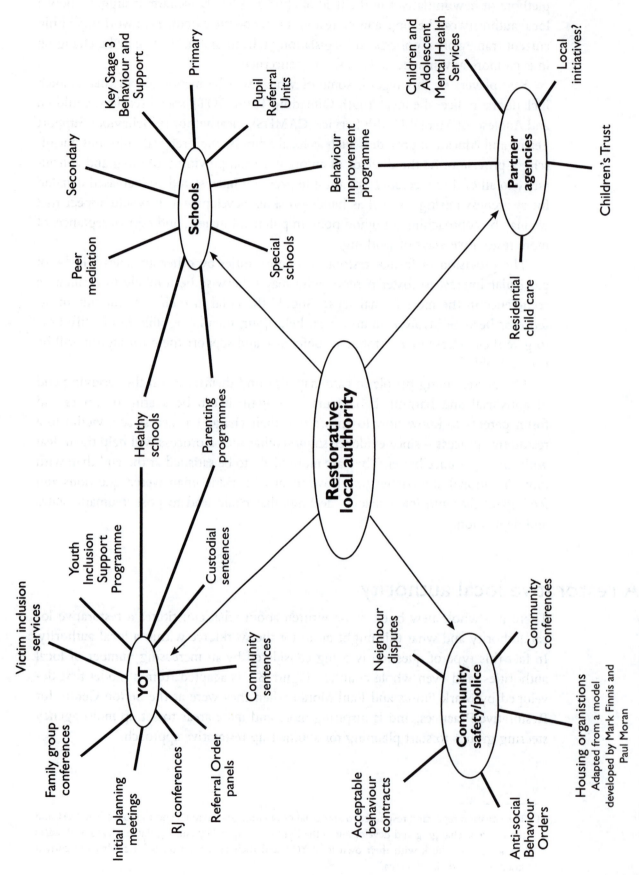

Figure 8.1 Restorative local authority

Schools
- Key Stage 3 Behaviour and Support
- Primary
- Secondary
- Peer mediation
- Pupil Referral Units
- Special schools
- Healthy schools
- Behaviour improvement programme

Partner agencies
- Children and Adolescent Mental Health Services
- Local initiatives?
- Children's Trust
- Residential child care

YOT
- Victim inclusion services
- Youth Inclusion Support Programme
- Family group conferences
- Initial planning meetings
- RJ conferences
- Referral Order panels
- Community sentences
- Parenting programmes
- Custodial sentences

Community safety/police
- Neighbour disputes
- Community conferences
- Acceptable behaviour contracts
- Anti-social Behaviour Orders
- Housing organisations

Restorative local authority

Adapted from a model developed by Mark Finnis and Paul Moran

This will involve not just working restoratively with clients, but reviewing internal procedures, looking at management style, team building, collaborative working, conflict resolution strategies, discipline and grievance procedures and even inter-agency and inter-company conflicts and disagreements. For the purposes of this chapter, however, I am going to limit myself to the current situation, with hints at what is to come and what could be achieved.

The Children's Act 2004 and *Every Child Matters*

In 2004 the Children's Act established Children's Services Authorities in England, now Children's Trusts (DCSF 2008), whose task is to promote partnership working between all agencies and institutions working with children and their families, in order to achieve the five outcomes for children identified in the government Green Paper *Every Child Matters*:

- making a positive contribution

- being healthy

- achieving economic well-being

- enjoying and achieving

- staying safe.

These partners include the police, youth offending teams, probation services, schools and other educational providers, health authorities and social services. Specified agencies, including YOTs (multi-agency teams already) and staff in secure accommodation, are also tasked with the duty of safeguarding children and promoting their welfare (DCSF 2008).

The *Every Child Matters* agenda is informing all aspects of partnership working and is in fact providing the *raison d'être* for partnership working. A new department to bring together all aspects of caring for children and their families was created in 2007 – the Department for Children, Schools and Families. A new construct emerged shortly afterwards – the Children and Families Workforce, a nationwide grouping of people who, it is hoped, will work together so that no child in need slips through the net.

Within a local authority the Children and Families Workforce has joint responsibility for young people in care in what has been called a corporate parenting role. NACRO (2005, p.13) describes a successful corporate parenting culture as one that has:

- a shared understanding of the outcomes sought for looked-after children

- shared ownership of issues relating to looked-after children

- positive problem-solving cultures in inter-agency planning for looked-after children

- active involvement from all relevant agencies and individuals responsible for providing services to looked-after children.

NACRO's research identified that in many areas agencies with corporate parenting responsibilities were not necessarily working together, nor sharing an over-arching set of shared values, principles and practices. Could it be that a restorative approach across the authority might begin to provide this shared ethos and value base – and even provide some shared principles and practice that could benefit not only the client group but the workforce itself?

The role of the police

As Chapter 1 identified, when residential staff feel overwhelmed by incidents occurring in the home, or when the situation becomes dangerous, they are likely to ring the police. What happens when the police arrive may vary greatly across the country. Although the role of the police in dealing with incidents affecting young people in care may be about to change dramatically (see below), existing legislation and past policy and procedures continue to cast a long shadow on local practice.

Crown Prosecution Service (CPS) guidelines about addressing offending behaviour in residential children's homes acknowledges the extra challenges facing children in care and their increased vulnerability to conflict, bullying and peer pressure. There is a recognition that the police are more likely to be called to a children's home than a domestic setting, but the guidelines state:

> A criminal justice disposal, whether a prosecution, reprimand or warning, should not be regarded as an automatic response to offending behaviour by a looked after child, irrespective of their criminal history. This applies equally to Persistent Young Offenders and adolescents of good character. A criminal justice disposal will only be appropriate where it is clearly required by the public interest.
>
> Informal disposals such as restorative justice conferencing, reparation, acceptable behaviour contracts and disciplinary measures by the home may be sufficient to satisfy the public interest and to reduce the risk of future offending.

The guidelines state that when reviewing the cases of young people who have offended, the CPS will want to know why the police have been involved, what action the home has already taken, whether there have been opportunities for apology and reparation, whether those harmed have been involved and whether there is scope for reparative work between those harmed and those responsible for the harm. The whole tenor of this kind of advice is restorative, and encourages the home to go down the restorative road before involving the police.

In the past, and to some extent even now, if a police officer is called out to a residential home, school or foster setting, although they have discretion, they may feel bound to arrest the young person – so as to be seen to be doing something to calm the situation down and, in many cases, to remove the young person temporarily from the environment where they are causing others some kind of harm. The impact of this intervention has already been described in Chapter 1 (pages 16–18).

In order to minimize the extent to which young people are criminalized as a result of police call-outs, some areas have developed their own local protocols. In Hertfordshire, for example, where restorative training has been carried out in all local authority residential homes, Hertfordshire County Council Children Schools and Families (CSF) have developed a joint protocol with the police. They have identified three categories of response for incidents occurring in children's homes: low, medium and high. The 'low' response would not involve police at all, and be addressed restoratively by staff in the home, and not necessarily even involve management. A 'medium' response may also involve internal restorative approaches, but the incident is reported to the registered manager and monitored. The 'high' response, involving serious assault or when either staff or young people are in immediate danger, would be an occasion for immediate police involvement.

In other areas police call-out still involves an immediate arrest – sometimes to the dismay of staff who had not realized that their call for help would be dealt with in this way.

> I am particularly glad you have pointed out the issue of police being called means a crime has been reported and they then have a duty to investigate and record an outcome, i.e. 'crime it'. Many people I come across are not aware of this. Had they been, then they would have thought twice about calling police in the first instance. Parents and children's home staff in particular have fallen foul of this when just wanting a situation calming – what often results is a charge of resisting arrest for the young person and no charges brought for the initial 'offence' to which they were called.[22]

However, the situation may be about to change with the advent of the Youth Restorative Disposal. This new police power could make a significant difference to the way in which incidents are dealt with if police are called out to deal with an issue in a residential home, school or foster home. The new approach has come out of a significant new policy document called the 2008 *Youth Crime Action Plan*.

Youth Crime Action Plan (2008) and the new Youth Restorative Disposal

The *Youth Crime Action Plan* (Home Office 2008) sets out what the Home Office describes as

> a 'triple track' approach of enforcement and punishment where behaviour is unacceptable, non-negotiable support and challenge where it is most needed, and better and earlier prevention.

From this plan one new initiative in particular – the Youth Restorative Disposal – is set to make a huge change in the way local beat officers address low-level disruption

---

22 Private correspondence with a restorative justice worker in a YOT in northern England.

and minor offending behaviour. This disposal gives police officers the power and the permission to address lower level disruptive and antisocial behaviour that they come across or are called to deal with, using a restorative approach – often there and then. It is gratifying for those of us who have been offering training in this type of 'on the spot' response to teachers and residential staff since the very early days of restorative justice in the UK to find them being more widely accepted. (We had to put up with a lot of criticism in the early days that what we were doing was not 'real' restorative justice.) At the moment the YRD, as it is called, can only be used in cases involving first-time offenders, but in some areas of the country more flexibility, particularly in cases involving young people in public care, is being negotiated. As ever there is the anomaly that it will be a matter of luck whether the person being victimized gets the chance of a restorative response – the decision to use one depends on the other person's record!

There is now increasing recognition that lower-level restorative responses that can nip issues in the bud and prevent them escalating. In a recent edition of *YJ*, the newsletter for the Youth Justice Board, Inspector Paul Cox of the Avon and Somerset Police welcomes the new YRD because it keeps many young people out of the criminal justice system and spares them from a damaging criminal record, reduces bureaucracy and frees up youth justice professionals to deal with more serious cases (Perry 2008). As Inspector Cox writes:

> In recent times police performance targets – particularly for offences brought to justice – have resulted in a drive to boost levels of arrest, massively increasing the number of young people being criminalised.

At the time of writing, the YRD initiative is in its pilot stage, being trialled by police forces in Avon and Somerset, Cumbria, Greater Manchester, Lancashire, Metropolitan, Norfolk, North Wales and Nottinghamshire. Other police forces around the country are recognizing its merits, welcoming the approach as a return to common-sense policing, and developing their own version.[23] This is a time of change, as the government is moving away from insisting on detected sanctions as a measurable target for police officers, and preferring measures based on public satisfaction and positive outcomes. It is a highly significant development which is likely to have a dramatic impact for young people in general, and for young people in care in particular.

---

23 I have a concern, based on my own experience of training 'instant restorative interventions', that at present the training for police officers to use a Youth Restorative Disposal is too short – in many cases only a day. Given that for many police officers this new approach amounts to a paradigm shift in their thinking, as well as their behaviour, I believe that there is a risk that if it is done badly and is not as successful as it could be, the whole approach might be dismissed. These 'instant RJ' or 'corridor/ street conferences' require a high level of skill, and I believe the training should be delivered at an advanced level after the initial 35 hours of basic restorative skills training. Integrating the approach into initial police training may be the pragmatic and the most time-efficient way forward here.

Safer School Partnerships

This section on the role of the police would not be complete without a mention of the Safer Schools Partnership (SSP) – a partnership of the Association of Chief Police Officers (ACPO), the Department for Education and Skills (DfES, as it was known at the time), the Youth Justice Board (YJB) and the Home Office. The concept of Safer School Partnerships arose from a Youth Justice Board proposal to develop a new policing model for schools and aimed to provide a very focused approach to address the high level of crime and antisocial behaviour committed in and around schools in some areas – crime committed *by* and *against* children and young people.

Although the project grew out of concern for rising street crime, the aims of the project extend beyond crime reduction, and include:

- to reduce the prevalence of crime and victimization amongst young people

- to provide a safe and secure school community, thereby enhancing the learning environment

- to ensure that young people remain in education, actively learning and achieving their full potential

- to deliver a partnership approach to engage young people, challenge unacceptable behaviour, and develop a respect for themselves and their community.

Thanks to Graham Waddington, the police officer who pioneered restorative approaches in schools, and Charles Pollard, ex-Chief Constable of the Thames Valley Police, who championed this approach, the original, school-based SSP police officers around England and Wales were trained in a range of restorative approaches to dealing with day-to-day challenging situations.[24] The SSP project was underpinned by restorative principles and, following pilot projects in an original 100 locations, the approach is now gradually being mainstreamed. Those in post have reported that they have been able to work most effectively in schools where the senior management team is also committed to this approach, so that staff and police are working together sharing a similar philosophy. The mainstreaming guidelines emphazise that schools working with an SSP officer are expected to review their behaviour policy and introduce a restorative approach (Hopkins 2006).

The reason I mention the SSP project is that, in England at least, there are a significant number of police officers already working in restorative ways with schoolchildren in local schools and neighbourhoods, and although their remit does not necessarily extend to looked-after children once they are off the school premises, there may be scope for some more joined-up work between SSP schools, children's homes and foster families wanting to offer a consistent approach.

---

24 I was very involved in the two first tranches of training for SSP officers. I acted as a consultant on the first, delivered by a team of Thames Valley Police trainers, visiting every course and delivering a half day input on informal restorative responses (an early YRD training, in effect). On the second, delivered on behalf of NACRO, I developed the training course and offered many of my training team as facilitators.

The role of Youth Offending Teams

The Audit Commission's seminal report *Misspent Youth: Young People and Crime* (1996) found that the existing system for dealing with youth crime was inefficient and expensive, and that services were failing both young offenders and their victims. Over the following four years three new government Acts[25] created the framework for dealing with youth offending in a completely different way. A national Youth Justice Board (YJB) was created to oversee initiatives in reducing offending and preventing re-offending amongst young people. Multi-agency Youth Offending Teams (YOTs) were established in all of the 154 local authorities in England and Wales (in some larger authorities there are several YOTs) to carry out this work (Davies 2005). The YOTs were a local manifestation of the new joined-up approach, comprising team members seconded from education, probation, the police, social services and health, all of whom work with, and support, young people who have offended or are at risk of offending. Much of the pioneering restorative work done in schools is being instigated by YOTs and they are also beginning to take the lead in introducing restorative approaches into care settings (Hopkins 2006).

This is why, when I began research for this book, the first thing I did was to contact every YOT in England and Wales by e-mail and to ask them if they were aware of the extent to which restorative approaches were being used in their local residential homes. Not everyone responded, but from those who did, responses varied. Some explained that no restorative work was being done in their local homes (which presumably meant by them, as a YOT, either as outside facilitators or within the homes themselves); some responded with a lot of useful information and contacts; and then there were the excellent people who not only offered information and contacts but diligently read each chapter as it was written, offering valuable advice, case studies and their own experiences and thoughts for me to use as quotations. These people are mentioned in my acknowledgements, and without them this book would not (and indeed should not) have been written by someone like myself, coming from outside of the field.

Many YOT staff all over the country are pioneering restorative projects with care homes all over the country, and many have a designated officer tasked with reducing offending with looked-after children (ROLAC). In addition to this specific role, YOT involvement with young people in care will range from crime prevention schemes involving sport and other recreational activities at one end (initiatives open to all youth at risk of offending), to the Referral Panel at the other.

The Referral Order and the Referral Panel

Even if a YOT has no specific schools-based or residential home restorative initiative in place, all YOTs around the country are obliged to be involved in supporting

---

25 Crime and Disorder Act 1988; Youth Justice and Criminal Evidence Act 1999; The Powers of Criminal Courts (Sentencing) Act 2000.

young people following a Referral Order. Whilst a young person is serving this sentence they are obliged to attend a number of Referral Panels and these panels are restorative in conception, if not always in practice. They can be more or less restorative, depending on the quality of facilitation and the degree to which both victims and the wrongdoer feel empowered to take a part in the decision-making. Regrettably, preparation for these meetings can sometimes be minimal, not always involving the type of preparation described as restorative enquiry in Chapter 3 of this book. In addition YOTs sometimes contract out the preparation, and so there is not the consistency of practice and the safety and trust that develop when a single facilitator (or a pair of co-facilitators) follow through the whole panel process, from preparation to facilitation and follow-up. As a result, victim involvement is much lower than it should be.

Some people would argue that without the victim present, the meeting barely deserves the description of 'restorative' (McCold and Wachtel 2002) There is widespread dissatisfaction with the way the Referral Panel structure has watered down the key restorative principles enshrined in the 2004 National Practice Guidelines. However, these are challenging issues, not least because a potential, very positive, element of Referral Panels is the involvement of volunteers from the local community. But this strength – involving local people in addressing local issues and offering support to the young people in their area – can also be a challenge, since volunteers do not always have the time or inclination to commit more hours than those required by the panel meetings themselves.

There is also much confusion about the difference between restoration and reparation. As readers of this book will have realized, the essential purpose of a restorative encounter between people is to restore connection, develop empathy and restore self-worth on both sides. Of course there are also issues of accountability and responsibility, but these emerge in parallel to the essential elements already listed.

This act of making amends has an almost symbolic function if the meeting itself has been successful – and indeed, sometimes the victim is more than willing to accept nothing more than an apology once they have seen genuine signs of recognition and remorse. However, for those people not centrally involved, this almost magical encounter between wrongdoer and wronged is often misunderstood. Panel members who are there to represent the community of the victim and wrongdoer may not have fully understood the restorative ideal, and may be seeking to impose sanctions – or reparation that has a punitive element. They may believe that the tangible act of reparation is what makes the meeting restorative, not what goes on in the meeting. And indeed, if the meeting is not facilitated sensitively, or if the victims are not even present, it is hard to see how restoration at the symbolic, and profound level, can occur. Community pay-back is all we are left with – the most distorted version of which would have sought to impose public humiliation on the wrongdoers by forcing them to wear brightly coloured jackets (an idea suggested at one point by the government). What could be further from restoration I do not know. Nevertheless, despite my reservations, many Referral Panels work well and these provide a further opportunity for restorative work even after a matter has gone to court.

Police and YOT partnership

Whilst the police may be called in to address a serious issue in a children's home, YOT officers may also occasionally be called in when the residential staff have not yet gained the confidence to use their own restorative skills or have not yet been given the training for themselves. However, there are also ways in which the role of the YOT and the police can complement each other, as in the example provided by one rural YOT (Figure 8.2).

In this model the more traditional role of the police, leading to the arrest and charging of a young person, might nevertheless provide the YOT with an opportunity to approach the home and offer an opportunity for a restorative disposal.

As already mentioned, even if the matter does go to court the local magistrate may sentence the young person with a Referral Order, during which the Referral Panel may offer a restorative opportunity. As can be seen, then, even with current guidelines there is already scope for some consistency of response, from informal, proactive, restorative interaction in the care setting, to formal responses at both pre- and post-court level, involving both police and YOT officers.

The role of Scottish Youth Justice services

Most Youth Justice services, which exist in all local authorities in Scotland, offer some form of restorative intervention (with 'person-harmed' involvement, as appropriate), as well as various support programmes for young people who have been charged. This can mean that a young person who has been charged may increasingly be able to benefit from a restorative approach since, when their case has bee referred to the Reporter of the Children's Panel, he or she may make a diversionary referral to a Youth Justice service for appropriate support or intervention. Even if it goes first to the Panel itself, one of the disposals may be to the Youth Justice service.

It is worth noting that Government Youth Justice Guidelines published in June 2008 now allow for direct requests to be made by residential settings to Youth Justice services for restorative interventions. This is in keeping with an increasing emphasis on the value of early, proportionate intervention and joined-up, inter-agency working. It is still early days in this new development – insufficient evidence of uptake and impact to date, but clearly, as adopted, this will reduce the number of charges being brought against looked-after young people.

The role of Northern Ireland Youth Justice Services

The Northern Ireland Youth Justice system has been reformed to reduce the use of detention and to offer a restorative response to offending on the basis of consent. Consequently young people who offend in residential units are unlikely to be given a custodial order. They will be offered a restorative caution by the police or, if they have offended before, a diversionary conference delivered by the Youth Conference Service. If they persist in their offending, they will be summonsed to the Youth Court, which will again offer a restorative conference. This process has

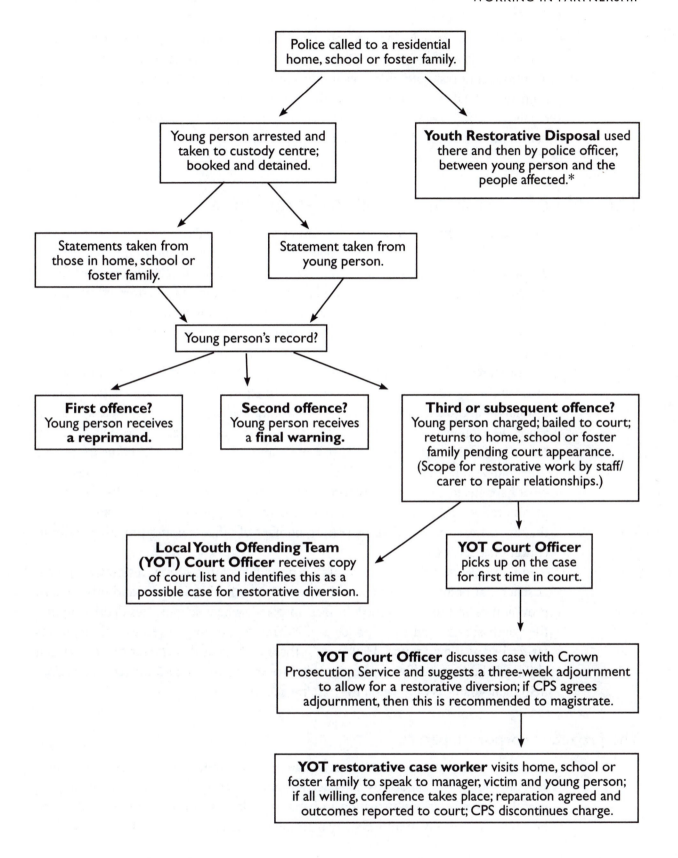

Figure 8.2 From police call-out to Youth Offending Team: one example of restorative practice in a rural YOT

*See pages 163–164 for more about the Youth Restorative Disposal

proved effective in reducing offending and keeping young people out of the custodial centre (Juvenile Justice Centre). Barnardos has also had a great deal of success in introducing restorative approaches to children's units in Northern Ireland. They train residential workers in day-to-day restorative practices and offer to facilitate conferences for more serious incidents. Evaluations have demonstrated improved behaviour and reduced involvement by the police.[26]

The role of schools and Pupil Referral Units

Consistency of approach is not only important at the sharp end, when behaviours spill out of the home and involve police and YOTs. It is also important on a day-to-day level for those children in public care who attend local schools or other forms of educational provision. Indeed, residential schools adopting a restorative approach would surely be ensuring that care staff as well as teaching staff would all be trained to use restorative approaches, and that there would be a consistent policy day and night.

An increasing number of schools around the UK are introducing restorative approaches along the continuum already described in this book. This 'whole school restorative approach' was first described in my book *Just Schools* (Hopkins 2004). Since then other excellent books on the subject have appeared (Morrison 2007, Newton and Mahaffey 2008, Thorsborne and Vinegrad 2002, Thorsborne and Vinegrad 2004, Warren 2004, Warren and Williams 2007). Readers interested in what happens in a restorative school are encouraged to read these books. The range of restorative approaches recommended in this one are exactly the same as those that my team at least, and an increasing number of other training providers, offer in educational settings.

In an ideal world children would be growing up in a totally restorative milieu, at school, at home, and out and about, whether engaging in sport and other youth provision or in the community. In fact, in places where schools, residential homes, the youth service and local police and YOTs are working together, this is not as far-fetched as it may sound. However, in these early days this is a rarity. So how can children's homes and foster families who are trying to act restoratively themselves help their young people when they attend school?

The proactive corporate parent

Acting as corporate parents, care staff can, as any parent can, approach their local schools asking the school to consider adopting a restorative approach. It may be useful to have certain information to hand, to help schools new to the approach to be open-minded. The books already mentioned, especially the excellent publications

---

26 This section was provided by Tim Chapman of CTC Associates, and now lecturer in Restorative Practices at Ulster University, and again I am very grateful.

from the local authority in Lewisham – *Restoring the Balance 1* and *2* (Warren 2004, Warren and Williams 2007) – describe the impact of restorative approaches in primary and secondary schools.

Schools are now obliged to deliver a curriculum on social and emotional aspects of learning (SEAL), and it may be useful to point out that the five key restorative themes address the five main SEAL themes (Table 8.1). I think there is probably some very useful work that can be done across the educational and residential sectors looking at the key outcomes of the social pedagogy agenda and of the SEAL agenda, and at how restorative ways of working can help staff to deliver on both.

Table 8.1 The five key restorative themes and the five main SEAL themes

Theme	Question	SEAL theme
1. Unique stories	What happened?	• awareness of self and others • empathy
2. Thoughts and feelings	What were you thinking? And so how were you feeling?	• managing of feelings (thoughts affect feelings) • self-awareness
3. Effect, affect and harm	Who has been affected by what has happened?	• empathy • social skills
4. Needs	What do you need for the harm to be repaired, so that you can move on?	• empathy • motivation
5. Accountability; empowerment; collaborative problem-solving	So what needs to happen now? (If appropriate: 'And what can you do?')	• social skills of cooperation and problem-solving • motivation (empowerment and goal setting) • self-awareness

Schools are increasingly concerned about tackling bullying and again, Lewisham is leading the way, publishing the first borough-wide anti-bullying policy, informed throughout by restorative principles and approaches (Lewisham Borough Council 2008). The national Anti-Bullying Alliance is also very keen on using a restorative response, and a recent book on bullying (Cowie and Jennifer 2008) recommends restorative approaches at varying levels of formality for varying degrees of seriousness. (See Chapter 9 for similar models of grading response.)

A third way to persuade schools new to restorative approaches to consider them is to share evidence of their impact (Kane *et al.* 2007, Youth Justice Board 2002). There is no evidence that punitive responses to bad behaviour have a long-term successful impact, and care staff know all too well how often the behaviours they experience from young people stem from their life experiences. This is not to condone such behaviour, but to appreciate that the punitive route misses the point and can be counter-productive. Once care staff have experienced for themselves how successful the restorative approach can be, they will be keen to promote the approach in their children's schools to ensure they get the best possible chances there.

The role of the Designated Teacher

Designated Teachers (DTs), staff designated with a specific responsibility for the welfare of looked-after children in their school, may be able to play a part in ensuring continuity of care and of response if they are included in the training in restorative skills. Their role is a significant one and includes:

- liaising with social service departments

- promoting inclusive policies and robust pastoral systems in the school

- encouraging communication across agencies

- building links with parents and carers and overseeing each child's Personal Education Plan

- helping to promote a climate of high expectation of attainment and behaviour

- being aware of any difficulties the young person may be experiencing

- acting as a resource for staff and students on issues relevant to young people in care. (Holland and Randerson 2005)

Given these roles, the designated teacher would be the ideal person to take a lead on ensuring that children in public care are responded to in a restorative way. He or she will know better than most the challenges that these children are facing in the school, and will be able to advocate for sensitive responses. In their book *Supporting Children in Public Care in Schools*, educational psychologists John Holland and Catherine Randerson (2005) indicate how much of the behaviour of young people in care can be a response to their experience of loss – of home, family, security, community, friends, pets, possessions, freedom, trust, love, sense of self-worth – the list is endless. Their emotional responses (again, a long list) can lead to much behaviour that, in some schools where staff do not understand their situation, could be identified as disruptive and 'naughty'. Mood swings, anger, violence, attention-seeking, poor concentration, restlessness, school refusal – these are only some of the many behaviours that can result in gradual, mutual alienation, resulting in young people finding themselves increasingly pushed out of mainstream schooling into specialist provision, and even out of school completely.

For these young people alone (and how much of this description of loss and the resultant behaviours also applies to a large number of young people who may still be living in challenging circumstances with their natural parents?), the adoption of a restorative approach would seem vital. It could provide ways in which accountability and responsibility are encouraged at all times, for the benefit of those causing harm, and also for those whom these behaviours are affecting.

Personal Education Plans (PEPs)

These plans, required at school for every child in care, need to be informed by restorative principles if the young person is not to become confused. The first PEP meeting must, by law, be held within 20 days of the child being admitted to a nursery or school. The partners in supporting a young person to develop their PEP (who are likely to include, at the very least, their social worker, their Designated Teacher [DT], their carer and their mentor in the school) will need to be used to working with this young person rather than imposing decisions on them or taking decisions for them (cf. the social discipline window in Chapter 2, page 43). The five key restorative questions may be useful (Chapter 3), and in fact the whole process of drawing up and reviewing a PEP could be done using a restorative circle, with a talking piece (Chapter 7).

Holland and Randerson point out that there are many other people who could potentially be taking an interest in the child's education and be involved in developing and reviewing the PEP – including their parent, Connexions staff, the special educational needs coordinator (SENCO) in the school, their class teacher, the head of year, the child protection coordinator, the educational welfare officer (EWO), the educational psychologist (EP) and staff from the Children and Adolescent Mental Health team (CAMHS). This list serves to point out just some of the agencies who need to be aware of and encouraging restorative approaches in schools and residential sectors. In my recent experience people from all of these teams have recognized the value of the approach and in some areas are amongst the pioneers, sitting on local and regional steering groups. Their influence and championing of the approach could also be a factor in encouraging schools themselves to adopt a school-wide approach, since it is not just the looked-after young people who stand to benefit.

Reducing exclusions

The issue of school exclusion is a particularly important one for young people in care. Francis points out that young people in care are ten times more likely to be excluded than their peers and that up to 60 per cent of children and young people in public care have a history of school exclusion. This is a staggering and distressing figure. As Francis writes:

> Clearly, when children are excluded from school they are not likely to make good progress with their studies and, in the longer term, permanent exclusion from school is associated with wider social exclusion from society. (Francis 2008, p.26)

Not only are excluded young people at risk of social exclusion. We also know there is a high correlation between excluded young people and offending behaviour

(Flood-Page *et al.* 2000, Graham and Bowling 1995) – the reason why early initiatives introducing restorative justice into schools were often led by youth justice professionals and the police, who focused on reducing exclusions first and foremost. (In fact the history of the development of school-based work from restorative justice to restorative approaches is very similar to this development in care settings, and for very much the same reasons [see Chapter 1 and *Just Schools* (Hopkins 2004].)

Once again, a whole-school restorative approach would increase the likelihood that even more serious wrongdoing by a young person in public care could be addressed in the first instance by a restorative conference, to the benefit of all concerned.

The role of health professionals

Ever since restorative justice began to be talked about in the UK, there have been educational psychologists taking a lead in promoting its philosophy and principles in settings where their clients were living and studying. Many of them have either been trained in restorative approaches themselves, or at least become sufficiently aware of what they involve to act as messengers to schools and residential settings.

Generally speaking, educational psychologists understand the value of using a consistent framework and consistent language with young people in public care, many if not most of whom have attachment disorders and struggle with building relationships, feeling empathy and expressing genuine emotions. Their role as advocates for the approach around the country is set to grow, in my view, and I would certainly see them as allies in local authority developments. Those educational psychologists who have been trained in restorative language and interactions have attested to how the five questions and the framework in which they are used make sense to them and how this has enhanced their already highly developed active listening skills.

Many young people in care are likely to be in a relationship with, and in regular communication with, other staff from the Child and Adolescent Mental Health Service. These staff will need to be aware not only of how conflicts and disagreements are being dealt with in the home setting, but also of the commitment to involving the young people in decision-making – neither imposing decisions on them (doing *to*), nor doing things *for* them (cf. the social discipline window in Chapter 2, page 43).

Conclusion

It is inevitable that with any book of this nature it is not always possible to cover all that I might ideally wish to, and I am aware that I have touched only briefly on the many issues to be considered in moving forward restoratively in a multi-agency partnership. However, I believe that this chapter has at least mentioned some of the key players who in many cases around the country are already working together in a restorative way to improve the life chances, and indeed the current quality of life, for young people in public care.

The main point being made in this chapter is that a residential home or school, or a foster family, are not sealed units, cut off from the rest of their community – fortunately! The young people living in these environments interact with and are cared for by a whole host of adults working in different settings themselves. Apart from the benefits to each of these agencies themselves of adopting a restorative approach amongst their staff and with other clients (another book or even a series!), the restorative approach provides a common framework, a common language and a shared ethos which all can work with when engaging with children in public care. Differences of opinion can be approached from the restorative viewpoint, and decisions can be measured against a restorative checklist. Of course, restorative criteria are not the only ones informing many decisions about the safety and well-being of young people, but they are fundamental, and a good place to start.

Chapter 9

Implementation and Sustainability

Introduction

Although it would be a shame to deter an individual residential home from going it alone in introducing a restorative approach, I would highly recommend that this venture be done in conjunction not only with all the partner agencies working with that home (for reasons addressed in Chapter 8), but also with the other children's homes in the authority. In this way staff can share training, share best practice, support each other as they develop frameworks and protocols – and also ensure there is continuity across the district, if and when young people move between placements. This chapter therefore considers implementation from an authority perspective, as well as within a single institution.

Sustaining good practice relies in large part on honestly reviewing what is working well, what is not working so well, and what improvements need to be made. Informal and formal monitoring and evaluation are therefore an integral part of the successful implementation and sustainability of any new initiative. This chapter suggests that an action research framework is built into the development plan, so that each new phase of the initiative builds on critical review and feedback. It also reports on how some of the early pioneers have been evaluating their progress, and how they too have been engaging in ongoing reflective practice. It shares some of the challenges that have been met and how these challenges are being tackled and overcome.

Finally the chapter considers the importance of ongoing monitoring and evaluation, not just to ensure that the initiative develops to best meet the needs of those involved, but also to produce local and national evidence to bring more people on board, attract further funding and impact on policy and legislation.

Getting started

I have recently come across an excellent model for implementing change, which I intend to use here as the basis for considering implementation of a restorative approach, whether in a single environment or across an area. It suggests that effective change depends on five key ingredients coming together: vision, skills, incentives, resources and an action plan (Knoster 1991). When all are in place, change will happen. If one ingredient is missing, things can go wrong (Table 9.1). Anticipating and planning for each ingredient maximizes the chances of the change process being successful.

Table 9.1 The five key ingredients for successful change

Vision	Skills	Incentive	Resources	Action plan	Result
✓	✓	✓	✓	✓	Change
✗	✓	✓	✓	✓	Confusion
✓	✗	✓	✓	✓	Anxiety
✓	✓	✗	✓	✓	Resistance
✓	✓	✓	✗	✓	Frustration
✓	✓	✓	✓	✗	False starts

Developing the vision

Every successful restorative initiative needs its champions. These will be people who somewhere, somehow, have heard about restorative justice or restorative approaches, either from colleagues in their own field or from other contexts where it is working well, and who can immediately see its value in the work they do. These people are the 'sparks' – to use a metaphor I first came across in the excellent training manual *Playing with Fire* (Fine and Macbeth 1992). They are the ones who start to share their excitement and their vision with like-minded people, 'firing' them with their enthusiasm so that, like kindling, these people in turn literally warm to the vision. Once the original sparks set alight the kindling, the small fire begins to smoulder and burst into flame. As more and more people come on board the small fire becomes a bonfire, more sparks fly off and adjacent leaves, twigs and small branches ignite, flames start to shoot higher and higher, and soon a full-blown conflagration spreads across a whole area.

Initial research can encourage those with initial curiosity to attend relevant conferences. (There are now many books and articles published about restorative justice in general, and an increasing number being written about restorative approaches in specific contexts.) The next step might be to invite someone with experience and expertise to come and run an awareness-raising event locally, to test the water and the local interest. Such early events will identify those already inclined to work in restorative ways, although they may not have given this name to what they were doing. These are the initial allies, often excited to have some kind of external validation for what they have been doing all along and pleased to have some framework for what they do, and maybe an opportunity to develop their skills further.

Will the vision be one for the whole local authority (see Figure 8.1 on page 160), a joint initiative across all residential care establishments and the foster care service in an area, or just for one institution in the first instance? What will it mean to be 'restorative' for each of these institutions? How can this best be captured? Figure 9.1 represents a model of restorative practices working at three different levels.

Figure 9.2 may help people to understand the extent to which a restorative approach can inform both proactive and reactive practice. This model is merely a suggestion and every residential community will make their own adaptations to suit their own context. Residential schools may like to have two versions – one for during the school day and one for out-of-school situations.

It could be useful to develop, amongst staff and residents, an agreed definition of restorative practice that draws from the five key restorative themes, encompassing proactive relationship and community-building as well as responses to conflict and wrongdoing, rather than relying on outdated definitions based on victim–offender practices and limited to the single model of the conference. The following activity encourages people to think about how they would like the home to be – reflecting first on what things are like on a very bad day, how it could be on an excellent day, and what factors might make the difference.

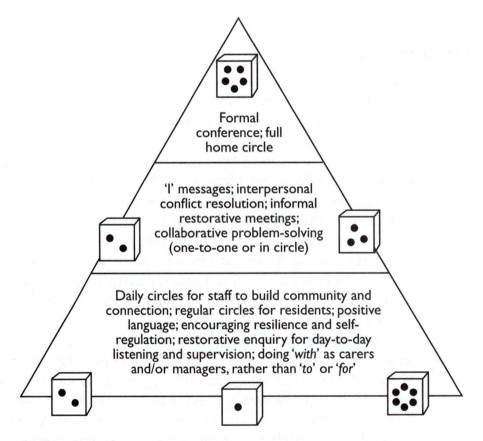

Figure 9.1 Three levels of restorative practice

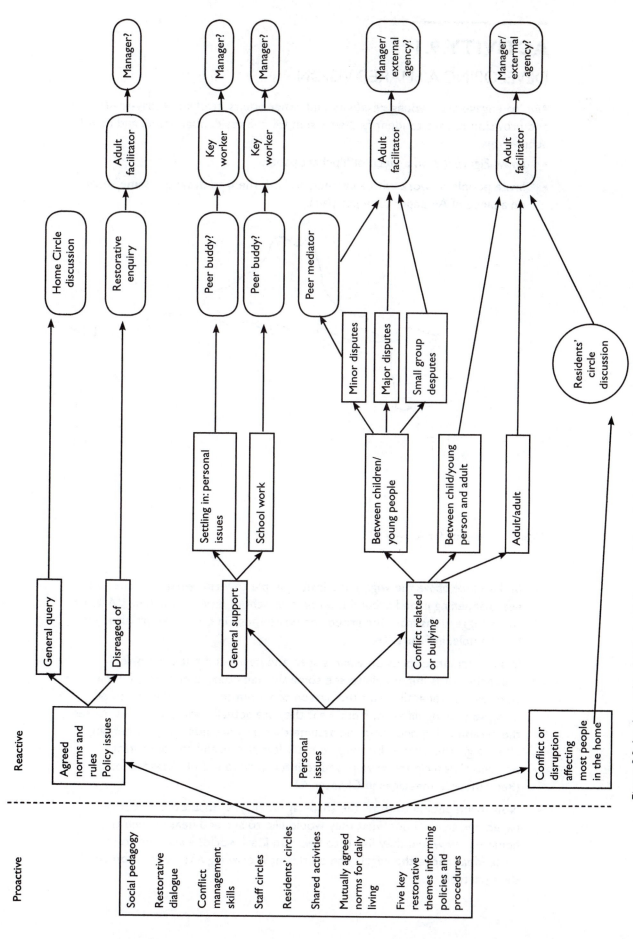

Figure 9.2 A relationship management framework based on restorative principles

Source: Transforming conflict, www.transformingconflict.org Original version SMILE, Stoke-on-Trent, http://get-me.to/smileteam; Adapted by Hamish Young; Adapted for residential settings by Belinda Hopkins.

ACTIVITY 9.1

DEVELOPING A SHARED VISION

Aim: to engage staff, young residents and other adults involved in day-to-day life and provision of care to identify their vision for the residential home, and how to achieve this.

- Draw Figure 9.3 on a piece of flipchart paper.

- Invite people to work with a partner, and ask them to draw the same shape on a piece of A4 paper (one per pair).

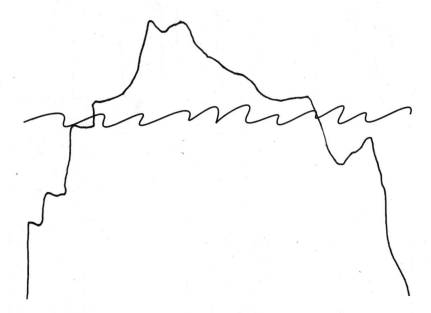

Figure 9.3 Template for Activity 9.1

- In the space *above* the wiggly line invite people to write what they see and hear happening in and around the home or school on a very bad day. Ask for some suggestions from the group and write these in on the big picture – as, for example, in Figure 9.4.

- It is important to focus on what is seen and heard and not what *isn't* happening. (It is impossible to see someone 'not doing' something. People who say this generally want the person to whom they are referring to be doing something different from what they are actually doing, or else they see the person doing one thing and assume that they are not doing something else – e.g. 'You are not listening to me.') It is also useful to concentrate on neutral description as opposed to interpretations and exaggerations. (Remember 'I' messages in Chapter 4.)

- Now invite people to draw the shape again, maybe on another sheet of paper, and think about what they would like to see and hear around the home – how would they like it to be, in an ideal world? Ask them to write these ideas above the wiggly line on this new drawing after discussion with their partner.

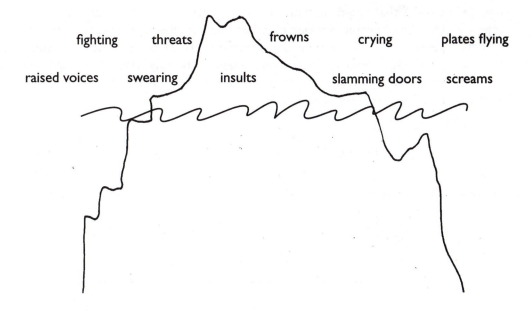

Figure 9.4 What things are like on a very bad day

- Ask for some suggestions from the group and write these in on the big picture – as, for example, in Figure 9.5.

- Now return to your first diagram and explain that what people see and hear is, of course, only the surface behaviours, and that beneath the surface people have hidden thoughts and feelings (cf. Restorative Theme 2). However, this model is going to illustrate what may be contributing to the lack of harmony and safety on a bad day and suggest ways to transform the bad days into better days, when what is happening is closer to people's vision. These are things that are hidden beneath the surface – like the bulk of an iceberg hidden from view beneath the surface of the waves.

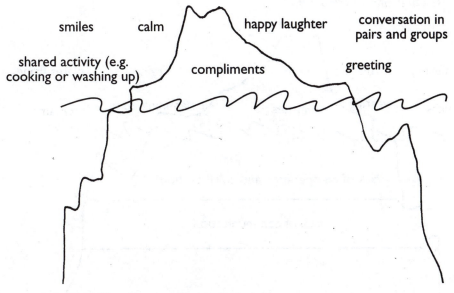

Figure 9.5 What things are like on an ideal day

- Suggest that one thing that is definitely absent in this unhappy picture is any sign of people working together, sharing jobs, helping each other and generally pulling together as a community. There is also a lack of respect, and no attempt to involve everyone in decision-making. Write the words 'lack of cooperation and collaboration' just below the waves (Figure 9.6) and check that this resonates with people.

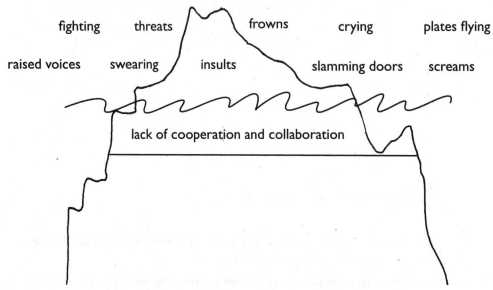

Figure 9.6 Lack of cooperation and collaboration

- Suggest that another thing missing on a bad day is effective communication – people are unable to talk reasonably together, unable to express what is really going on inside, and do not feel really listened to. This may be because it does not feel safe, because the skills are missing or because it has just become the way things are. Write the phrase 'lack of communication' below the first phrase (Figure 9.7).

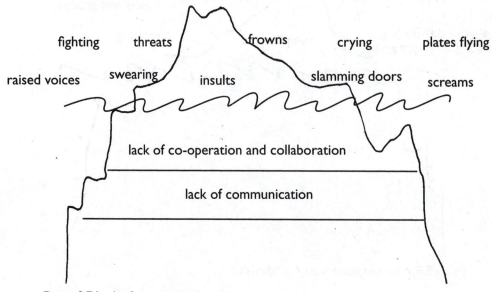

Figure 9.7 Lack of communication

- Fundamentally what can be missing in these unsafe and even dangerous environments is a lack of self-esteem and self-worth, amongst adults and young people. There is therefore a lack of mutual respect and a culture of put-downs, rather than one of affirmation where people acknowledge and praise each other for their achievements and offer compliments and congratulations for things well done. Write the phrase 'lack of self-esteem, mutual respect and affirmation' at the base of the iceberg and check whether this makes sense to people (Figure 9.8).

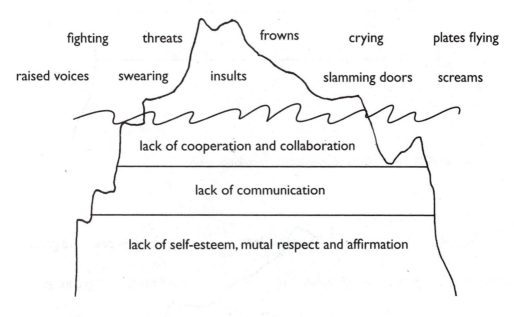

Figure 9.8 Lack of self-esteem, mutual respect and affirmation

- The group may want to discuss how such a situation has come about but it is important to reassure everyone that, despite the backgrounds of many of the young people and other factors, such situations can be changed. The key lies in offering more of the very things that are missing on a bad day.

- Reflecting on the good day – the happy iceberg – it can be beneficial to think about what does work and why. On such days there are signs of co-operation and collaboration: people working together, doing things together and maybe planning together for future events and activities. Write the words 'cooperation and collaboration' just below the waves on this diagram. (Figure 9.9).

- Incidentally, it is worth reflecting on the influence of social pedagogy, which emphasizes the importance of care staff simply doing day-to-day activities with the young people in their charge, teaching them how to relate to each other by their pro-social modelling.

- Another element that makes the good days successful is when people are able to talk and feel heard. These are days when communication has been effective. Write the words 'effective communication' on the diagram (Figure 9.10).

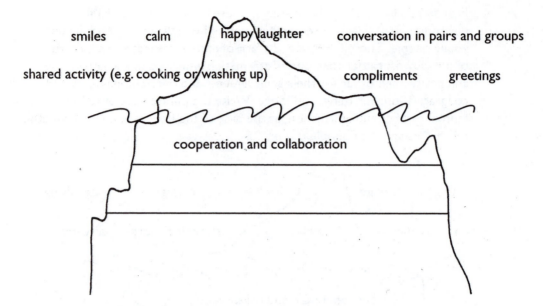

Figure 9.9 The bedrock of cooperation and collaboration

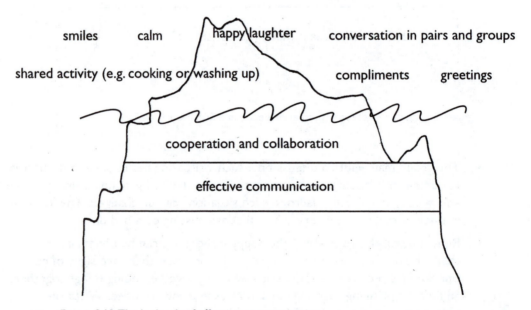

Figure 9.10 The bedrock of effective communication

- Finally – the most significant factor affecting what happens on a good day, and what can contribute to a positive atmosphere, is the extent to which people are feeling good about themselves, giving and receiving respect, and ready to give and accept compliments, praise, recognition and acknowledgement for who they are, and things they do. Write 'self-esteem, mutual respect and affirmation' at the base of the iceberg (Figure 9.11).

- Invite reflection on how to move from the unhappy iceberg to the happy one. I like to think of the second one not as an iceberg (too cold!) but as an island built on the firm rock of mutual respect and affirmation.

- The point to make is that it is not possible to move from the kind of environment described in Figure 9.3 to the one in Figure 9.5 by using a system of punishments and rewards. Building the foundations described in Figure 9.11 is the way to develop the vision.

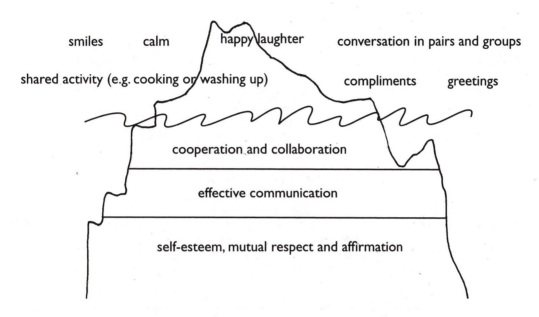

Figure 9.11 The bedrock of self-seteem, mutual respect and affirmation

Developing the skills

The significance of the iceberg activity described in the previous section cannot be underestimated. Sharing a vision of what everyone, adults and young people, would like their good days to be like, and identifying the factors that can contribute to this, creates the beginnings of a shared plan for developing skills. The fact is that the five key restorative themes depend on cooperation and collaboration and effective communication skills. By integrating these key themes into daily life on a consistent basis, self-esteem, mutual respect and a climate of affirmation will inevitably develop, because everyone's perspective is valued and recognized, and everyone is encouraged to contribute to problem-solving and repair when things go wrong. As one residential social worker from Hertfordshire has said about restorative approaches:

> An effective skill, but more importantly a set of values that underpin relationships and how to nurture and build them. It's about empowerment and has gone much further in helping young people to develop a voice about their views than anything before or since.

Although all five themes apply to everyone in the home there is a hierarchy of restorative responses requiring different levels of expertise, and not everyone need be able to facilitate the most formal restorative meetings (conferences and circles involving everyone in the home community in the event of a serious incident). Figure 9.1, on page 178 may be a useful starting point in identifying who needs what level of training, depending on who is likely to be doing what within a residential team. This could inform a second model representing roles within the team (Figure 9.12).

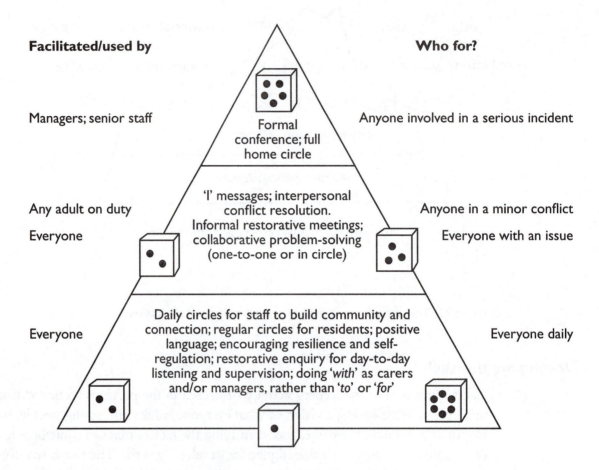

Facilitated/used by

Managers; senior staff

Any adult on duty

Everyone

Everyone

Formal conference; full home circle

'I' messages; interpersonal conflict resolution. Informal restorative meetings; collaborative problem-solving (one-to-one or in circle)

Daily circles for staff to build community and connection; regular circles for residents; positive language; encouraging resilience and self-regulation; restorative enquiry for day-to-day listening and supervision; doing 'with' as carers and/or managers, rather than 'to' or 'for'

Who for?

Anyone involved in a serious incident

Anyone in a minor conflict

Everyone with an issue

Everyone daily

Figure 9.12 Restorative responses – who by and who for?

The relationship management framework illustrated in Figure 9.2 might also be useful in identifying training at different levels – including the possibility of developing the mentoring and mediation skills of some of the young people themselves, to 'buddy' each other, act as peer mediators for lower level conflicts and share in the facilitation of residents' circles. In my experience it is best to allow a day of training for each stage of the restorative approach – perhaps using ideas from each of Chapters 2–7 as the basis for a five-day course (or five separate days spread over several weeks, depending on the availability of staff – Table 9.2.

Table 9.2 Six-day training programme

	Stage of training	See:	Focus
	Day/Module 1	Chapter 2	The restorative mindset
	Day/Module 2	Chapter 3	Restorative enquiry – for • active listening • developing empathy • encouraging communication and cooperation
	Day/Module 3	Chapter 4	Restorative enquiry – for use in interpersonal conflict
	Day/Module 4	Chapter 5	Mediation or mini-conferencing – semi-formal approaches
	Day/Module 5	Chapter 6	Conferencing – formal approaches
	Day/Module 6 (or stand-alone day at any stage)	Chapter 7	Circles of various types

The important point to make, as is evident from this book, is that each level of intervention of response builds on the skills of the previous one, and so participants need to have done each previous stage before beginning the next. The only exception might be the use of circles, which could possibly be developed as a stand-alone day of training, perhaps after one or two days of initial training and practice with restorative enquiry (although I would suggest that only someone with experience of the full training runs a community circle in response to a serious issue).

Developing the incentives

Persuading staff and young people to engage in a restorative way of living and working inevitably involves addressing the WIIFM factor – 'What's in it for me?' Other people's stories and evidence from other residential contexts can be persuasive. The case studies in this book are offered to encourage those new to the approach to consider it.

Staff in Hertfordshire (the first county to train all residential care staff), when asked what they would like to say to those new to restorative approaches, wrote that they would want:

to emphasize the positive aspects of the approach, the feeling of empowerment it can prescribe to all involved and the feelings that come from a successful intervention changing behaviour and attitudes.

They also wanted to stress:

how effective this can be for both staff and young people and the positive results for young people

and

that it is a great way for young people to make things better without the use of negative sanctions.

One person wrote:

This is not about using a skill with a young person who has caused harm; it is about everyone, relationships, respect, no matter.

Although research evidence is still thin on the ground there has been an external evaluation carried out in Hertfordshire (Littlechild 2003). The Hertfordshire study, carried out after six months of using restorative responses in one residential home, noted that there had been a 39 per cent reduction in police call-outs and that relationships between staff and young people were significantly improved.

In a subsequent report based on his evaluation, Littlechild (2008) identifies the following advantages of working restoratively mentioned by care managers and staff he spoke to.

- Children and young people are helped to deal with their anger.

- They gain a greater sense of responsibility and remorse for wrongdoing.

- They are acknowledged and given a voice.

- They are included in the process.

- They learn more about the consequences of their actions and learn more positive ways to resolve difficulties, conflicts and problems.

- They develop empathy and learn to build relationships.

- They learn how to behave in a mature, adult way.

- Mutual respect is developed.

In addition to the Hertfordshire evaluation informal, unpublished, evaluations carried out by project managers in Derbyshire and Bedfordshire also mention positive outcomes in a similar vein.

I was unable to find any other published reports but this situation is bound to change as more and more projects are begun. The importance of ongoing monitoring and evaluation cannot be underestimated – not only to help assess next steps (see the section on action planning below), but also to encourage those involved to continue and to learn.

Accreditation

Another incentive for staff, and perhaps even young people as well, is the possibility of having the hard work they put into training and developing their restorative practice recognized in terms of accreditation. The development of accreditation for restorative practice is currently being led by a body called Skills for Justice. Aside from its work developing awards in the youth justice and police sector, this body has now been tasked by the Children's Workforce Network to develop national occupational standards for restorative practice for use in justice, health and school settings (Skills for Justice 2008).

Skills for Justice is identifying learning objectives, performance indicators and assessment criteria for good practice based on the *Best Practice Guidelines for Restorative Practitioners and Their Case Supervisors and Line Managers* (Home Office 2004). Many of us on the original Home Office working party developing these guidelines wanted to ensure their generic nature so that they would be relevant beyond the criminal justice context. Nevertheless, I think they do tend to focus on the more serious 'victim–offender' type scenarios. Practice and thinking has developed since then, and there is more work to be done to identify awards more relevant to restorative institutions, with a restorative ethos and not just awards focused on reactive practices. It is important that the residential sector informs those developing these new awards what skills they believe to be of value in restorative work, and ensure that accreditation is awarded for the appropriate skill set.

In the meantime I think there is probably local work to be done in conjunction with local accreditation providers (local universities, perhaps?) who may well be interested in developing accreditation suitable for the workforce in residential settings – at certificate, diploma and even graduate and post-graduate level. There may also be opportunities for identifying awards meaningful to young people in restorative practices such as conflict resolution, mentoring and mediating in conjunction with local schools or youth services.

Identifying the resources

The resources required for bringing about effective change along restorative lines include people, time and money. In the early days, and to some extent even now, those planning restorative initiatives and tasked with applying for funding have underestimated the importance of all three of these resources.

People

Identifying the right people to lead the initiative forward is vital – these people will become the champions. However, some people are more suited to championing a cause than others. In his book *The Tipping Point* Gladwell (2000) discusses what makes some people excellent communicators and networkers. They are the ones who can best spread a message – they are able to share their enthusiasm, and by virtue of their relationship-making capabilities they have huge networks of contacts which they can activate to spread the word. In the early days of implementing restorative approaches across an authority, such people are gold dust. Hall and Hord (2001) report that one of the most important factors in successful innovation programmes in the US was the use of what they call 'one-legged interviews' – brief exchanges by managers with those implementing the innovation as they meet in corridors to see how things are going. (Another phrase to describe the brief nature of the exchange might be 'on the hoof'.) It is interesting that the process they describe – asking what is happening and what people's thoughts and feelings are about the innovation – sound very much like 'restorative enquiry' – an example of how a restorative process can contribute to the implementation stage itself.

However, these people need nurturing – with on-going support and refreshment. They will need to be stimulated with new ideas, on-going skill development and opportunities for sharing the challenges and the opportunities. Change work sometimes makes the error of focusing too much on winning over new advocates and forgets to nurture and support those already on board – a fatal mistake. As Shapiro (2003) points out in her excellent book *Creating Contagious Commitment*, if as many previous advocates of restorative approaches drop out as are recruited, then the situation will remain static. The key to the tipping point is for the number of new advocates to outstrip the number of those disillusioned people giving up their advocacy efforts. Shapiro sums this up very simply by saying that the challenge is to (1) get advocates, (2) keep advocates and (3) grow advocates.

The senior management team, at authority level and within the residential service, can impact on what the rest of the staff do and think by their own example, publicly recognizing and honouring the achievements of those successful in implementing the new changes and, crucially, ensuring that there are structures in place to allow the innovatory new idea and practices to happen.

Time

Allowing enough time for the implementation process is crucial. In educational settings the general view now is that it will take between three and five years for an institution to have fully absorbed the approach. As one commentator (Reynolds 2001) from the field of school improvement remarks:

> Change is only successful when it has become part of the natural behaviour of teachers in the school. Implementation is not enough.

I suspect that this observation applies to residential settings as well. The adoption of restorative approaches in the residential child care sector is still relatively new. The very first home to introduce restorative practice systematically into its behaviour management policy did so in 2002.[27] Time will tell how long effective and thorough

---

27 This was Stanfield Home in Hertfordshire, championed by the manager at the time, Veronica (Ron) Hart. Several years earlier I trained staff in an Oxford residential children's home in informal restorative approaches which resulted in a 100 per cent decrease in police call-outs – staff literally stopped calling out police because they felt empowered to address the situations competently themselves. This was before I had developed my ideas on a home-wide restorative framework.

change takes – and it probably depends on many different factors – with progress involving steps forward and steps back as staff and young people come and go.

Money

Ensuring adequate funding for a restorative initiative is vital – an underfunded project could cause more damage than one that does not even get started. Initial training will enthuse and inspire, and then people will expect a clear plan and ongoing opportunities for development. The sooner local capacity for training and planning is developed, the better, since no project will want to depend on outside consultancy for too long. However, local support also necessitates resourcing – in terms of local training fees, cover costs to pay for replacement staff during training and refresher meetings, investment in publications to spread good practice, such as brochures and booklets and perhaps a newsletter. A significant and important consideration would be whether to appoint a full-time Restorative Approaches Coordinator – or even go to the extent that Hull and Sefton have, and establish a Restorative Approaches Centre, offering consultancy training and hands-on service delivery across the authority or borough.

My recommendation would be to plan for an initial three-year project and then, as the initiative develops, assess what on-going maintenance costs the initiative will require. How to plan is the topic of the next section.

Developing an action plan

The most important point about implementing a restorative approach is that it must be done in a restorative way. In other words, right from the outset people need to be 'walking the talk' and those in positions of more authority will need to be modelling a restorative leadership style – working *with* their teams, and not imposing new ideas (doing *to*) or taking decisions on behalf of (doing *for*) those who will be affected by the changes planned.

In my experience of implementing restorative approaches in schools, there is no one formula at every stage, because as people learn more and more about the potential of the approach they will evolve a plan that fits local needs and integrates local initiatives and local circumstances. The most useful way to address implementation, in my view, is to consider it like an action research project – one based on action research guru Kurt Lewin's (1946) four-stage action research framework: plan, act, observe, reflect – then adjust the plan according to the feedback and experience.

The whole venture is akin to the Chinese meditation practice of walking backwards. We can see where we have come from and how we have got to where we are now, but we cannot predict exactly where we are going or how to get there. This is not a recipe for chaos. It is in fact a very thorough, and very restorative way to work – and essentially much more realistic than imposing a staged procedure that is resistant to feedback suggesting that the original plan may have been misguided or may need to be adapted.

My expertise and experience lies more with effecting whole-school change[28] and I think there is much to be learnt from experts in this field. Changing a culture means changing people, and that this is a delicate business. Indeed, as one guru of organizational change, Peter Senge (Senge *et al.* 1999) has said:

People do not resist change: people resist being changed.

Stoll and Fink (1996), for example, emphasize the need to share perceptions and ideas, rather than imposing a single version of change; the importance of each person finding out for themselves what the change means for them; the recognition that change is a personal and emotional process, with the potential for bringing stress and anxiety; the acceptance that conflicts are inevitable; the importance of on-going help and encouragement – a judicious mixture of pressure and support; the integration of both 'top-down' and 'bottom-up' change; the recognition that change has an inevitable ripple effect in what is a connected system; allowing enough time – between three to five years, if not longer; the acceptance that not everyone will accept the change but that resistance may have many reasons; and finally, that change is a journey for which there is no pre-ordained roadmap (and nor should there be):

No amount of knowledge ever makes totally clear the action needed to be taken. Development is evolutionary. It is not beneficial to lay down precise plans. Rather, it is important to get started and constantly make amendments. This requires people to 'trust the process'. (Stoll and Fink 1996)

Next steps

Training

Following initial planning and consultation, a provisional action plan will be useful. I tend to work with the one in Figure 9.13, knowing that it will begin to evolve and change as soon as we get started, for all the reasons identified above. However, some kind of initial plan is helpful. Most initiatives, after some initial awareness raising, start with some early training for the pioneers – either at the authority level (future members of a steering group perhaps) or in the residential homes themselves. If the training is going to be rolled out to foster carers as well, then potential trainers for this group will also be on the early training.

Some areas decide to offer training to several representatives from each home, and expect these pioneers to share their training with colleagues; or run a series of courses, involving more and more people from each team on every course. Other

---

28 Much of this chapter draws on my doctoral research about implementing a restorative approach in educational settings, which by extension involved my learning about organizational change more generally. (See Hopkins 2006.)

Figure 9.13 Implementing of a restorative approach in a local authority

Step 1: Authority level
Awareness raising for senior managers of authority's children and family services, local schools, Pupil Referral Units, children's homes, Youth Offending Team, police and probation services – to generate interest and identify pilot projects.

Step 2: In-house level – individual schools/units/homes/services
Targeted training for pilot projects – one-day awareness raising; identify participants for the steering group who will participate in the first five-day training.

Step 3: In-house training for the Steering Group

Step 4: Individual project development
In-house steering group develops an implementation plan for their particular school/unit/ home/service – looking at necessary policy changes; implementing referral protocols; establishing a regular support group to review how they are doing in their day-to-day use of restorative dialogue; implementing evaluation and monitoring procedures.

Step 5: Review of progress
After several months of skills development by trained individuals using what they have learnt, progress is reviewed and next steps are planned by the Steering Group.

Step 6: Sustainability
Training for trainers; evaluation and monitoring procedures need to be kept in place and regularly reviewed; Steering Group continues to meet regularly.

initiatives identify the benefit of training whole teams. This poses the challenge of how to reach everyone in the team without taking people away from their daily duties in the home. The existence of dedicated restorative justice coordinators working at the local YOT (often with ROLAC funding) means that there may be a local person who can offer modular training at times when staff can be more easily available.

Following initial training, the best way to ensure that everyone is making the connection between what they learnt on the course and what they do and say in 'everyday' life is to start straight away – using the language, introducing regular circles and addressing daily issues in a restorative manner. It may be only a matter of days, or it could be weeks, before something more serious occurs, needing the more formal interventions – but by then staff will already know how effective the language and the approach can be.

> ## Case study: Implementing a restorative approach
>
> In a children's home in Derbyshire staff began having their own circle every day, with a talking piece, to check in, share what had been happening, and how they had dealt with any issues that arose. The very act of 'circling' and the language in which issues are addressed ensured that the language of thoughts, feelings and needs soon became common currency. This same home has regular house meetings, in which the staff and young people sit around the kitchen table and discuss the week. If things get a bit heated, a talking piece is introduced so that everyone gets a chance to have their say. The manager attests to the fact that now, after about 18 months, the young people tend to use the language themselves. If someone does something they do not like, rather than swearing or lashing out, as they might have done in the past, they explain, in affective language inspired by the 'I' message, how they feel when someone acts in a particular way, and what they would prefer instead.

Policy and procedure reviews

I think it is difficult to predict what policies and procedures will need to be changed until people have become familiar and confident with the full range of restorative approaches. There will inevitably be a time when practice runs ahead of existing policy. Strong leadership at this stage will be crucial so that staff – and especially staff who have yet to go through training – do not get confused. The young people too will need to know about the changes and why people are using new language and different ways to address issues. I imagine that the sooner the use of regular circles starts to happen, the better, so that worries and confusion can be talked about. It would be unrestorative for a staff team to pretend all is well when in fact they themselves are struggling – the teething problems can be shared and the young people themselves may be able to play an important part in the way their home adopts restorative practice.

It will certainly be necessary to review the existing behaviour management policy as soon as possible so that the evolving practice is in line with established policy, or else newly trained staff will be confused. Existing systems, if based on rewards and sanctions, will cease to be appropriate and this will need discussion (Kohn 1999).

All the language and the range of restorative processes described in the book will need adapting to be accessible to those involved. This is an equal opportunities issue – restorative meetings are for all sides involved in a conflict or harmful incident. If, for whatever reason, a restorative response is deemed unsuitable for either the person responsible for the harm or those affected, then the others involved miss out on the positive benefits of the meeting. All sides have needs, and without the restorative meeting those needs are still there and, if unaddressed, could lead to further unrest, conflict or harm.

This book is a basic introduction to restorative approaches in care settings. I have touched on the potential benefits of the process, the language and the consistent framework for young people with attachment difficulties, but there will be other issues affecting children in care that are outside the scope of this book. In fact many of these issues are ones facing schools as well, and there is development work and research to be done here too. I will simply mention areas in which I believe more work needs to be done – and I will also say that where the basic practices and principles of a restorative approach have been introduced, practitioners in more challenging situations have been determined to make the process accessible to their particular community.

I anticipate and welcome specialist advice on making restorative opportunities available for those with:

- complex learning needs[29]

- hearing impairments

- first, and strongest, language other than English

- different cultural expectations with regard to conflict and wrongdoing.

I personally have not experienced extra challenges when using restorative approaches with boys (as distinct from girls) but I think there is work to be done in this domain. In fact, I think working restoratively with boys can do much to develop their supposed particular deficit as far as emotional literacy is concerned.

Challenges and opportunities

It is useful to anticipate the challenges of implementing a restorative approach and also to learn from those a bit further on in their journey. That said, there is also, as mentioned in the last section, something to be said for regular review of progress by those involved, since a restorative belief is that those with the problems are the ones best placed to resolve them.

In recent months my team has been working with Walsall's residential care staff, and after initial training and a chance to try out new skills a refresher day was offered, during which the following activity was carried out. It is one that other teams relatively new to the restorative approach could also use as a way of identifying what is working well, what not so well, and how to overcome any problems arising.

The activity is not only a useful interactive and constructive way for a team to assess how they are doing, but it can also serve as a data collection tool – a chance to review progress midway through the implementation process. I designed it for my own doctoral research and have used it many times when working with schools on implementation.

---

29 Iffley Mead School in Oxford is leading the way in this field and staff there are very happy to offer advice and support.

ACTIVITY 9.2

SNAKES AND LADDERS

Because we use this activity a lot for refresher training, we have had some snakes and ladders boards made up for us and laminated (size A1 card). We have also made some snakes and ladders and had these laminated as well. However, when I first began, I drew them up by hand and cut out snakes and ladders myself.

Resources

- laminated boards (one per group of 5–6 people)
- a pack of (laminated) snakes and ladders per table
- a pile of white (laminated) strategy cards per table
- several fine-tipped coloured markers per table (water-soluble if using laminated materials, so that they can be wiped clean for re-use)
- Blutak.

1. Participants divide themselves into groups of about six around tables on which has been placed a game board divided into 100 squares numbered 1 to 100. Each group is also given a selection of cardboard snakes and ladders, in three different lengths – short, medium and long. The first stage of the activity is for participants within each group to share what their vision for their home or school is, write a joint statement on a white strategy card, and then stick this in the '100' square – so that they agree what they are working towards.

2. Next they are asked to share their experiences of using and implementing restorative approaches, and to identify things that have set them back (a) a little, (b) quite a bit and (c) a lot, and to write these down in water-soluble pen on snakes of the appropriate length, in a few clear words. They are then asked to attach these snakes to the board with Blutak.

3. The next step is to share experiences of factors that have *helped* them (a) a little, (b) quite a bit and (c) a lot, and to write these on the ladders of appropriate lengths and place these on the board.

4. The fourth stage of the activity is to move around the room slowly, stopping at each group's board. On each group's table is a set of blank white strategy cards on which participants are invited to write suggestions to the group that 'owns' the board for coping with, or avoiding, their particular snakes. These are then stuck with Blutak next to the relevant snakes, for the group to find when they return to their own board. One comment has been that it is easier to come up with strategies for someone else's problems than it is for one's own.

5. Finally the groups return to their own board and read and reflect on the strategies they have received from everyone else.

6. The activity can be concluded by the group sharing their snakes, ladders and strategies on three sheets of flipchart paper. Their contributions can be recorded and used for evaluation purposes to inform next steps.

With permission from Walsall restorative approaches champions Alison Glover and Wendy Thompson, I reproduce just a sample of the challenges the teams there have been meeting, and some of the strategies they suggest to overcome or anticipate these challenges.

The factors they identify that have helped move the project forward include:

- initial practical, appropriate training in communication and mediation skills

- an enthusiastic team

- willingness to change

- working together as a team – good communication

- commitment to making it work – positive attitude

- use of circles

- consistency of practice across team

- having the support of the ROLAC worker and the multi-agency team

- integrating other models (e.g. Transactional Analysis and attachment theory).

Table 9.3 lists some of the challenges the teams have met and the strategies they are trying out to overcome these challenges. I am very grateful to Walsall staff for being

Table 9.3 'Snakes and ladders': overcoming challenges to implementation

Challenge ('snake')	Suggested strategy
Lack of communication across whole team.	Everyone from team implementing restorative approach together.
Initial scepticism; negativity.	Team discussions and shared planning.
Unrealistic goals.	Common objectives from management.
Different shifts and time scale to deal with issues.	Structures and guidance needed.
Resistance to getting started after initial training.	Positive role modelling from management. On-going personal development. Support during supervision.
Lack of guidance or support from management.	Managers must be part of initial training.
Institutionalized habits.	Commitment to using conflict resolution every day.
Non-compliance; resistance to change.	Persevere; offer refresher training.
Lack of appropriate place for restorative meetings.	Recognition of the value of this – creative thinking.
Not seeing opportunities for restorative approach – not understanding its applicability.	Daily/weekly circles and day-to-day conversations modelled by others can illustrate the everyday nature of the approach.

willing to share their teething problems. It is important to recognize that there will inevitably be some of these and to welcome them as opportunities to review practice together and learn together – thereby modelling effective restorative circle work.

Monitoring and evaluation

Earlier in this chapter I referred to the advantage of approaching planning in the spirit of an action research project – involving everyone in reflecting on each new stage of implementation, and using their learning and experience to plan the next stage of the project. Some initiatives decide to buy in independent evaluators, and this has the advantage of ensuring a degree of objectivity and a chance to benefit from the experience and expertise of professional researchers. However, I would still recommend engaging with an evaluation team who prefer an action research approach, working *with* all participants in ways that are congruent with restorative practice.

My own research background is one that favours working with participants and, through encouraging them to share their stories, gradually developing a shared frame of reference (Hopkins 2006). I would suggest that everyone who is likely to be affected by the restorative approach discuss what outcomes they would like to see from the initiative, and that these desired outcomes be used to measure progress and success.

As Les Fletcher, a manager of a residential home in Walsall says,[30] it is important to be patient when assessing the impact of introducing restorative approaches – to focus on the minutiae, and not expect dramatic changes overnight. He has realized that he and his staff need to value the small changes that are happening – such as the improvements he has noticed in the young people's listening skills as a result of using circle time regularly with each other.

Whatever research methodology is adopted, the important thing is to start the evaluation at the very beginning with a base-line audit so that you know your starting point.

Whatever changes are going to be measured, it is important to assess how the situation is before any training is offered. This base-line audit could take the form of a questionnaire, filled in by young people and staff alike. My preference would be for one that was common across the UK, but with some local variation so that people feel that their own needs and perspective are being taken into account. If there is some common ground then this paves the way for a national data collection tool that can give a bigger picture than a local study can.

The evaluation is an in-house resource, to ensure the on-going fine-tuning of how an initiative is developing; a local district-wide resource for evaluating progress and identifying further training needs; and a national resource to share with those who have yet to be convinced that restorative approaches are so important in residential settings. Local and national data can also be used for lobbying purposes to

---

30 In a private telephone conversation.

ensure that policy at national level supports restorative developments. Greater commitment to developing restorative approaches is also likely to affect the availability of funding for such initiatives.

In the short term a case study pro forma like the one in Appendix G might be useful, if everyone who was recording cases for their own in-house use also recorded cases for a national database. I think we are at an early stage with this type of data sharing, but I mention it as an issue that needs further consideration.

Conclusion

No one area, unit, school or family will have the same implementation journey. However, there is much to be gained from sharing experiences within a team, across teams and across areas. The implementation of restorative approaches in communities, institutions and organizations is still relatively new, although the individual elements in this approach are probably all familiar. This is what makes it all so attractive to people when they really understand it all – it just makes so much sense and allows people to get back in touch with why they began to work with young people in the first place.

I like to use a gardening analogy for the task of implementation – initial awareness raising is like planting seeds. The prospects of these seeds putting down roots will depend in part on the quality of the soil into which they are sown. The readiness of the environment to embrace change is an important consideration.

Once the seeds have been sown and then watered with some initial training, the tender plants need plenty of care to begin with. Good management of individuals and sensitive and knowledgeable supervision will help the tender plants put out shoots. There is nothing like the fertilizer of success to boost growth and strengthen roots, so sharing stories is crucial, and regular opportunities for refresher meetings will also help.

Things will not always go well – occasionally plants undergo the stress of not enough nourishment or a drop in temperature; sometimes things get too hot. However, the good gardener (the manager or the project worker) checks regularly to see how each plant is getting on – and does not expect them to survive without constant care.

Eventually the plants will be strong enough to plant out and fend for themselves in the open air. They will still need the odd bit of fertilizer, though – meetings to develop skills; new ideas; conferences to meet others around the country. In time they will produce seeds too, or have cuttings taken from them – and so the garden grows.

Epilogue

There comes a moment in writing a book when it is time to stop. There is always more to write and always more to learn. This is the first book to be written about using restorative approaches in residential and foster care settings, but it will not be the last. I hope that by describing restorative approaches in terms of key themes, informed by essential values and principles, I have made it easier for people to feel able to adapt what they find in this book to their own particular circumstances.

In England and in Scotland we are at the beginning of a very exciting time as more and more residential children's homes adopt restorative approaches. The experiences from these homes and from the restorative developments in mainstream schools will, I hope, encourage more residential schools to consider the approach. Initiatives will be evaluated, and experts in particular areas will add their understanding, so that we become better at making restorative process accessible to those for whom the 'basic model' is too challenging.

There are issues that I have not considered in this book, such as the needs of young people as they face the prospect of leaving care – a particularly vulnerable time for many.

> Several times, I have seen a young person develop uncharacteristically disruptive behaviour, and in the worse instance, detach completely from staff, partly because of anxiety about where they will be living in three months' time. Then the young person gets prosecuted. This action is seen as the ultimate, in order 'to show them the consequences, in the real world', whether prior restorative practice has taken place or not.
>
> (YOT Restorative Justice Coordinator in West Midlands)

A whole new area for development would be the sheltered housing that young people find themselves in when they do leave care. There are a few lone restorative pioneers in this field but there is much work still to be done there.

Another area which I have not explicitly dealt with is the needs of those in secure residential accommodation. I hope that there is material in this book to help those wanting to work restoratively in such settings, but the secure estate is one that requires specialist consideration. Kimmett Edgar and Tim Newell have considered what a restorative prison might be like in their book *Restorative Justice in Prisons – Making It Happen* (Edgar and Newell 2006).

I know that some of those involved in the training of residential staff are also working with foster carers – and so the word spreads. What works for foster parents will almost certainly be valuable for any, and every, parent. Maybe families who struggle to offer a safe, supportive home for their children can be given more skills to do so with some training in restorative parenting – which may help some families to stay together who would otherwise be unable to. And maybe the children who are benefiting now from these restorative approaches will be better able to care for their own children in the future. I hope so.

Belinda – what's been happening?

I've been writing this book for over two years – talked to so many people, learnt so much. It's transformed the way I think about restorative approaches myself.

What have you been thinking? And so how have you been feeling?

As the deadline for submitting the manuscript has loomed I've realized how much more there could be in the book – and as a result I've been feeling anxious.

But I've also been telling myself that this is only the beginning. Others will write new books that will build on these basic foundations – and this thought has reassured me and made me feel excited and optimistic.

So who has been affected by what's been happening?

All those around me – my family who have taken over most of the cooking, the washing, my office manager who has been holding the fort when I stay at home writing, my training team, whom I may have been less in touch with than usual – and all the good people who have been reading chapters and giving me feedback.

So what do **you** need now to feel better?

Well, I need a return to normality, a good rest and the opportunity to show my gratitude – I imagine everyone I've mentioned needs appreciation and reassurance that it's all been worthwhile – and needs me back to normal and pulling my weight!

So what needs to happen now – and what are you going to do?

I'm going to show my gratitude in various ways to everyone I've mentioned, and make sure people know that although I actually wrote the book, it's been a team effort – and I want to do as much as I can to support readers of this book so that we all carry on learning together.

And right now – it's time for a coffee...

Figure 10.1 Epilogue

✓

Appendix A

Restorative enquiry one-to-one

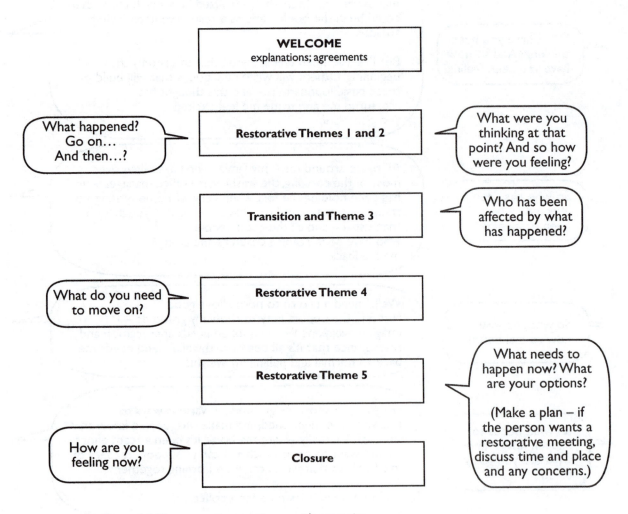

WELCOME
explanations; agreements

What happened?
Go on...
And then...?

Restorative Themes 1 and 2

What were you thinking at that point? And so how were you feeling?

Transition and Theme 3

Who has been affected by what has happened?

What do you need to move on?

Restorative Theme 4

Restorative Theme 5

What needs to happen now? What are your options?

(Make a plan – if the person wants a restorative meeting, discuss time and place and any concerns.)

How are you feeling now?

Closure

Figure 6.1 The restorative meeting: an aide memoire

Appendix B

The restorative meeting

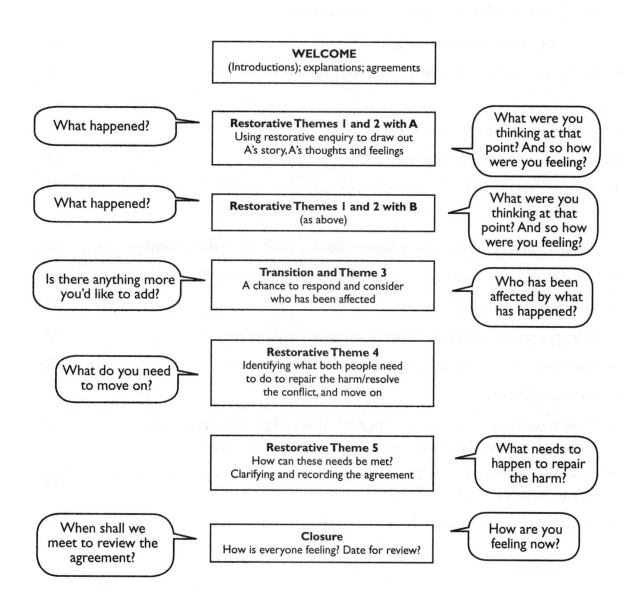

WELCOME
(Introductions); explanations; agreements

What happened?

Restorative Themes 1 and 2 with A
Using restorative enquiry to draw out
A's story, A's thoughts and feelings

What were you thinking at that point? And so how were you feeling?

What happened?

Restorative Themes 1 and 2 with B
(as above)

What were you thinking at that point? And so how were you feeling?

Is there anything more you'd like to add?

Transition and Theme 3
A chance to respond and consider
who has been affected

Who has been affected by what has happened?

What do you need to move on?

Restorative Theme 4
Identifying what both people need
to do to repair the harm/resolve
the conflict, and move on

Restorative Theme 5
How can these needs be met?
Clarifying and recording the agreement

What needs to happen to repair the harm?

When shall we meet to review the agreement?

Closure
How is everyone feeling? Date for review?

How are you feeling now?

Appendix C

Checklist for preparing for a restorative conference

- Are the venue and the room easy to find for visitors? ☐
- Have maps been sent if necessary? ☐
- Have instructions or directions been posted on walls if necessary? ☐

- Temperature of room – not too hot or too cold? ☐
- Sunlight – not dazzling anyone? ☐
- Privacy – do curtains or blinds need to be drawn? ☐

- Are all chairs the same height, with no wobbly legs or other distractions? ☐
- Are the chairs arranged in a circle, not to close together or too far away? ☐
- Have you agreed the seating plan? ☐
- Is it appropriate to label the chairs or pin up a seating plan? ☐
- Are there water and tissues available? ☐
- Are the toilets easy to find? ☐
- If the room has a phone, is it switched off? (Remind participants to do the same with their mobiles. This might need to be discussed beforehand.) ☐
- Once the meeting starts, will there be a notice on the door, or even someone outside to prevent interruptions? ☐
- Is there paper and a pen handy for any written agreement? ☐

Appendix D

How things were put right – restorative enquiry

Name of young person

Date   *Time*

Staff on duty

Role	**Full name**
Shift leader	
Staff member involved	
Other staff on shift	

What happened?

Brief, neutral description (would everyone agree with this description?)

Events leading up to incident?

Incident?

✓

Checklist for restorative enquiry

Young person asked to give their version of events? ☐

Young person asked about their thoughts and feelings during these events? ☐

Young person invited to reflect on who has been affected by the events? ☐

Young person's plan for putting things right

Specific? ☐

Measurable? ☐

Achievable? ☐

Realistic? ☐

Time-bound? (When? For how long? When by?) ☐

Action plan

Review

Action	Date and people involved
Action plan to be completed by:	
Meeting to discuss between staff member and young person (and person affected if requested):	

Young person's experience

Did you feel the process was fair?   Did you feel listened to?   What will you do differently in the **future**?

Signature of facilitator   **Signature of young person**

Appendix E

How things were put right – restorative meeting

Names of people involved

Date   *Time*

Staff on duty

Role	Full name
Shift leader	
Meeting facilitator	
Other staff on duty	

What happened?

Brief, neutral description (would everyone agree with this description?)

Events leading up to incident?
Incident?

✓

Checklist for restorative enquiry

Each person asked to give their version of events?	☐
Each person asked about their thoughts and feelings during these events?	☐
Each person invited to reflect on who has been affected by the events?	☐

Plan agreed for putting things right

Specific?	☐
Measurable?	☐
Achievable?	☐
Realistic?	☐
Time-bound? (When? For how long? When by?)	☐

Action plan

```
┌──────────────────────────────────────────┐
│                                          │
│                                          │
│                                          │
└──────────────────────────────────────────┘
```

Review

Action	Date and people involved
Action plan to be completed by:	
Meeting to discuss between staff member (and those affected if requested):	

Participant's experience

Did you feel the process was fair?

Did you feel listened to?

What will you do differently in the future?

Signature of facilitator   **Signature of participants**

Appendix F

How things were put right

Date and time of meeting

Between   *and*

Who will do what? When? When by? How? How will we know?

Review time and date?

Where?   Who will be there?

✓

Appendix G

Case study form

Name of school/residential home/unit:

Facilitator(s):

Please answer the questions below to submit a case study for sharing good practice.

Please remember not to use the real names of people involved. Refer to people by different names, or alternatively use A and B, etc. (Please indicate their role, i.e. student; teacher; parent; resident; staff member.)

If possible, please give an example of a regular type of restorative meeting and one that presented you with challenges or was unique.

Question 1: What happened?

Question 2: How was the incident referred to you?

Question 3: What preparation do you have to do?

Question 4: What restorative approach did you use?

Question 5: What happened at the meeting or during the interaction?

Question 6: Did any key moment happen to bring the parties together or keep them apart?

Question 7: Did the meeting find a resolution? If so, what was it?

Question 8: How have things been since the meeting/conversation?

Question 9: What benefits were there of using this approach for the people involved?

Question 10: What benefits were there for the school/residential home?

Question 11: Would you do anything differently next time?

Question 12: Is there anything else you would like to add?

Form adapted from one developed by Luke Roberts

Appendix H

Further Reading about Restorative Justice

General background

Johnstone, G. (2003) *A Restorative Justice Reader*. Cullompton: Willan Publishing.

Liebmann, M. (2007) *Restorative Justice: How It Works*. London: Jessica Kingsley Publishers.

Restorative Justice Consortium (RJC) (2004) *Principles of Restorative Processes*. London: RJC. http://www.restorativejustice.org.uk/?Resources:Best_Practice:Principles

Sullivan, D. and Tifft, L. (2001) *Restorative Justice – Healing the Foundations of our Everyday Lives*. Monsey, NY: Willow Tree Press.

Wachtel, T. and McCold, P. (2001) 'Restorative justice in everyday life.' In H. Strang and J. Braithwaite (eds) *Restorative Justice and Civil Society*. Cambridge: Cambridge University Press.

Zehr, H. (1990) *Changing Lenses*. Scottdale, PA: Herald Press.

Restorative approaches in schools, residential homes and prisons

Edgar, K. and Newell, T. (2006) *Restorative Justice in Prisons – Making it Happen*. Winchester: Waterside Press.

Hopkins, B. (2004) *Just Schools*. London: Jessica Kingsley Publishers.

Hopkins, B. (2008) *Restorative Approaches in Residential Child Care*. http://www.ncb.org.uk/ncercc/ncercc%20practice%20documents/restorative_approaches_highlight.pdf

Littlechild, B. (2003) *An Evaluation of the Implementation of a Restorative Justice Approach in a Residential Unit for Young People in Hertfordshire. Final Report*. Centre for Community Research, University of Hertfordshire.

Morrison, B. (ed) (2007) *Restoring Safe School Communities*. Sydney: The Federation Press.

Thorsborne, M. and Vinegrad, D. (2004) *Restorative Practices in Classrooms*. Buderim, Queensland: Marg Thorsborne.

Warren, C. (2004) *Restoring the Balance*. London: Lewisham Action on Mediation Project LAMP.

Warren, C. and Williams, S. (2007) *Restoring the Balance 2*. London: Lewisham Council Restorative Approaches Partnership.

Appendix I

Useful websites

This is not a definitive list but provides some useful points of contact for those seeking more information, training, or help with implementation. A far more extensive list of relevant websites can be found in Marian Liebmann's excellent book (2007): *Restorative Justice: How It Works.* London: Jessica Kingsley Publishers.

Transforming Conflict – the National Centre for restorative approaches in Youth Settings

0118 933 1520

www.transformingconflict.org

I offer my own organizational website first – if you like what I have read and you want to know more, visit our site or give us a ring. We have a team working with residential staff, and we are also supporting multi-agency development across all children's services.

NCERCC – the National Centre for Excellence in Residential Child Care

020 7843 1168

www.ncb.org.uk/ncercc

The National Centre for Excellence in Residential Child Care, based at NCB (National Children's Bureau), is a major collaborative initiative to improve standards of practice and outcomes for children and young people in residential child care in England. It strongly supports the development of restorative approaches with children in public care.

RJC – the Restorative Justice Consortium

0207 653 1992

www.restorativejustice.org.uk

The Restorative Justice Consortium is the national voice for restorative justice. It provides independent information about restorative justice to the public, and support and resources to members who deliver restorative justice; and promotes the development and use of restorative justice.

Although I very much hope readers looking for further training will come to my organization, I also value and respect the work that my colleagues do in the field, and I believe people need to make an informed choice. Listed below are other training providers for the residential sector. Apologies to others who feel left out – let me know who you are and I can always pass on your details to enquirers if we cannot help.

International Institute for Restorative Practices

01706 810201

www.iirp.org.uk

The UK branch of this organization offers training and consultancy. The NCERCC website has a useful piece written by IIRP staff giving a useful summary of what restorative justice means to them.

SACRO – Safeguarding Communities, Reducing Offending

0131 624 7270

www.sacro.org.uk

This Scottish-based organization offers training in conferencing and mediation.

Walker Research and Training

01869 277633

www.researchandtraining.co.uk

This organization is one of the major providers of training in the residential sector and specializes in this area. They are highly regarded and have a wealth of experience.

Netcare

028 3025 6469

www.netcare-ni.com

This Northern Ireland-based company offers training in restorative approaches and has worked with organisations like Barnardos and the YMCA who support young people in care and leaving care.

CTC Associates

799 069 0854

www.ctcassociates.co.uk

Another Northern Ireland-based company with extensive experience working with young people in the residential sector.

Bibliography

Audit Commission (1996) *Misspent Youth: Young People and Crime.* London: Audit Commisssion.

Barton, C. (2003) *Restorative Justice – The Empowerment Model.* Sydney: Hawkins Press.

Bentley, C., Bentley, M., Conchie, J., Liebmann, M., Musgrave, R. and Williams, P. (1998) *Mediation Works.* Bristol: Mediation UK.

Blood, P. (2002) Personal communication.

Braithwaite, J. (1989) *Crime, Shame and Reintegration.* Cambridge: Cambridge University Press.

Cherry, S. (2005) *Transforming Behaviours: Pro-social Modelling.* Devon: Willan.

Christie, N. (1977) 'Conflicts as Property.' *British Journal of Criminology 17,* 1, 1–15.

Consedine, J. (1995) *Restorative Justice: Healing the Effects of Crime.* Lyttelton: Ploughshares Publications.

Cornelius, H. and Faire, S. (1993) *Everyone Can Win.* East Roseville: Simon & Schuster.

Cowie, H. and Jennifer, D. (2008) *New Perspectives on Bullying.* Buckingham: Open University Press.

Davies, L. (2005) 'The development of restorative justice in the United Kingdom: a personal perspective.' Building a Global Alliance for Restorative Practices and Family Empowerment, Part 3. Paper presented at the Sixth International Conference on Conferencing, Circles and other Restorative Practices. Penrith, NSW Australia.

De Shazer, S. (1988) *Clues: Investigating Solutions in Brief Therapy.* New York: W.W. Norton and Co.

Department for Children, Schools and Families (DCSF) (2008) *Children's Trusts: Statutory guidance on inter-agency cooperation to improve well-being of children, young people and their families.* http://www.everychildmatters.gov.uk/_file s/48459BE8717A3D2E3C71501D44FA60BF.pdf

Department for Education and Skills (DfES) (2003) *Every Child Matters.* London: The Stationery Office..

Department for Education and Skills (DfES) (2006a) *Care Matters: Transforming the Lives of Children and Young People in Care.* London: The Stationary Office.

Department for Education and Skills (DfES) (2006b) *Safer School Partnerships.* London: The Stationery Office.

Department for Education and Skills (DfES) (2006c) *Youth Matters: The Next Steps.* London: The Stationary Office

Edgar, K. and Newell, T. (2006) *Restorative Justice in Prisons – Making It Happen.* Winchester: Waterside Press.

Faber, A. and Mazlish, E. (1980) *How to Talk so Kids will Listen and Listen so Kids will Talk.* New York: Rawson,Wade Publishers, Inc.

Fine, N. and Macbeth, F. (1992) *Playing with Fire.* Leicester: Youth Work Press.

Flood-Page, C., Campbell, S., Harrington, V. and Miller, J. (2000) *Youth Crime: Findings from the 1998/99 Youth Lifestyles Survey.* Home Office Research Study 209. London: Home Office.

Francis, J. (2008) 'Could do better! Supporting the education of looked-after children.' In A. Kendrick (ed) *Residential Child Care – Prospects and Challenges.* London: Jessica Kingsley Publishers.

Gilligan, R. (2000) 'Promoting resilience in children in foster care.' In G. Kelly and R. Gilligan (eds) *Issues in Foster Care: Policy, Practice and Research.* London: Jessica Kingsley Publishers.

Gladwell, M. (2000) *The Tipping Point: How Little Things Can Make a Big Difference.* Boston, MA: Little, Brown.

Golding, K. S. (2008) *Nurturing Attachments.* London: Jessica Kingsley Publishers.

Graham, G. and Bowling, B. (1995) *Young People and Crime.* Home Office Research Study 145. London: Home Office.

Kane, J., G., Lloyd, G., McCluskey, G., Riddell, R., Stead, J., Weedon, R., Maguire, R. and Hendry, R. (2007) *Restorative Practices in Three Scottish Councils: Final Report of the Evaluation of the First Two Years of the Pilot Projects 2004–2006.* http://www.scotland.gov.uk/Publications/2007/08/24093135

Hall, G. E. and Hord, S. M. (2001) *Implementing Change: Patterns, Principles and Potholes.* Needham Heights, MA: Allyn and Bacon.

Hicks, L. Gibbs, I., Weatherly, H. and Byford, S. (2007) *Managing Children's Homes: Developing Effective Leadership in Small Organisations.* London and Philadelphia: Jessica Kingsley Publishers.

Holland, J. and Randerson, C. (2005) *Supporting Children in Public Care in Schools.* London: Jessica Kingsley Publishers.

Home Office (2004) *Best Practice Guidelines for Restorative Practitioners and Their Case Supervisors and Line Managers.* London: The Stationery Office.

Home Office (2008) *Youth Crime Action Plan.* http://www.homeoffice.gov.uk/documents/youth-crime-action-plan

Home Office and Association of Chief Police Officers (2002) *National Crime Recording Standard.* http://www.homeoffice.gov.uk/rds/recordedcrime1.html

Hopkins, B. (1999a) 'Restorative approaches in the community.' *Mediation 15*, 3, 3–4.

Hopkins, B. (1999b) 'Restorative justice in schools.' In: TV Partnership (ed) *Restoring the Balance – a Handbook of Restorative Approaches in Community Safety.* Thame: Thames Valley Partnership.

Hopkins, B. (2004) *Just Schools.* London: Jessica Kingsley Publishers.

Hopkins, B. (2006) 'Implementing a restorative approach to behaviour and relationship in schools – the narrated experiences of educationalists'. Reading: University of Reading.

Hopkins, B. (2007) *Peer Mediation and Mentoring Trainer's Manual.* London: Optimus Education.

Hopkins, B. (2008) *Restorative Approaches in Residential Child Care.* http://www.ncb.org.uk/ncercc/ncercc%20practice%20documents/restorative_approaches_highlight.pdf

Johnstone, G. (2003) *A Restorative Justice Reader.* Cullompton: Willan Publishing.

Kingston Friends Workshop Group (1996) *Ways and Means Today.* Kingston upon Thames: Kingston Friends Workshop Group.

Knoster, T. (1991) 'Managing change.' TASH Conference, Washington DC.

Kohn, A. (1999) *Punished by Rewards.* New York: Houghton Mifflin.

Leeds Youth Offending Service, West Yorkshire Police and Leeds Children and Young People's Social Care (2007) 'Protocol between Leeds YOS, West Yorkshire Police and Leeds Children and Young People's Social Care in respect of incidents in looked after placements which might result in police intervention.' Leeds: Leeds Youth Offending Service.

Lewin, K. (1946) 'Action research and minority problems.' *Journal of Social Issues 2*, 34–36.

Lewisham Borough Council (2008) *Anti-Bullying Policy.* http://www.lewisham.gov.uk/NR/rdonlyres/09710847-154F-4661-A33A-11C596D4C5BB/0/AntiBullyingPolicy.pdf

Liebmann, M. (2007) *Restorative Justice: How It Works.* London: Jessica Kingsley Publishers.

Littlechild, B. (2003) *An evaluation of the implementation of a restorative justice approach in a residential unit for young people in Hertfordshire. Final Report.*

Littlechild, B. (2008) *Conflict Resolution, Bullying and the Introduction of Restorative Justice Approaches in Young People's Residential Units.*

Marshall, T. (1998) 'Restorative justice: an overview.' In G. Johnstone (ed) *A Restorative Justice Reader.* Cullompton: Willan.

McCold, P. (2001) 'Primary restorative justice practices.' In A. Morris and G. Maxwell (eds) *Restorative Justice for Juveniles.* Oxford: Hart.

McCold, P. and Wachtel, T. (2002) 'Restorative justice theory validation.' In E. G. M. Weitekamp and H.-J. Kerner (eds) *Restorative Justice: Theoretical Foundations.* Cullompton: Willan Publishers.

Mindell, A. (1997) *Sitting in the Fire – Large Group Transformation through Diversity and Conflict.* Portland, OR: Lao Tse Press.

Moore, D. B. and O'Connell, T. A. (1994) 'Family conferencing in Wagga Wagga' (extract). In G. Johnstone (ed) *A Restorative Justice Reader.* Winchester: Willan Publishing.

Morrison, B. (ed) (2007) *Restoring Safe School Communities.* Sydney: The Federation Press.

NACRO (2003a) *Reducing Offending Behaviour by Looked-after Children.* London: NACRO.

NACRO (2003b) *Youth Crime Briefing. Looked-after Children Who Offend: the Quality Protects Programme and YOTs.* London: NACRO.

NACRO (2005) *A Handbook on Reducing Offending by Looked-after Children*. London: NACRO.

Nathanson, D. L. (1992) *Shame, Pride, Affect, Sex, and the Birth of Self*. New York: W. W. Norton.

Newton, C. and Mahaffey, H. (2008) *Restorative Solutions – Making It Work*. Nottingham: Inclusive Solutions.

Peachey, D. E. (1989) 'The Kitchener experiment.' In M. Wright and B. Galaway (eds) *Mediation and Criminal Justice*. London: Sage Publications.

Perry, H. (2008) 'The right balance.' *YJ* (September/October).

Petrie, P., Boddy, J., Cameron, C., Wigfall, V. and Simon, A. (2006) *Working with Children in Care: European Perspectives*. Buckingham: Open University Press.

Pranis, K. (2001) 'Telling our stories and changing our lives.' *The Texas Mediator 16*, 3, 1–4.

Quill, D. and Wynne, J. (1993) *Victim and Offender Mediation Handbook*. London: Save the Children/West Yorkshire Probation Service.

Redl, F. (1966) *When We Deal with Children*. New York: The Free Press.

Reynolds, D. (2001) 'Beyond school effectiveness and school improvement?' In A. Harris and N. Bennett (eds) *School Effectiveness and School Improvement*. London: Continuum.

Restorative Justice Consortium (RJC) (2004) *Principles of Restorative Processes*. London: RJC. http://www.restorativejustice. org.uk/?Resources:Best_Practice:Principles

Rosenberg, M. (1999) *Nonviolent Communication*. Encintas, CA: PuddleDancer Press.

Senge, P., Kleiner, A., Roberts, C., Ross, R., Roth, G. and Smith, B. (1999) *The Dance of Change*. London: Nicholas Brealey.

Shapiro, A. (2003) *Creating Contagious Commitment*. Hillsborough, NC: Strategy Perspective.

Shapland, J., Atkinson, A., Atkinson, H., Chapman, B., Colledge, E., Dignan, J., Howes, M., Johnstone, J., Robinson, G. and Sorsby, A. (2006) *Restorative Justice in Practice*. London: Ministry of Justice.

Shapland, J., Atkinson, A., Atkinson, H., Chapman, B., Colledge, E., Dignan, J., Howes, M., Johnstone, J., Robinson, G. and Sorsby, A. (2007) *Restorative Justice: the Views of Victims and Offenders*. London: Ministry of Justice.

Sherman, L. W. and Strang, H. (2007) *Restorative Justice: the Evidence*. London: The Smith Institute.

Skills for Justice (2008) *National Occupational Standards for Restorative Practice*. http://www.skillsforjustice.com/ template01.asp?PageID=609

Stoll, L. and Fink, D. (1996) *Changing Our Schools: Linking School Effectiveness and School Improvement*. Maidenhead: Open University Press.

Stone, D., Patton, B. and Heen, S. (1999) *Difficult Conversations*. New York: Michael Joseph.

Sullivan, D. and Tifft, L. (2001) *Restorative Justice – Healing the Foundations of our Everyday Lives*. Monsey, NY: Willow Tree Press.

Thorsborne, M. and Vinegrad, D. (2002) *Restorative Practices in Schools*. Buderim: Marg Thorsborne.

Thorsborne, M. and Vinegrad, D. (2004) *Restorative Practices in Classrooms*. Buderim, Queensland: Marg Thorsborne.

Wachtel, T. and McCold, P. (2001) 'Restorative justice in everyday life.' In H. Strang and J. Braithwaite (eds) *Restorative Justice and Civil Society*. Cambridge: Cambridge University Press.

Wallis, P. and Tudor, B. (2009) *The Pocket Guide to Restorative Justice*. London: Jessica Kingsley Publishers.

Warren, C. (2004) *Restoring the Balance*. London: Lewisham Action on Mediation Project (LAMP).

Warren, C. and Williams, S. (2007) *Restoring the Balance 2*. London: Lewisham Council Restorative Approaches Partnership.

Whitehouse, E. and Pudney, W. (1998) *A Volcano in My Tummy: Helping Children to Handle Anger*. New Society.

Willmott, N. (2007) *A Review of the Use of Restorative Justice in Children's Residential Care*. London: National Children's Bureau

Yantzi, M. (2004) Private conversation.

Youth Justice Board (2002) *Restorative Justice in Schools*. London: Youth Justice Board. http://www.yjb.gov.uk/ Publications/Scripts/prodView.asp?idProduct=207&eP=YJB

Zehr, H. (1985) *Retributive Justice, Restorative Justice. Occasional Paper No 4*. US Office on Crime and Justice.

Zehr, H. (1990) *Changing Lenses*. Scottdale, PA: Herald Press.

Zehr, H. and Mika, H. (1997) *Fundamental Concepts of Restorative Justice*. US Office on Crime and Justice.

Zehr, H. and Mika, H. (1998) 'Fundamental principles of restorative justice.' *The Contemporary Justice Review 1*, 1, 47–55.

Subject Index

Au_____